THE JAPANESE ECONOMY IN INTERNATIONAL PERSPECTIVE

THE JAPANESE ECONOMY IN INTERNATIONAL PERSPECTIVE

Edited by Isaiah Frank

Haruhiro Fukui

Donald C. Hellmann

Leon Hollerman

J. J. Kaplan

Yoichi Okita

William V. Rapp

C. Tait Ratcliffe

Kozo Yamamura

M. Y. Yoshino

A SUPPLEMENTARY PAPER
OF THE COMMITTEE FOR ECONOMIC DEVELOPMENT

THE JOHNS HOPKINS UNIVERSITY PRESS
Baltimore and London

The Johns Hopkins University Press, Baltimore, Maryland 21218
The Johns Hopkins University Press Ltd., London

Library of Congress Cataloging in Publication Data
Frank, Isaiah, 1917–
    The Japanese economy in international perspective.

    (A Supplementary paper of the Committee for Economic Development)
    Includes index.
    1. Japan—Economic conditions—1945–   2. Japan—Economic policy—1945–   I. Fukui, Haruhiro, 1935–   II. Title
HC462.9.F7   1975   330.9'52'04   74–15567
ISBN 0–8018–1629–7
ISBN 0–8018–1630–0 pbk.

CONTENTS

THE JAPANESE ECONOMY IN INTERNATIONAL PERSPECTIVE

INTRODUCTION

Isaiah Frank

In 1973, the Japanese economy entered a new and troubled phase marked by tight supplies of energy and raw materials, soaring inflation, a slowdown in growth, a deteriorating balance-of-payments position, and a weakened yen. How long this situation will persist and how it will affect Japan's relations with the United States and the rest of the world remain to be seen. This volume was written, however, against the background of the quite different set of conditions prevailing in the late sixties through 1972—a phenomenal rate of economic growth, comparatively moderate price increases, and mounting balance-of-payments surpluses. Paradoxically, this honeymoon period for the Japanese economy was at the same time the period of severest strain in Japan's economic relations with other countries, particularly the United States.

Many of the problems in Japan's external economic relations stemmed from a combination of three sets of circumstances: an unprecedented rate of economic growth and structural change over a period of two decades that was reflected in a sharp increase in Japan's international competitiveness; a set of Japanese foreign economic policies that became increasingly out of tune with the reality of Japan's economic strength; and an international framework of institutions and rules that proved incapable of inducing the kinds of adjustments that in the end were forced upon Japan.

To describe Japan's growth performance as an economic miracle may be a cliché, but it is hardly an exaggeration. Never in history has any major country even closely approached the sustained rate of increase in gross national product achieved by Japan since the early fifties. U.S. output, for example, increased during this period at a per capita rate of 2.1 percent, a rate that would result in doubling in thirty-three years. At Japan's per capita growth rate of 8.6 percent, however, the increase in thirty-three years would be almost sixteenfold. Prior to Japan's current economic difficulties, the expectations were that the absolute levels of per capita incomes in the two countries would converge early in the eighties.

Economic Growth

How has Japan achieved its unparalleled economic growth? It is not possible to assign numerical weights to the closely interrelated factors involved. But the key ones can be identified as a rapid rate of technological innovation, a high rate of savings and investment, an educated and highly motivated labor force, and a set of government policies explicitly designed to stimulate growth and structural change.

Technology imported from the West, and particularly from the United States, has been basic to Japan's rapid productivity gains in the postwar era. Because the expensive and risky research and development costs were borne by others, Japan was able to acquire this technology cheaply through purchase, licensing arrangements, and technical links with foreign firms. The latter were willing to sell the technology since the marginal costs to them were minimal; at the same time, the option of maximizing returns on the technology through direct foreign investment in Japan generally did not exist because of the consistent opposition of the Japanese government. Much of Japan's own technological effort took the form of ingenious adaptation of imported technology through improvements with quick commercial payoffs.

Closely related to the rapid rate of technological innovation was the extremely high level of fixed capital formation (more than 30 percent of GNP) maintained by Japan during the 1950s and 1960s. Expenditures on new plants and equipment contributed to higher productivity not only by increasing the capital-labor ratio but also by serving as the main vehicle through which new technology was introduced into the production process. High rates of investment were encouraged by the profitability of the new ventures and by the determination of businessmen to maintain their shares in rapidly growing markets. In addition, however, the government provided an environment conducive to investment by making funds available through the banking system at low interest rates and on a priority basis, and through highly favorable tax provisions and depreciation allowances which helped to provide sizable internal sources of funds.

Two features of the Japanese economy are especially noteworthy in explaining how the resources were generated to support the massive scale of productive investment in Japan. One was the low claim on the nation's resources made by the government: Only 19 percent of GNP was taken in the form of taxes as compared to 27 percent for the United States and 35 percent for the United Kingdom. This was reflected in a relatively low rate of expenditure on housing and social infrastructure and, most dramatically, in the low level of defense expenditures. Throughout the postwar period, Japan has relied on the U.S. security umbrella: Its expenditures on defense have amounted to less than 1 percent of GNP as compared to 6 to 9 percent for the United States.

The other factor facilitating a high rate of investment has been a personal savings level of almost 20 percent of disposable income or almost three times that of the United States. To some extent, this high rate of abstention from current consumption may reflect a traditional frugality such as can be seen in the simple austerity of a Japanese home. But certain institutional factors are no doubt also at work. With an underdeveloped social security system and with retirement typically at age fifty-five on small private pensions, the Japanese save voluntarily to provide for their own welfare in sickness and retirement. The large bonus payments in the wage system and the limited availability of consumer credit are additional inducements to save. And there is some evidence of a natural lag between the rate of increase of consumption expenditures and the steep advance in personal incomes.

Also contributing to rapid economic growth have been certain aspects of the Japanese labor force. Well-educated and highly motivated, the Japanese worker is industrious, adaptable, and receptive to change. Technological innovation of the laborsaving variety poses no threat to his job under the lifetime employment system characteristic of many

Japanese firms. Workers tend to identify their welfare with that of the enterprise, loyalty to the firm is strong, and worker organizations have tended to take the form of cooperative enterprise unions. And despite the slowdown in the growth of the total labor force in the sixties, the supply of labor for the expanding manfacturing sector proved ample as Japanese industry was able to call upon a large reservoir of workers from agriculture and other lower-productivity sectors.

The role of the government in Japan's growth process has been a matter of some dispute. The image of a centrally directed "Japan Incorporated" in which the government, in close consultation with business, virtually determines the allocation of resources among productive activities is certainly overdrawn. At the same time, the government did place the highest priority on rapid economic growth and on the expansion of exports, acting as lubricator and stimulator of the process. Its five-year projections have served as targets in guiding business decision making. And in addition to macroeconomic policies aimed at full employment and price stability, it has adopted a coordinated set of microeconomic policies designed to accelerate structural change in favor of promising high-growth sectors. Among the instruments of the Japanese government's 'industrial policy" have been credit allocation, import controls, export incentives, tax provisions, and policies with respect to cartels and industrial concentration.

Until well into the 1960s, the rapid growth of Japan's GNP was not accompanied by a decisively favorable international trade balance. Indeed, in the decade immediately following World War II, the cumulative balance was negative to the extent of almost $3 billion. From 1955 to 1964, the trade balance fluctuated between deficits and surpluses of several hundred million dollars while Japan's international reserves varied around an average of about $2 billion. It was not until the mid-1960s that it became apparent that Japan's international competitive position had greatly strengthened across a broad range of industrial products and that the country had unequivocally moved into the position of structural surplus on trade account.

This shift in Japan's external economic position came about despite a rate of inflation through the 1960s substantially higher than that of the United States or other industrial countries. How could Japan's international competitiveness improve in the face of prices that were rising faster than those of her trading partners? The answer lies in the differences in the behavior of the consumer price index on the one hand and the wholesale price index on the other. While the consumer price index is the conventional measure of inflation, the wholesale price index is the more relevant for comparisons of international competitiveness.

Until 1972, industrial countries tended to show more rapid long-term rates of increase in the consumer price index than in the wholesale price index. The reason is that the former is heavily weighted with services, including distribution services at the various stages of delivering the product to the consumer. On the whole, these services are labor-intensive and show a slower growth in productivity than manufacturing. They are also by and large nontraded and therefore sheltered from the cost-reducing effects of international competition.

In the case of Japan, the gap between the movement of the consumer price index and the wholesale price index was greater than in any other industrial country. While consumer prices rose faster for Japan than for its trading partners, wholesale prices lagged behind those of other countries; in fact, they did not increase at all during the period 1955–1965. The excellent performance of Japan's wholesale price index until 1972 was due in large part to the very rapid rise in labor productivity in manufacturing, particularly in the high-growth industries (e.g., steel, chemicals, shipbuilding, autos, electronics), which made it possible for wages to increase by about 13 percent per year with only minimal effects on costs. Additional factors were the stability of the prices of imported raw materials and the effectiveness of monetary policy in restraining demand when the economy became overheated.

In Japan, we find a dual structure in which highly efficient, rapidly growing, large-scale enterprises have coexisted with low-productivity, slowly growing, small-scale production units, the latter concentrated not only in services and agriculture but in certain branches of manufacturing as well, such as clothing and food processing. From the standpoint of the international competitiveness of Japanese industry, one of the interesting aspects of the dual structure is the limited extent to which the rising standard of wages in high-growth industries forced up wages in the lagging sectors, at least until the mid-sixties. To a large extent, the wage gap reflected the redundancy of the supply of labor in the low-productivity sectors. Undoubtedly, the lifetime employment system and the docility of Japanese trade unions also had something to do with this phenomenon. Whatever the reasons for the wage differential, however, it served to restrain cost and price increases in the low-productivity, import-competing sectors, thereby providing Japan with a natural resistance to imports.

In sum, Japan's quick expansion of exports of manufactured products and its resistance to imports can be largely explained in terms of market forces underlying the price behavior of Japanese goods under conditions of rapid economic growth. Even without explicit government export aids and import restrictions, Japan would probably have emerged as a trade-surplus country by the mid-sixties. And the heavy concentration of her rapidly expanding exports in particular products of increasing sophistication (e.g., from textiles to steel to electronics) would in any event have had disruptive effects, particularly in the United States, which constituted overwhelmingly the largest single market for Japanese goods. After 1965, the competitive position of Japanese goods in the U.S. market received an additional boost from the American inflation associated with the war in Vietnam.

International Framework

As the force of Japanese competition made itself felt in one product after another, American business reacted sharply. Until the end of the sixties, however, its complaints tended to center not so much on the general change in underlying price and cost relationships between the two countries, suggesting that the yen was undervalued, but rather on certain features of Japanese economic policy and organization, including the government-business relationship, that together added up to a charge of unfair competition. In other words, American business tended to see its problems largely in microeconomic rather than macroeconomic terms.

The complaints of unfair competition often failed to distinguish among three sets of conditions: explicit government restrictions on imports and incentives to exports; the more general close relationship between government and business, including industrial policy and administrative guidance; and certain inherent features of Japanese economic organization, such as the financial structure of business or the internal distribution system, that were believed to encourage excessive exports or restrain foreign access to the Japanese domestic market.

Throughout the fifties and sixties, Japan maintained a complex apparatus of export incentives and restrictions. At various times, export incentives took the form of tax concessions on export income or sales, liberal depreciation allowances for exports, liberal write-offs for the expenses of export development, preferential credit terms, and comprehensive government export insurance. The most important of these was the system established in 1953 that exempted from income tax substantial proportions of export income or sales. By 1964, this incentive was terminated, and by the end of 1972 virtually all export incentives had been eliminated. Even in their heyday, however, the total impact of export-related tax incentives was quite small compared to other developments including structural changes and rapid productivity increases in Japanese industry.

Japan's import policy remained basically protectionist well beyond 1963 when the government acknowledged that its quantitative restrictions could no longer be justified under the General Agreement on Tariffs and Trade (GATT) on balance-of-payments grounds. Although substantial reductions in nominal tariffs resulted from the Kennedy Round, effective rates of protection remained high, particularly on consumer manufactured goods, because of the sharp escalation of tariffs from the raw material to higher processing stages. Moreover, few significant steps toward the removal of quotas were taken until late in the sixties and then only in response to heavy pressure from the United States. While trade liberalization proceeded rapidly beginning in 1969, the lag in the removal of import quotas in the face of a rapidly strengthening international competitive position accentuated the tensions associated with Japan's dramatic export penetration of the U.S. market for manufactured goods.

To the extent that Japan's import barriers and export incentives were overt, her trading partners could at least invoke specific GATT provisions with respect to quantitative restrictions and export subsidies. Much more frustrating were the various other forms of Japanese government support for particular industries that fell outside the scope of GATT commitments. Among these nontariff distortions were the allocation of cheap credit for industrial expansion through the government's administrative guidance to the commercial banks and government sanction for various types of cartel arrangements. The latter included arrangements to curtail competition and maintain prices in the domestic market during periods of slack home demand, thereby facilitating sales abroad at lower prices.

While supply-oriented exports were encouraged by government sanction of cartel practices, much of the pressure for expanding sales abroad during domestic recessions arose from two elements of fixed cost inherent in Japanese industry. Because investment is financed chiefly by loans rather than equity capital, Japanese firms generally carry a high fixed interest cost. In addition, a high fixed labor cost results from the lifetime employment system. These overhead costs have generated tremendous pressure to push products out of the sluggish domestic market so long as variable expenses are covered and some contribution made toward fixed costs.

The institutional stimuli to exports had their counterpart in inhibiting factors on the import side. The archaic and fragmented internal Japanese distribution system acted as a deterrent to potential American exporters even after formal import liberalization had taken place. And more specifically, the sole-agent system conveyed monopoly import privileges to trading companies acting as agents for foreign suppliers. Such companies, commonly linked to large domestic conglomerates, imposed their private quota decisions on imports.

Monetary Issues

While institutional factors and specific government policies contributed to Japan's rising trade- and current-account surpluses, they were hardly the crucial elements. It was becoming increasingly apparent by 1970 that the basic problem was more pervasive, namely, the undervaluation of the yen. Nevertheless, the government resisted pressure for revaluation and sought desperately to meet the problem through a variety of ad hoc measures. In June 1971, the Japanese adopted a plan entitled Eight Items of Urgent Policy Measures to Avoid Yen Revaluation. Included in the plan were unilateral tariff cuts, further quota liberalization, enlargement of the preferential tariff scheme for imports from developing countries, orderly marketing of exports, and promotion of the export of capital.

By the time this plan was announced, however, the Canadian, German, Dutch, and Swiss currencies had floated upward, accentuating further the yen's undervaluation. It was only after the "Nixon shock" of August 15, 1971—suspending the convertibility of the dollar into gold and imposing a 10 percent import surcharge—that the yen was forced to float. Following several months of floating, the yen was revalued by 17 percent against the dollar in December 1971 as part of a general currency realignment.

The 1971 exchange rate correction was not only long delayed; it also proved inadequate. Despite another series of ad hoc measures adopted in 1972 to restrain exports and promote imports, the surplus on current account rose steadily. By the end of 1972, Japan's foreign-exchange reserves had swollen to more than $18 billion (as compared to less than $5 billion two years earlier) as the Bank of Japan tried to defend the new yen rate of 308 to the dollar. As speculation against the dollar mounted, the United States announced in February 1973 a further devaluation of the dollar, and Japan allowed the yen to float to 265, a rate which amounted to a further 15 percent revaluation against the dollar.

The combination of Japan's rigid exchange rate policy until 1971 and its long delay in eliminating quantitative trade restrictions and tight controls on the movement of long-term capital proved to be extremely disturbing elements to the world economy. They lent strength to protectionist policies in Western Europe as well as in the United States, often in the guise of orderly marketing arrangements or "voluntary" export controls by Japan. At the same time, however, they contributed to the growing consensus that the postwar monetary and trading systems needed fundamental overhauling if they were to respond to the new realities of the 1970s.

The world of the 1970s differs from the world of Bretton Woods and Havana in at least three fundamental respects: the radical shift in the relative economic positions of the United States, Japan, and the countries of the European Community; the much higher degree of integration among the economies of the industrial world; and the greater responsibility assumed by nation states for the welfare of their citizens. Each of these changes has generated severe tensions in international relations and has profound implications for the nature and management of the international economic system.

Despite the attenuation of its relative economic power, the dollar continued at the center of the world monetary system at least until 1971, and the United States has continued to assert its leadership forcefully in international affairs. The Nixon shocks of 1971 are examples of the exercise of U.S. initiatives which were deeply resented in Japan, more for their unilateral character than for their substance. At the same time, the international economic policies of Japan and the European Community have been viewed by the United States as reflecting parochial conceptions of self-interest, ill befitting major economic powers which by now should be assuming substantial responsibility for world economic order. European and Japanese reactions to the oil crisis are regarded as but the latest example of this inward orientation.

Need for Basic Reforms in Economic Relations

More fundamental is the set of problems flowing from the high degree of integration that has been achieved among the economies of the noncommunist industrial states. As a consequence of the revolution in transport and communications, the steady erosion of government barriers to international trade, the emergence of a world market for liquid funds, and the enhanced role of the multinational corporations, national economies have become much more interdependent, yielding enormous benefits to all in terms of a more efficient use of the world's resources. But the concomitant high degree of exposure of nation states to external economic forces has tended to accentuate two types of adjustment problems. The first is the macroeconomic problem of how the general level of costs and prices in one country can be kept in line with that of others so that a country can, over time, maintain equilibrium in its balance of payments. The second is the microeconomic problem of how individual countries accommodate to the shifting international competitiveness of particular industries within each country. Most of the economic conflicts with Japan of the past decade have been instances of one or the other of these problems of adjustment.

Finally, governments in highly industrialized societies are increasingly intervening in domestic processes for purposes going beyond the traditional goals of high employment, price stability, and economic growth. More and more, governments are taking on responsibility for additional social and economic objectives including an improved environment, more equitable distribution of income, reduction of regional disparities in growth, and the encouragement of technology-intensive industrial development. More extensive government economic intervention at home has important consequences for foreign trade which must be reconciled internationally if the benefits of an open trading system are to be realized.

Taken together, these changes in the economic environment imply the need for some basic reforms in the rules and institutions that have governed economic relations among the noncommunist states since the end of World War II. Although sharp divergences remain as to the specifics of the reforms, a broad consensus exists among the United States, Japan, and Western Europe with respect to its essentials.

On the monetary side, the most urgent change—greater exchange rate flexibility—has already been accomplished de facto. With the floating of the world's major currencies, the burden of balance-of-payments adjustment is increasingly being borne by the exchange rate mechanism, with a lesser need to resort to trade and capital controls on the one hand or extreme domestic deflation or inflation on the other. But the floating regime is a managed one and therefore likely to be sustainable only if the major economic powers can agree on a set of principles or rules for official intervention in the exchange markets. Without such an agreement, countries may attempt to use the exchange rate mechanism as a means of exporting their domestic problems of unemployment or inflation through competitive depreciation or appreciation of their currencies.

Another objective of monetary reform on which there is broad agreement is the reduction in the role of the dollar as a reserve asset in order to impose upon the United States the same discipline to which other countries are subject in balancing their external accounts. The recent strengthening of the dollar in the wake of the oil crisis is likely to make the attainment of this objective, however, even more elusive than before.

Trade

On the trade side, three major problems need to be confronted: nontariff distortions to trade; safeguards against market disruption; and the problem of worldwide scarcity or surplus of basic commodities. Japan's stake in how these problems are resolved internationally is at least as great as that of any other major country.

Nontariff distortions comprehend not only intentional protective devices such as import quotas but many other government actions directed to perfectly legitimate social objectives which may have unintended distorting effects on trade. Examples are health and safety regulations, assistance for the economic development of backward regions, and environmental controls financed in ways that do not reflect the cost of the controls in the price of the product. As Japan shifts its priorities away from rapid economic growth toward greater concern with the quality of life, the government will increasingly be involved in activities of this type and will have a major interest in international efforts to minimize their distorting effects on trade. As part of this endeavor, an attempt will also need to be made to cope with informal nontariff distortions, such as those resulting from the Japanese government's "administrative guidance" to domestic firms.

Safeguards against market disruption take on particular importance as further advances are made in trade liberalization. The resulting changes in the flow and composition of trade entail structural shifts in the composition of output which can have profound effects on workers and firms in particular industries and localities. In recent years, the pace of structural change has accelerated not only because barriers to the international movement of goods have progressively been removed but also because productive factors, including capital, technology, and skills, move more freely across political boundaries, often through the vehicle of the multinational corporation. Safeguards would permit governments to impose temporary protection as a means of facilitating structural change and alleviating its social consequences. In the past, such protection has typically been imposed unilaterally, often taking the form of voluntary export controls or orderly marketing arrangements in the case of Japan. The object of an international negotiation would be to establish multilaterally agreed criteria, procedures, and surveillance with respect to the use of safeguards and to ensure that resort to such mechanisms is of brief duration.

The third problem concerns the availability and price of basic raw materials. As a country almost totally dependent on foreign sources for energy and raw materials, Japan has always been preoccupied with this subject. But the issue was dramatized in 1973 when the United States unilaterally imposed temporary controls on the export of soybeans and later, more profoundly, when the Arab oil producers reduced their shipments and announced a fourfold price increase within a period of three months. These two events have had an even more traumatic effect on Japan than the Nixon shocks of 1971.

In its acute form, the problem of energy and materials scarcity came on so suddenly that it was not even on the agenda when the present negotiations on trade and monetary reform were launched. Nor do any international rules or institutions exist which seriously address the relevant issues or even provide an agreed framework within which to deal with them. Yet the international economic and financial repercussions of the oil crisis are so profound and far-reaching that some cooperative international approach has become necessary to deal with the supply and payments consequences of the new situation in the world oil market.

Of all the industrial countries, Japan has the greatest stake in a smoothly functioning international economic system subject to agreed norms and rules. Its dependence on foreigners for the necessities of life is greater than that of any other major industrial country. And it still suffers from a legacy of discriminatory trade restrictions in many parts of the world. Moreover, the worldwide phenomenon of inflation has struck Japan with particular force. At the beginning of 1974, its wholesale price index stood 30 percent higher than a year earlier, and the Tokyo consumer price index was up 17 percent. As put by Finance Minister Takeo Fukuda, Japan is "engulfed in a flame of extraordinary price spirals, to which the oil problem is adding fuel." How the oil problem is managed internationally will be a test of the capacity of the United States, Japan, and Western Europe to act cooperatively on the broad range of their common interests.

Understanding the Japanese Economy

Closer and more far-reaching cooperation among the United States, Western Europe, and Japan requires in the first instance a mutual understanding of how the economy of each of the partners functions. In this respect, the situation is asymmetrical. While many Japanese appear to have a lively familiarity with economic institutions and policies in the West, the reverse is hardly the case. This volume is intended to help rectify this imbalance by illuminating a number of aspects of the Japanese economy that affect its external relations in a major way.

Japan's postwar economic capabilities and policies have been heavily conditioned by the low claim on its resources for purposes of national defense. Never in history has a major economic power existed with such a minor military establishment. In the first chapter, Donald C. Hellmann examines the prospects for a continuation of this anomalous situation in the light of the changing American security role in Asia and the rapidly expanding Japanese links with the rest of Asia through trade, aid, and foreign investment.

Industrial policy in Japan consists essentially of a set of microeconomic measures to encourage structural change and development along predetermined lines in contrast to macroeconomic policy aimed at full employment and price stability. William V. Rapp describes the evolution of the government's industrial policy from its priority on rapid growth by promoting industrial investment and exports to greater emphasis on the provision of social overhead and improving the quality of life. Rapp explains why the government is likely to encounter greater difficulties and increased tensions as it attempts to translate the new goals into a concrete set of policy measures.

Kozo Yamamura presents a critical examination of Japanese policy on cartels and industrial concentration during the period 1960–1972. Yamamura places special emphasis on the harmful effects at home and abroad of government sanction or encouragement to mergers and collusive practices which shielded Japanese firms from domestic competition in order to strengthen their competitive ability in foreign markets. As Japan's trade position moved into increasing surplus, such policies accentuated the imbalance and contributed to a heightening of international tensions.

The Japanese distribution system is often cited as contributing, on the one hand, to the difficulties experienced by foreign manufacturers in attempting to penetrate the Japanese market and, on the other hand, to the success of Japanese manufacturers in selling abroad. In analyzing the system, C. Tait Ratcliffe explores the relationship between fragmentation in production and retailing and the length of the distribution chain. He also pays particular attention to the multifaceted role of the Japanese trading company as a unique institution combining the functions of selling, finance and risk absorption, and organizing overseas projects.

Japanese agriculture has been deeply transformed in the last two decades. Haruhiro Fukui describes the recent changes and explores their relationship to agricultural policies and to the structure and style of farmers' political activities. Special attention is given to the traditional identification of rural interests with the Liberal Democratic Party.

Leon Hollerman analyzes the relationship between Japan's economic structure, her export-oriented growth, and her international position during the transition from a balance-of-payments deficit to a surplus country. In discussing the sources of Japan's competitive power, particular attention is given to government policy, the phenomenon of supply-oriented exports, and the role of trading companies. Hollerman also reviews traditional Japanese import policy as well as the various methods adopted to deal with the payments surplus in the period 1968–1972, including the revaluation of the yen and the promotion of Japanese investment abroad.

What was the scope and significance of the various forms of export-related tax incentives in stimulating Japan's export growth? Yoichi Okita describes the different systems and attempts quantitatively to evaluate their importance. He concludes that none of the individual measures seems to have had a great significance, although the system as a whole did have some impact. The high rate of increase of exports was more the consequence of the structure and pace of industrial development than a result of export subsidies. In Okita's view, monetary policy played a larger role than fiscal policy in the government's contribution to Japan's export success.

Jacob Kaplan's chapter on raw-materials policy assesses the position of Japan and the United States with respect to the adequacy of material supplies and identifies the principal policy issues in this field. Among the areas of collaboration suggested are: intergovernmental study groups to develop a common view of the market outlook for each major raw material; coordination of materials policies; international agreements to facilitate expanded production abroad; better use of multinational institutions to facilitate the expansion of materials production in developing countries; and a joint approach to the energy problem, including concerted efforts to develop alternative sources and standby arrangements for allocating available supplies.

The emergence of Japanese firms in recent years as major investors in other countries has added a new element to the world economy. M. Y. Yoshino examines the outward flow of Japanese capital and the different roles played in the Japanese economy by foreign investment in basic materials and in manufacturing. Japanese investment in the exploration and development of natural resources abroad reflects a deep concern with the vulnerability of continued reliance on foreign-controlled sources. Direct investment in manufacturing is motivated by a desire to offset the loss of export markets and to take advantage of the cheap labor supplies in developing countries. But the ability of Japan to realize projected rapid increases in foreign investment will depend on the ability of Japanese management to adapt more smoothly to conditions abroad and to overcome the serious difficulties already being experienced in a number of host countries.

In the final chapter, Yoshino discusses Japan as host to the international corporation. The various phases of postwar government policy on inward foreign investment are reviewed, from the tight restrictions of the early period to the sweeping fifth liberalization put into effect in 1973. Although the progressive removal of restrictions was strongly influenced by external pressures, particularly from the United States, the ultimate decisions reflected a redefinition of Japan's national interest by its own leaders.

The background papers included in this volume were of great benefit to the Committee for Economic Development in formulating its joint policy statement with Keizai Doyukai on the reform of the international economic system. The papers deal with subjects that have aroused serious controversy in U.S.–Japanese relations and, at times, strong passions. While the authors have tried to lay out the issues fairly, they have not been asked to be neutral. The only requirement was that they shed light on an aspect of Japanese policy critical to the economic relations between the two countries. This they have admirably succeeded in doing.

1.

CHANGING AMERICAN AND JAPANESE
SECURITY ROLES IN ASIA:
Economic Implications

Donald C. Hellmann

IT IS DOUBTFUL THAT THE CLOSE and comprehensive security alliance between Japan and the United States can endure in the new era of international politics now dawning in East Asia. The Nixon Doctrine and related moves toward diplomatic recognition of the People's Republic of China signal a fundamental change in American policy and an end to a pattern of international relations that has prevailed for a quarter of a century. In the future, the U.S. military role in Asia will be greatly reduced, the criteria for intervention will purposefully remain indeterminate, and conventional defense responsibilities will increasingly devolve upon the East Asian states themselves. U.S. retrenchment in the region, no matter what its ultimate form, challenges the very foundation of Japan's postwar security policy, which has depended to an extraordinary extent on the American alliance. Barring the sudden emergence of a new and stable regional power balance or the establishment of permanent peace, these changes in U.S. policy will ultimately force the Japanese to confront the internally divisive issues of broadened security goals and expanded defense capabilities. Because there tends to be a direct connection between alliances among states and the structure of the international economy, the way in which the two nations approach new strategic roles in Asia is important not only to the creation of a stable East Asian power balance but also to the establishment of viable new international economic relationships on both regional and global levels.

This chapter will focus on the economic implications of the security dilemmas facing Washington and Tokyo. This approach emphasizes the need to reconsider bilateral and regional foreign policies. Government and business leaders of both the United States and Japan have tended to misperceive or even to deny the integral ties between economic and political-military policies, thereby serving, as it were, as diligent tailors to a naked emperor. Continued failure to appreciate fully the direct relationship between economic and security matters will impede efforts to build a new alliance suited to the realities of the current international situation.

Postwar Security Relations

Since 1945, the basic security aims of Japan have been effectively established by the United States. The roots of this policy grew out of the special aims and conditions of the Occupation period (1945–1952) and the general efforts of the United States to contain communism throughout East Asia. The Occupation provided a singularly favorable occasion for implementing policies designed to bring about a transformation of Japanese international behavior in keeping with the Wilsonian vision of democracy and peace on behalf of which World War II had been fought. This experience placed bilateral relations on a uniquely close and comprehensive plane and established the ideals on which Japan's foreign policy still rests. As the cold war developed, Japan was brought into the global security bloc and the international economic system created under American leadership in response to the communist challenge. A broad review of the actual security arrangements will serve as a helpful preface to understanding the changed nature of the current strategic situation and the relevance of bilateral economic conflict.

The Occupation. In the initial efforts by the American Occupation authorities to demilitarize and democratize the country, not only were the Japanese military forces completely dismantled, but Article

Nine of the new constitution (drafted by the United States) renounced "war as the sovereign right of the nation and the threat or use of force in settling international disputes." This utopian gesture, giving unprecedented legal sanction and symbolic dignity to pacifism, was seen at the time as a realistic aim by its principal architect, General Douglas MacArthur, who grandly announced, "Japan today understands as thoroughly as any nation that war does not pay. Her spiritual revolution has probably been the greatest the world has known."[1] Concrete actions were taken to ensure that this spiritual rebirth was not transitory. In keeping with the reformist zeal characteristic of the early years of the Occupation and with the Wilsonian notion that defects in the internal political structure of states are the basic cause of war, a full-scale democratization of economic and social as well as governmental institutions was undertaken in ways that were "deemed likely to stress the peaceful disposition of the Japanese people."[2] Thus, from the beginning, the Japanese-American alliance was placed on a unique level, standing as a kind of test of the most basic beliefs in the American diplomatic tradition. This has given a peculiarly paternalistic and moral cast to U.S. relations with Japan, which are not unlike America's relations with China in the years prior to the triumph of the communists. Any future economic conflicts with the Japanese will be colored by this posture, which has an inherent potential for rigidity and sanctimonious overreaction that has on occasion characterized U.S. cold war policies.

Moreover, the pacifist idealism of Article Nine continues to be a potent force in Japanese politics and will affect any effort by Japan to play an expanded security role in Asia. Although it is doubtful that the Japanese people have become resocialized as pacifists or have developed a permanent nuclear allergy, the peace clause has become the most dramatic symbol of the postwar constitution. Furthermore, the left-wing parties have given concrete political meaning to this issue by making it the main slogan of their attacks on the American security alliance and all government programs for defense. Consequently, any major move toward rearmament or even overt acceptance of the principle of realpolitik would precipitate a bitter internal struggle that would implicate the very foundations of the postwar political order. The emotional and political legacies of Article Nine stand as major impediments to a controlled, pragmatic decision on behalf of a significantly expanded defense policy.

Security alliance. The ink had scarcely dried on the new constitution when a series of international events, which grew out of the global cold war, led to an abrupt reversal of the reformist policies of the early Occupation period. From the outset, specific American security arrangements regarding Japan had been cast, not simply in bilateral terms, but in terms of the broader American goal of meeting the general threat of communist expansion in Asia. The triumph of the communists in China and the outbreak of the Korean War led to policies that treated Japan as a major and essential ally, not as a primary threat to regional peace.

Because of the sudden expansion of U.S. security interest in a strong Japan, two new policies were initiated: one military, the other economic. A cautious step forward toward rearmament was made with the establishment of a small "police reserve" (later the Self-Defense Forces). At the same time, a major effort paralleling the Marshall Plan was launched to hasten the country's economic rehabilitation.[3] The integral relationship between American security policy in Japan and general strategy in Asia was clearly manifested in the 1952 peace treaty, in which the central objective was, not settling issues related to the Pacific war, but securing an alliance with Japan in order to check the spread of communism in Asia.[4] Moreover, the American-Japanese Mutual Security Treaty (and the accompanying Administrative Agreement), which was made effective simultaneously with the peace treaty, emphasized use of the substantial American forces deployed in Japan in any way that Washington felt would "contribute to the maintenance of international peace and security in the Far East." Thus, Japan returned to international politics a passive and dependent partner in an alliance created by the United States, totally committed to and dependent on the Western bloc.

The security treaty was revised in 1960 before the Sino-Soviet split and was again predicated on cold war assumptions that the communist monolith posed the security threat in Asia and that the United States bore the full responsibility of meeting and containing that threat. Despite some basic concessions, especially the agreement to prior consultation with Tokyo regarding combat deployment of Japan-based American troops, Japan remained a military protectorate of the United States and a critical cog in the general American military posture in the Far East. However, rapid and dramatic changes in the strategic realities in East Asia in the 1960s—changes centering on China's development of nuclear weapons and the escalation of the Vietnam War —led the United States to prod Japan into fuller participation in the region's international affairs. On the most general level, the aim was to move Japan into a leadership role in Asian economics and, to a lesser extent, in political affairs under a one-sided military partnership featuring an American nuclear umbrella. This policy assumed that the United States would continue to remain deeply engaged militarily in the region on both nuclear and conventional levels, that there was and would continue to be a basic identity of Japanese and American security interests, and that the economic and political dimensions of policy could be effectively separated from the security dimension. All these assumptions are now being subjected to serious challenges.

The war in Vietnam ultimately forced basic changes in America's strategic policies toward Asia and the world. The enormous U.S. military and political investments in escalating the war, an extreme extension of cold war globalism, created the kind of implausibly exorbitant commitment to Asian security implied in U.S. policies toward Japan during the 1960s. This prolonged Japan's withdrawal from all concerns of realpolitik and allowed the measured but steady expansion of Japan's own conventional forces to occur free from any tangible security threats. The stalemate in the war demonstrated that the United States lacked the capacity effectively to control conflict in the region, shattered the bipartisan internationalist consensus on American foreign policy, and made any military ventures in East Asia in the near future singularly improbable. Thus, Vietnam at once ensured the short-term success of U.S. policy toward Japan and demonstrated the long-term infeasibility of America's general Asian policy of serving as a policeman in conflicts in the region.

In the shadow of the comprehensive U.S. strategic commitments in East Asia throughout the 1960s, it is not surprising that Japan's security policy assumed a rather stunted and distorted form. Security has been defined in the narrow sense of preserving territorial integrity, and government defense measures have been aimed, first, at maintaining *internal* order and, second, at supplementing American forces to cope with a conventional invasion, a contingency that has been singularly implausible since the early 1950s. Appropriations for the Self-Defense Forces have steadily grown, but their increase has been determined essentially by budgetary criteria rather than by strategic objectives. Moreover, the level of expenditure (less than 1 percent of GNP) remains completely out of line with levels in all other industrial powers. Although the Japanese have in fact become the leading economic force in East Asia and have highly vulnerable shipping lines to critical resources, they have steadfastly refused to dispatch forces abroad or even to acknowledge the need for an overseas security role. Up to now, there has been no linkage between overseas economic interests and military capabilities. The pressures for this strategic option cannot but grow in the future, and there are no real technical or material barriers to the development of a military force (including nuclear arms) adequate to defend Japan's growing foreign interests in the region.

Japan's approach to the issue of security has been that of an expanding international trading company, not that of a nation-state. Japanese international activities have concentrated on maximizing national economic well-being, and all matters of power politics have been scrupulously avoided. In view of the scope and intensity of American military involvement in East Asia and the salutary international economic relations that have prevailed among the Western industrial powers during the past two decades, this policy posture was highly appropriate. However, the uniquely favorable international conditions that permitted this unusual role collapsed with the American recognition of a multipolar world political order and the end of the postwar international monetary system. Tokyo must now devise a new formula that will be appropriate to different and still fluid circumstances in the areas of international economic policy and political-military strategy.

Two major barriers stand in the way of appropriate new Japanese policies: (1) the demonstrated inability of the postwar governments to make major foreign policy decisions in which political considerations are central and (2) the difficulties inherent in establishing a domestic consensus linking security and international economic policy. Contrary to popular wisdom and to the remarkable achievements of Japan in establishing a flexible and effective economic foreign policy, the Japanese have played a passive role in international politics. Serious domestic political conflict has accompanied those few decisions that external events led the government to make (e.g., normalization of relations with the Soviet Union, South Korea, and the People's Republic of

China and extension of the American Security Treaty). This passivity is due partly to the fragmented structure of the ruling conservative party and a style of decision making that inhibits bold leadership and partly to the absence of a national consensus (which would include the opposition parties) on the basic goals of the country's foreign policy.[5] The essentially immobilist character of the process by which Japan makes foreign policy decisions will impede the formulation of any new strategic policy and will leave substantial latitude for American influence in shaping the direction of any such policy.

An equally serious block in the way of any major new Japanese political-military policies is the rationale for the trading-company approach, which has a deep-seated legitimacy within Japanese political and business worlds. According to the vision of global affairs that still prevails in Japan, economics and politics are seen as separable, and armaments and realpolitik are not believed to be critical to a successful foreign policy. Instead, the augmentation of international trade is seen as the primary guarantor of peace.

The substitution of commercial for political relations between states is not a novel concept. It was most fully developed by nineteenth-century economic liberals, especially Richard Cobden,[6] but it has also long been a conspicuous part of the American liberal ideal of world order, an ideal promoted during the U.S. occupation of Japan.[7] Thus, no matter how compelling the external events (e.g., American pressure and Chinese competition) for Japanese rearmament and/or participation in international politics, there will be powerful resistance from within Japan to any change. The transition from the security policy of a trading company to that of a nation will mean all the substantial domestic political traumas and uncertainties that are involved when any nation abandons the values of one diplomatic tradition and establishes a radically new foreign policy consensus. As the meaning of the Nixon Doctrine has unfolded over the past two years, the seeming imperative for a broadened military role that is implicit in the vision of a competitive multipolar world has proved such a distasteful challenge that the Japanese government has self-consciously sought to avoid directly confronting the issue.

Nixon Doctrine and Japan. The Nixon Doctrine, the first fundamental reordering of American foreign policy priorities since the onset of the cold war, rests on a vision in which Japan has a conspicuously expanded but highly uncertain place as one of the world's five major powers. This doctrine, like the containment strategy it replaces, had its initial impetus in changes that occurred in the high politics of political-military affairs. Progress in strategic arms limitation with the Soviet Union, the opening of channels of communication with the People's Republic of China, and the laying of a basis for reduced American military involvement in the Third World have been the most visible and most important items in establishing an American posture suited to the needs of a multipolar world. However, there is an economic dimension to this policy that is essential to its successful implementation. The economic position of the United States has changed greatly since the late 1940s, when the containment strategy was initiated. Today, the United States faces an uncertain and highly competitive international economic situation. Washington is struggling with a host of problems, including structuring a new international monetary system, coping with serious and seemingly chronic balance-of-payments deficits, and meeting mounting domestic pressures (especially from labor) for trade policies that are nationally assertive, if not protectionist. Japan has emerged as the primary economic target of concern and competition for the United States in ways that inevitably touch the security relationship of the two nations. Indeed, the success of American diplomacy in Asia in the years immediately ahead depends to a great extent on how Japanese-American economic and strategic interests are kept in proper balance.

The full strategic meaning of the Nixon Doctrine for Japan and Asia is still unfolding, but several fundamental points of departure from past policy will shape the future pattern of development no matter what the short-term exigencies. First, in the new multipolar global order, the United States will not intervene militarily to "contain communism," as it did in the past two decades. Despite the affirmation that existing alliances will be honored, the President has made it clear that "we are not involved in the world because we have commitments; we have commitments because we are involved. Our interest must shape our commitments, rather than the other way around."[8] Thus, the certitude of the containment era has been replaced by conditions of what has been aptly labeled *indeterminacy*.[9] Secondly, under the new concept of "realistic deterrence," there is a notable shift from the globalist ideals of cold war policy to an emphasis on more narrowly defined national security interests and a concomitant assumption that East Asian nations can and will assume fuller responsibility for their own defense. Finally, there is a clear expectation that a stable new international order (a "generation of peace") will be created in the region through policies stressing diplomatic maneuver with the other great powers rather than through the far-flung alliances and direct U.S. military intervention that characterized the "era of confrontation."[10]

America's new economic policy, which in Asia is directed primarily toward Japan, displays changes paralleling those in the area of strategic policy. There has been an implicit shift toward concentrating on national interests rather than attempting to play the pivotal role for the economic well-being of the entire noncommunist world. Basic to this change is the fact that the government is responding more fully to domestic economic and political pressures that are increasingly geared to the protection of American industries, to the restriction of overseas investment, and to the confrontation of the problems of unemployment and social welfare. Moreover, the country now lacks the resources to retain its preeminent economic position in the Western world, just as it no longer has capabilities to play global gendarme. Until the late 1960s, the United States saw economic relations with Japan basically in terms of providing aid and markets to strengthen an ally and bring her into the club of industrialized noncommunist nations. Today, however, the United States regards Japan as a major economic competitor against whom pressures must be brought to rectify serious bilateral (and global) trade and monetary imbalances. Thus, the United States is assuming a competitive economic position vis-à-vis Japan at the same time that Tokyo is expected to take a more independent international political stand befitting a great power. Implementation of the Nixon Doctrine cannot but severely test the Japanese-American alliance, a fact that was readily apparent in the repercussions of recent bilateral economic problems on the security relationship of the two countries.

Bilateral Economic Relations and Security

The meaning of the Japanese-American Mutual Security Treaty hinges on the broader alliance, encompassing massive and close economic ties, between the two countries. Until the 1960s, America's economic policy toward Japan was essentially a function of strategic commitments in East Asia and a broader political-military stance in the world. This is no longer the case. The initial pronouncement of the Nixon Doctrine indicated a shift in American strategic priorities, and subsequent changes in international economic policy (including devaluation of the dollar) signaled that the United States could no longer subordinate economic concerns to security questions. Moreover, the timing of these changes exaggerated their importance for Japanese-American relations. At the very moment when a calculated U.S. challenge to the strategic assumptions of the cold war (most notably, the presidential decision to visit Peking) caught Tokyo by surprise, bilateral economic relations deteriorated with unexpected suddenness as a result of a host of problems associated with the enormous and seemingly chronic American trade deficit with Japan. Although the security issue has thus far remained in the background, the recurring conflicts over trade have taken on an increasingly political coloration. Domestic pressures within each nation have made compromise on economic matters increasingly difficult and have altered the mood in which the alliance itself has been approached. Consequently, economics and politics have become integrally related as a result of internal and international pressures beyond the easy control of leaders in both countries.

For Japan, the question is not really which economic issue at what time will force reconsideration of the security relationship with the United States. More basically, it is whether, in the context of a multipolar world, economic matters can be kept wholly separate from political-security matters. The Japanese government and business community will try to maintain this separation as long as possible, partly because of a generally pro-American orientation and partly because of enormous dependence on the United States for defense as well as for trade. However, a variety of domestic political factors will make this increasingly difficult. Above all, it is quixotic to expect Japanese governmental leaders to implement policies that draw fine distinctions between the political and economic aspects of the relationship when no consensus exists within the country regarding fundamental principles and priorities of a foreign policy appropriate to the new international setting. The uncertainties and fluidity of the external environment make the formation of such a consensus difficult, as does the diffuse process of foreign-policy making that virtually proscribes the emergence of the adroit leadership necessary for subtle diplomatic maneuver.[11] Moreover, despite close ties with the business world, the Japanese prime minister does not in fact have a free hand to bring policies of specific industries into line with political imperatives of foreign policy. This limitation was graphically illustrated in the recent prolonged textile dispute, in which Prime Minister Sato tried unsuccessfully for eighteen months to convince Japanese textile interests to accept the restrictive quota system that he had personally pledged to President Nixon at the conference that established the conditions for the reversion of Okinawa to Japan. America and all aspects of the Japanese-American relationship already have a salience within Japan that necessarily carries profound political and psychological implications.[12] In part, this is due to the sheer dominance of the American presence. However, the obsessively critical concern of the mass media and the opposition parties with all aspects of U.S. policies has heightened the intensity and narrowed the focus of the domestic foreign policy debate, so that a kind of bilateral myopia regarding the United States now prevails. Correspondingly, recent American efforts to redress the bilateral trade balance and to force revaluation of the yen have given rise to nationalistic responses from all strata of Japanese society. The line between economic nationalism and political nationalism will prove increasingly difficult to draw and to maintain in Japan in the next decade when the ruling party will be more and more hard-pressed to maintain its ascendancy. Consequently, to suppose in these circumstances that economic rationality alone will be the governing force in establishing a viable bilateral relationship is to disregard the influence of the Japanese domestic political system.

With one fundamental deviation, striking parallels do appear in the circumstances currently surrounding the American and the Japanese approaches to the alliance. Unlike Japan, the United States recognizes the necessity for establishing a power balance in East Asia that is ultimately rooted in military force. Thus, the United States sees Japan as a critical factor in regional security. However, there is no clear American or Japanese consensus regarding basic strategic goals beyond maintaining the alliance, and the resulting indeterminacy of the American posture is a major cause of apprehension for all countries in the region, including the People's Republic of China. Under the Nixon Doctrine, Japan is seen both as a security partner (albeit a strong and independent one) and as an economic competitor, and the United States has used the security commitment as a bargaining tool in the negotiations to adjust the bilateral trade deficit. Although politics and economics have come to be treated as inseparable by the Nixon administration, the U.S. economic position is rightly viewed to be as much a response to domestic pressures as a calculated maneuver by the government. These pressures are likely to increase. The mounting protectionist sentiment among many members of Congress, the labor unions, and much of the business community is likely to generate claims against Japan's remarkable success in the international marketplace to an extent that will challenge the foundations of the alliance. Despite the current trade imbalance and the seemingly irrepressible buoyancy of the Japanese economy, Japan remains by far the weaker and more vulnerable partner. Because Japan is more heavily dependent on trade with the United States than the United States is on trade with Japan, successful lobbying by American interest groups can generate an economic incident with much more serious and dramatic repercussions for the Japanese, as the protracted textile dispute well illustrated. Thus, the fluctuations of the American domestic economy and the attendant political pressures will have two important effects: They will serve to inhibit the President's flexibility in diplomatic maneuvers with Tokyo, and they will ensure that U.S. domestic policies will affect the status of Japanese-American relations to a greater extent than at any time since 1945.

Bilateral economic relations between the two countries, which currently stand as the most immediate area of conflict, are integrally related to the political-security aspects of the alliance. Moreover, the capacities of government leaders in both nations to deal with the economic issues have been limited because these matters have become politicized and because both nations have yet to establish consensus on foreign policy goals appropriate to the new international order. Japan can no longer ignore the question of an expanded security policy while concentrating on economic benefits, as it could during the American-dominated postwar period. However, the answer to that problem must take into consideration the enormous economic stake the Japanese now have in East Asia and how this relates to the new strategic needs of Washington and Tokyo.

An Economic Gulliver
in the Political Quicksands of Asia

Japan is an East Asian nation, and incentives for expanded defense capabilities will grow out of regional security problems, not out of the imperatives of participation in global power politics. Rather than conjecture about the virtually limitless scenarios that might lead to a decision for rearmament, it is more instructive to examine the fundamental assumptions of Japan's policy in light of the pattern of economic involvement in the region and the prospects for Asian peace in a multipolar world. To extend the trading-company policy of the past into the future by eschewing a military establishment commensurate with her economic capabilities and narrowly defining her security in terms of national territorial defense while expanding her material interests abroad, Japan is, in the words of the *Diplomatic Bluebook for 1971,* engaged in "a challenging experiment unprecedented in world history."[13] The success of this experiment has been primarily the result of the configuration of regional international politics that developed in an essentially bipolar world. Although a more complex multipolar world has now come into being, two important legacies remain from the past. First, the comprehensive alliance with America served as an international incubator, insulating Japan from the war and the upheaval that have convulsed East Asia; this will make adjustment to the harsh realities of the ensuing decade difficult for Japan. Second, the extensive economic (and political) ties Japan has cultivated in the region during the past two decades have been critically dependent on the alliance system and the far-flung political-military imperium maintained by the United States in Asia, a sphere of influence that will be radically altered as the Nixon Doctrine is implemented. From both an internal and an external perspective, the formulation of Japanese foreign policies suitable for the new East Asian international situation will be profoundly challenging if not destabilizing.

The current level of Japanese economic involvement in East Asia is startling. From 1958 to 1968, the Japanese increased their share of regional trade from 9.0 to 27.4 percent, displacing former colonial powers, completely overshadowing the People's Republic of China, and widely surpassing the United States.[14] Today, Japan is the leading trading partner of every major nation in the region except South Vietnam, and most Japanese projections see this trend continuing until 1980, when roughly 50 percent of regional trade will involve Tokyo. Beyond the network of trade ties generated largely by the forces of the marketplace, Japan has taken a leading role in the largely economically oriented, multinational organizations (such as the Asian Development Bank) that have sprouted among noncommunist Asian countries behind the smoke of Vietnam. All Japanese wartime reparations and the overwhelming proportion of its foreign aid are concentrated in the region. Japan already extends considerably more aid to East Asian countries except Vietnam than the United States does, and this amount is expected at least to double within the next several years. With the exception of South Korea and Indonesia, Japan has made relatively modest direct investments in Asia; nevertheless, the enormous annual trade surpluses and the massive exchange reserves these investments have produced assure that there will be a greatly augmented flow of investment funds into the region. From any viewpoint, it is evident that Japan will consolidate her position as the dominant economic force in East Asia.

Under these circumstances, how can Tokyo remain permanently aloof from international politics and its concomitant security responsibilities? There are three major ways in which this might come about: (1) Japan may simply write off all economic losses in Asia whenever politics intrudes; (2) an agreement among the major powers may make a stable peace possible in East Asia; or (3) political conflict may be mitigated, if not eliminated, through rapid economic growth spurred by a massive Japanese aid program concentrated in the region.

The first option seems, at first glance, a most plausible development because Japan remains quite independent of Asia economically. No single country in the region takes much more than 3 percent of total Japanese trade, and the investment level will also remain low enough to leave Tokyo wide room for policy maneuvers. Moreover, by cultivating multiple sources of raw materials on a worldwide basis, Japan has reduced the political pressures that might flow from economic ties of this sort. Despite this growing capacity to remain economically independent of East Asia, there are in fact severe limitations on the extent to which this autonomy can be extended. Unlike the United States and the Soviet Union, Japan is a peculiarly vulnerable economic superpower because of its almost total dependence on a number of raw materials (e.g., oil, iron ore, nickel, and bauxite) that are absolutely essential to a modern economy and for which there are no ready substitutes. If global competition for raw materials replaces the balance-of-payments problem as the most serious crisis in international trade, all sources of supply will take on greatly exaggerated importance for Japan. Even if there is no short-term economic *necessity* for Japan to become militarily involved in East Asia, it is all but inconceivable that any Tokyo government could for long ignore the *political* pressures (from other nations in the region as well as from world powers) that would inevitably result from major upheaval in the region.

As for the second option, it is singularly unlikely that peace will break out in Asia after the end of the Vietnam War, although this has been openly avowed by leaders of both the conservative and opposition parties in Japan—and by the President of the United States. A number of forces converge to produce deep instability in the region: the highly uncertain implications for international behavior of the profound economic and social changes occuring in all nations; the conflicts of interest tied to past and current national competitions that are aggravated by ideological cleavages between communist and noncommunist political groups; the virtual impossibility of a power balance, given the vulnerability to "people's wars" and Chinese intransigence to any attempt to freeze the status quo; the failure of both superpowers to articulate their short-term objectives in Asia, much less to build effective alliance systems or to lay the foundations for neutralization of the region; and the rivalry (currently muted) between the status quo–oriented Japanese and the Chinese Communists.

The third possibility involves the assumption, basic to Japan's aid program, that prosperity can indeed serve as the solvent of political conflict in the East Asian region. In the words of Prime Minister Sato, "By stabilizing a country economically, a way to coprosperity and coexistence will be opened. This is the way to abide thoroughly by peace. Japan wishes to move forward along this course."[15] However, there is no conclusive evidence that economic development leads to a peaceful pattern of domestic political development and to international harmony. The symbolic importance of economic progress may benefit the short-term political stability of a regime, but counterevidence suggests that rapid economic growth actually increases the level of social frustration and creates an environment in which extremist political movements prosper by undermining the traditional and familiar while failing to be of immediate benefit to the general populace.[16] Therefore, not only are we foolish to predicate domestic political stability on economic growth, but in a basic sense we are putting the cart before the horse because a substantial amount of political stability is a precondition of economic development. Even more mistaken is the assumption that regional economic cooperation will mitigate, if not eliminate, political rivalries among nations. Ultimately, the scope of East Asian economic cooperation will be the result of *political* decisions by the elites of the various countries, in which the benefits of economic rationality from a regionwide viewpoint represent only one consideration. As presently constituted, the web linking Japan to Asia cannot in itself bring international harmony or even serve as the basis for coping with the full range of diplomatic issues that will arise. Trade, aid, and investment have drawn Japan deeply and inextricably into Asia, but they cannot offer an immediate solution to political problems.

The peculiar prism in which Japan sees the world in largely economic hues has led to a major misapprehension regarding the implications of gradual American disengagement in Asia. Japan attained its current position of regional economic preeminence because of the military-political order maintained by the United States in East Asia. To suppose that, in the wake of Vietnam and the curtailment of the American role in the region, economic forces can fill the void is to ignore the lessons of history in Asia throughout this century. Political and security factors will continue to determine the basic structure of international relations, especially international economic relations, in Asia.[17] If Japan wishes to extend the pattern of economic involvement of the past two decades or even partially to fulfill the goals for aid repeatedly articulated by various prime ministers, a new and expanded security role is necessary. This strategic imperative is lodged in the scope of Japanese economic involvement in East Asia.

Japanese Business and Security Policy

When and how Japan decides to undertake an expanded security policy will be strongly influenced by the process of making foreign policy, in which the business world plays a prominent part. Despite the vision of intimate business-government collaboration conjured up in the image of Japan, Incorporated, the role of business foreign affairs decisions is ambiguous and varies widely from issue to issue. Japanese business leaders are closely tied to the conservative party through their overt and covert financial support, through a sharing of basic political values, and through continuous and intimate personal contacts. Ties between business and the Ministry of International Trade and Industry (MITI) and other government agencies exercising careful control over the day-to-day conduct of Japan's international economic activities are similarly close, which is inevitable, given the overwhelming economic emphasis of postwar foreign policy. Despite these connections and the establishment by the national business organizations of committees to deal with specific foreign affairs issues and continuing questions such as rearmament, there is no clear mutual understanding regarding the procedures through which business opinion should be brought into the policy-making process. Nor is there automatic agreement on the goals of the nation's foreign policy. The complexity and diversity of the Japanese business world are mirrored in the viewpoints of the various individuals and groups who speak out on international affairs. Consequently, when political and security considerations are involved in policies that were previously intended to maximize economic benefits, it is just as probable that the businessmen will become further divided among themselves as it is that they will rally around the flag.

The impact of organized business and of individual businessmen on major Japanese foreign policy decisions has varied. Regarding normalization of diplomatic relations with the Soviet Union in 1956 and the extension of the Mutual Security Treaty in 1960 (both issues involving essentially political questions), business was not able to make a decisive impact on the policy process. It played a somewhat more important part in the normalization of relations with South Korea and with China, but not in regard to the critical political decisions involved. As the links between politics and economics grow (as a direct result of Japan's commercial stake in East Asia and the world) and Japan moves toward full participation in power politics, the relationship between the business world and the liberal-democratic party will take on added importance *and* at the same time be placed under increasing strains, especially regarding security policy.

Japan has no equivalent of the much-maligned and vaguely defined American military-industrial complex. Needless to say, defense-related businesses have pressed hard to maximize their own profits by bringing about an expansion of the overall defense budget and promoting self-sufficiency in weapons production. Since 1961, *Keidanren* (Japanese Federation of Economic Organizations) has had a number of standing committees concerned with government programs for weapons procurement and the role of business in the various government defense plans. These committees now cover the full range of weaponry. Since the mid-1960s, their activities have enormously expanded in both research about and coordination of business policies, as well as liaison with relevant government officials.[18] The Japanese government has no center analogous to the Pentagon in which the interests of the active military and the civilian defense establishment are found in powerful concentration. The military has remained remarkably peripheral to the civilian-dominated policy-planning process within the Defense Agency, and the agency holds a comparatively weak position within the bureaucracy in bargaining for a slice of the annual appropriations. Because they have no strong locus of power within the government regarding defense, businesses are severely limited in bringing direct pressure for greatly augmented military expenditures. Once a decision to greatly expand military expenditures is made, a close business-government cooperative arrangement seems probable. Such an arrangement may well feed upon itself, thus giving momentum to a rearmament program. However, this cooperation will be the result, not the cause, of rearmament. The decision to rearm will grow not out of the machinations of a Japanese military-industrial complex, but out of a policy-making process dominated by the ruling party and broadly rooted in the prevailing climate of opinion.

To summarize, the security roles of the United States and Japan are now in the process of change. In part, this is a result of a calculated strategy of retrenchment initiated by the United States in order to cope more adequately with the problems of a multipolar world in the wake of the domestically divisive war in Vietnam. Partly, it is the result of the collapse of the postwar international monetary system, the spectacular success of Japan in the global economy, and the political implications of Japan's enormous economic stake in East Asia. The American alliance remains the key to future Japanese security policy, but the alliance itself is currently strained by mounting bilateral economic conflicts rooted in the domestic politics of both nations. On the whole, the internationally oriented business establishment in Japan objects to any change in the current security arrangement and opposes full-scale autonomous rearmament. However, the role of business in Japanese foreign-policy making is neither secure nor well articulated regarding major *political* decisions. The way in which Japan accomplishes the transformation from trading company to nation-state will severely test the stability of the international economic system and the still uncertain multipolar political order.

Notes

1/ Supreme Command for the Allied Powers. Government Section, *Political Reorientation of Japan: September 1945 to September 1948* (Washington, D.C.; U.S. Government Printing Office, 1959), p. 765.

2/ John M. Maki, *Conflict and Tension in the Far East* (Seattle: University of Washington Press, 1961), p. 129.

3/ For elaboration on the security consideration underlying the American effort to stimulate Japanese economic recovery, see Frederick S. Dunn, and others, *Peace-Making and the Settlement with Japan* (Princeton: Princeton University Press, 1963), chap. 7.

4/ Ibid., pp. 45–52.

5/ For elaboration, see Donald C. Hellmann, *Japan and East Asia* (New York: Praeger, 1972), chap. 3.

6/ For example, see Edward L. Morse, "Crisis Diplomacy, Interdependence, and the Politics of International Economic Relations," *World Politics*, vol. 24, Supp. (Spring 1972), pp. 123–150.

7/ Hellmann, *Japan and East Asia*, pp. 61–64.

8/ Richard M. Nixon, *U.S. Foreign Policy for the 1970s* (Washington, D.C.: Government Printing Office, 1971), p. 13. This same statement also appeared in the President's First Annual Report in 1970.

9/ Robert J. Pranger, *Defense Implications of International Indeterminacy* (Washington, D.C.: American Enterprise Institute for Public Policy Research, 1972), passim.

10/ This point is made in the best and most complete discussion of the military implications of the Nixon Doctrine for Japan—Robert E. Osgood, *The Weary and the Wary: U.S. and Japanese Security Policies in Transition* (Baltimore: Johns Hopkins Press, 1972), pp. 14–17.

11/ Hellmann, *Japan and East Asia,* chap. 3.

12/ See Hiroshi Kitamura, *Psychological Dimensions of U.S.-Japanese Relations* (Cambridge: Harvard University, Center for International Affairs, 1971), passim.

13/ Japan. Ministry of Foreign Affairs, *Diplomatic Bluebook for 1971* (Tokyo, 1972), p. 103.

14/ The statistics cited are derived from various issues of *Direction of Trade Annual,* published by the International Monetary Fund and the International Bank for Reconstruction and Development.

15/ *Yomiuri Shimbun* (Nov. 29, 1969).

16/ For example, see Mancur Olsen, "Rapid Growth as a Destabilizing Force," *Journal of Economic History,* vol. 23, no. 4 (December 1963), pp. 529–558.

17/ For an interesting discussion of the causal relationship of economics and politics in international relations, see Robert Gilpin, "The Politics of Transnational Economic Relations," *International Organization,* vol. 25, no. 3 (Summer 1971), pp. 398–419.

18/ For example, see Keidanren, Bōei Seisan Iinkai, *Bōei Seisan Iinkai Tokuhō* [Defense production committee special report] (Tokyo, 1970), pp. 1–14.

2.

JAPAN'S INDUSTRIAL POLICY

William V. Rapp

THE YEARS 1970–1972 MARK THE END of an era in Japanese economic history. After a hundred years, Japan has caught up with the West and achieved foreign-exchange self-sufficiency. Two manifestations of this are a large and continuing surplus and a 17 percent yen revaluation. Japan is now rethinking her economic goals and industrial policy. The emphasis is shifting markedly from a growth, industrial-investment, export-oriented policy to a social-overhead-investment, postindustrial, free-trading policy.

In the broadest sense, industrial policy deals with economic structure: the development of particular industries and resource allocation between sectors. In Japan, this policy has used market forces and has been complementary with overall economic policy, supporting and facilitating general monetary and fiscal policies. It has provided a basis for harmonizing programs in one sector with those of another, but has been indicative rather than compelling. The various elements of the economy have been helped to move together, making efficient and consistent use of available resources and promoting rapid growth and development.

Americans have often misunderstood the nature of Japan's industrial (structural) policy and the economic influence of the Japanese government. U.S. postwar economic policies have been chiefly macroeconomic, aimed at avoiding a repetition of the events of the 1930s. In addition, Americans often feel that an industrial policy requires centralized planning and control. Yet examination of Japan's postwar industrial policy clearly illustrates that an industrial policy can use market forces and can promote effective competition, is complementary with and supportive of macroeconomic policy, and is not dependent on centralized planning and control.

Policy Development

Historically, the Japanese government has taken an active interest in economic planning. At the end of the nineteenth century, Japan was a poor, weak country with little in the way of industry, technology, or natural resources. To maintain her independence, her leaders felt compelled to catch up with the West. For both military and economic reasons, industrialization was a necessity. This step resulted in early government involvement in promoting industry and early development of close relations between government and business. For example, the government imported and set up modern textile mills, which were later sold to private enterprise, but found that ventures were more profitable and successful when operated by entrepreneurs. As industry grew and major groupings, Zaibatsu, emerged, the government found it increasingly efficient to work with them in implementing policy. As the new business leaders had similar backgrounds to their bureaucratic counterparts, their relationships were often close and cooperative. But the Zaibatsu did not always agree with government programs. In the case of the automobile industry that MCI (predecessor of the Ministry of International Trade and Industry [MITI]) tried to develop during the 1930s, the major Zaibatsu expressed no interest. Thus Toyota and Nissan gained position by default. However, in general the two groups worked together. Yet, the government's power was weak relative to the large combines. It was the wartime controls and the postwar economic dislocations combined with the dissolution of the Zaibatsu that increased MITI's policy-making powers. Thus Japan's industrial policy was formalized and became effective during the postwar period.

At the end of World War II, Japan was confronted with the need for substantial economic development and rapid industrialization. After much discussion and analysis, the government, in cooperation with business leaders, targeted as strategic five basic industries: steel, shipbuilding, coal, power, and fertilizer. Japan's steel capacity was largely intact but needed repair and raw materials. Because there was a world steel shortage and steel was basic to industrial recovery, the industry's expansion was the key to industrialization and increased export earnings. Shipbuilding was required to rebuild Japan's shattered merchant fleet and to reduce the foreign-exchange drain of buying foreign ships and paying foreign shippers. Coal was needed for heating, power, and steelmaking. Power was a prerequisite for industrial expansion. Finally, fertilizer was needed to increase agricultural output to feed people, to reduce food imports, and to release people from the agricultural labor force.

These strategic industries received special government help in the form of duty-free equipment imports, accelerated depreciation benefits, loans from government banks (e.g., Industrial Bank of Japan, Long-term Credit Bank, Export-Import Bank, and Reconstruction Bank), raw-material quotas, and so on. Other industries such as automobiles, electronics, petrochemicals, and computers received no special government consideration until much later. In the case of the automobile industry, the Ministry of Finance (MOF), the Ministry of Transportation (MOT), and the Bank of Japan (BOJ) initially opposed its development as being high cost and contrary to the international division of labor. However, MITI, the chief architect of Japan's postwar industrial policy, finally obtained government assistance in terms of depreciation allowances, technical support, loans, and so forth for the industry. But this was not done until the early 1950s and only after considerable discussion. Computers in turn were not considered strategically important until the 1960s, after more basic industries were developed. It is always after some debate and as older industries become established that new ones are encouraged. Government policy shifts as the economy changes (e.g., in regard to steel, automobiles, and computers) and is dynamic in nature, looking toward future development.

These target industries have been limited in number, however, though they are indicative of the government's industrial policy. Policy with respect to most industries has left a great deal to competitive forces in the market. Indeed, even within the strategic industries, policy has been only indicative, and the relative success or failure of particular firms has been determined by competition.

Current Situation

Japan's industrial policy is becoming more inward looking, concerned with the benefits of growth and the quality of life. The reasons for this major policy adjustment are clear. The postwar economy has achieved previous long-term objectives: The industrial structure is modern and sophisticated, and current exports more than pay for the massive required imports of raw materials, fuel, and technology.[1] The chronic balance-of-payments deficit that constrained growth until 1965 is no more. A long-term, though not indefinite, surplus is the current problem.

The balance on current account surplus and trade surplus was about $5.9 billion and $7.9 billion, respectively, in 1971 and may increase in 1972. This situation has created severe external pressures, particularly from the United States. Japan has already been forced to revalue the yen about 17 percent, and another revaluation is being discussed. However, Japanese policy makers view currency revaluations and trade restrictions as temporary measures supportive of longer-term policies. More fundamental changes in economic structure are needed, they feel, to correct the long-term situation.

Even before the Nixon shock, Japan had begun to rethink her economic policies. Basic industries responsible for past growth (textiles, steel, shipbuilding, automobiles, and chemicals) were showing signs of maturity or decline. Excess capacity, sagging domestic demand, and—with the exception of automobiles—slow export growth were widely apparent. The effects of rapid industrial expansion at the expense of social-overhead facilities were also visible in pollution, congested roads, and so on. (Japan has the world's highest gross national product per square mile, $4,245, compared to $357 for the United States. Cars per square mile are 344 compared to 41 for the United States.) Recent public surveys show that the Japanese are less concerned with income growth than with pollution, housing, living space, rising food prices, and social security.[2] Conversely, people are satisfied with the availability of consumer durables (e.g., cars, television sets, and appliances). Successful development has created an internal atmosphere ready for change.[3]

The response of Japanese policy makers to these dual pressures, internal and external, has been to revise the hundred-year-old policy and to focus more on internal demands. Their plan is to reinflate the economy by increasing expenditures on long-needed social-overhead investments such as roads, improved harbors, parks, and pollution control. In addition, imports will be liberalized, the rate of industrial-equipment investment will be reduced, export expansion will be deemphasized, and overseas investment will be encouraged. The complexity of both the Japanese economy and the decision-making process has necessitated some lag between perception of the need for change, policy formulation, and implementation. The first two steps now seem fairly complete, but policy implementation is only beginning and is encountering some difficulties.

The recently published government white papers of the various ministries and agencies all address the common theme of their sector's future role within Japan's new economic context. Statements by various business leaders set forth their new goals and problems. An advisory council to the prime minister has been formed, headed by Yoshizane Iwasa, chairman of the Fuji Bank. Its mission is to study a plan for "remodeling" Japan,[4] with recommendations due by the end of the year (1972). These are significant indications that a general policy decision is being reached via the well-known consensus process. That is, opinions are solicited from various elements of society and the economy (big business, small business, agriculture, labor, various ministries, politicians, and academics) until an overall agreement and policy emerge. At this point, although resistance and disagreements may continue, the policies will usually be pursued and implemented as each sector makes its contribution. This process facilitates consistency and accommodation in establishing Japan's structural goals and in carrying through programs. As objections are dealt with ahead of time, obstacles do not arise—as they sometimes do in the United States—once the decision to go ahead has been made. Several differences in opinion remain to be worked out with respect to short-term implementation, but the long-term orientation is now clear.

Revision of Past Policy

Japan's new industrial policy represents a major change in goals but is still consistent with previous policy. Japan's old industrial policy basically followed a Western model of economic evolution. Major industries were targeted as growth opportunities based on previous European or U.S. experience. Unlike the centrally planned economies, Japan has moved sequentially from light, technically unsophisticated industries to more capital-intensive and technically advanced industries (textiles, steel, machinery, shipbuilding, automobiles, and computers). Strategic industries received government support and assistance, but as they became competitive they were left on their own to provide their contribution to growth and development along with other industries.

The new policy turned out to be quite logical. When a country is poor in capital, income, and technology, it should produce products for which there is a large internal demand and which require little capital and few labor skills. As a country develops, incomes grow, the capital stock increases, and labor skills improve, generating demand for and making possible production of more and more sophisticated products. Similar to many less developed countries (LDCs) today, in the late nineteenth century Japan was an exporter of primary products—copper, green tea, raw silk, rice, and fish. It also was starting to produce cotton textiles and was importing steel, ships, and machinery. Today Japan imports cotton, wood, iron, copper, coal, and food and exports machinery, ships, and steel. The government has favored this change and has looked ahead to the next stage of development.

In terms of international competition, Japan's product sequencing was also appropriate. Because higher wages and lower capital costs gave the United States and Europe a comparative advantage, Japan shifted toward even more sophisticated and capital-intensive products (see Tables 1, 2, and 3). What had begun as an ad hoc patterning of Western economic development became a structural policy of dynamic comparative advantage under which industries were developed in response to local demand and in anticipation of future competitiveness.

Japan's postwar economic policies were a continuation of this pattern. Japan needed to industrialize, had a balance-of-payments constraint, and wished to emulate the United States and Europe. Therefore, although the particular policies actually pursued in individual strategic industries such as steel, shipbuilding, automobiles, computers, and petrochemicals were often responses to specific events, Japan's general industrial policy consistently stressed growth, industry sequencing, export promotion, and rapid plant and equipment investment—a policy that

TABLE 1. Real Income, Wage-Interest Ratio, and Industrial Production in Japan, 1890 to 1975

Year	Real Per Capita Income (yen)	Wage-Interest Ratio (index)	Industrial Production (percent of GNP)	Heavy Industrial Production (percent of all industrial production)
1890	57	37.1	9.8	12.1
1900	81	37.0	29.8	17.5
1910	88	67.3	23.1	31.9
1920	112	58.7	27.0	46.0
1930	192	110.7	28.6	50.0
1948	128	40.9	30.8	56.0
1958	276	128.8	33.5	57.7
1968	750	241.1	38.0	71.0
1975ᵃ	1,500	480.0	—	74.4

ᵃEstimated

Sources: Japan. Ministry of International Trade and Industry, *New Economic Plan* (Tokyo); Bank of Japan, *100 Year Statistics of Japan* (Tokyo); W. V. Rapp, "Theory of Changing Trade Patterns," *Yale Economic Essays* (Fall 1967); Japan Economic Research Center, *Japan's Economy in 1980 in the Global Context* (Tokyo).

affected industrial development as a whole, that is, in both strategic and nonstrategic industries.

The success and the soundness of this policy are apparent in Japan's current economic position and in the growth, composition, competitiveness, and size of her exports. At the same time, the greater sophistication of her industries has raised the value added per unit of exports so that net foreign-exchange earnings per yen of exports have been increasing. These two effects, combined with a relatively constant composition of imports (food and raw materials), have changed Japan's traditional balance-of-payments deficit to a large surplus.

Government policy makers feel that the logical continuation of past development can ease the current situation but that a shift toward a postindustrial, knowledge-intensive economy is required to emphasize infrastructure investment, housing, pollution control, and social welfare facilities. In effect, Japan's new policy will continue to follow the U.S. and European economic models, while it simultaneously addresses mounting internal and external pressures. More sophisticated employment opportunities will be needed to justify higher incomes. Industries such as steel, chemicals, and automobiles, while continuing to provide employment and foreign-exchange earnings, are not fast growing. Areas such as computers, fashion, oceanography, research institutes, consulting, city planning, pollution, prefabricated housing, and social welfare facilities offer more logical investment and growth alternatives and are primarily domestic-demand oriented. As resources are redirected to these sectors, productivity in the major export industries will begin to decline, and their international competitiveness will decrease. The export surplus will decline, and the people's quality of life will rise. At the same time, Japan plans to import many more agricultural products, textiles, handicrafts, and other less sophisticated manufactured goods. This will also help to correct Japan's balance-of-payments surplus while upgrading her economic structure and lowering the cost of living.

Many economic and political problems must be solved in implementing this policy, but the economic and political logic is apparent. It is in fact a major conclusion of this paper (and also the opinion of many Japanese policy makers) that Japan's industrial policy has been successful because of its logic and consistency, which are the result of interaction and acceptance by various social elements. That is, it makes use of, rather than opposes, social and economic forces.

Japan's Postwar Policy and Changing Economic Structure: Product Cycles and Economic Growth

Japan's new industrial policy is important in assessing her future economic role and relations with the United States. But some appreciation of the Japanese economic system is required to place this new policy in perspective.

Japan's competitive environment is growth oriented, and this has been encouraged by government policy. Japan's per capita income in 1948 (Table 1) was equivalent to that of the 1920s, and not until 1957

TABLE 2. Japanese Industrial Production and Manufactured Exports, Selected Years and Projection for 1975 (percent)

Year	Manufacturing		
	Total	Heavy	Light
Production			
1928	100	35	65
1935	100	53	47
1950	100	50	50
1960	100	68	32
1969	100	71	29
1975 (projected)	100	74	26
Exports			
1928	100	7	83
1935	100	18	72
1950	100	33	67
1960	100	51	49
1969	100	70	30
1975 (projected)	100	78	22

Sources: Japan. Ministry of International Trade and Industry, *New Economic Plan;* Bank of Japan, *100 Year Statistics of Japan;* Rapp, "Theory of Changing Trade Patterns"; Japan Economic Research Center, *Japan's Economy in 1980 in the Global Context.*

did it again achieve its prewar highs. Thus, economic growth was a logical postwar priority. This growth required high rates of investment and export promotion if capacity was to be expanded rapidly and imports were to be financed. But Japan's capital stock was extremely small, and only the banks had the necessary funds. Therefore the government, through the Bank of Japan, encouraged the debt financing required for high investment rates. In addition, tax reforms continually altered the progressive nature of Japan's income tax to favor capital accumulation and high savings rates. Interest income was taxed at lower rates than was salary income, and capital gains were often not taxed at all (e.g., in the case of stock sales). Extensively used commodity taxes encouraged savings. Corporations were allowed to revalue their assets to compensate for the high immediate postwar inflation, and accelerated depreciation was given on purchases of new equipment. Companies also received favorable tax and interest-rate benefits for exports (e.g., even more favorable allowances on equipment depreciation and lower interest rates on export bills and on imports-for-exports). These and other measures encouraged industrial recovery, rapid investment, and export growth.

The program was particularly successful because it favored those firms that grew fastest and were effective exporters. The measures were growth incentives, not subsidies. The fastest-growing firms used the most debt and received the most tax benefits, and they could thus price lower relative to competitors and achieve the same return on equity even if costs were the same. They could then undersell competitors both domestically and overseas. As their volume increased, their unit costs became lower and they could further lower prices, grow faster, and benefit from government tax policies. Conversely, slow-growing firms had to repay loans and deferred taxes (i.e., had declining depreciation allowances).

The government itself favored private investment over public investment, which had a lower income payout. The government consistently underestimated growth rates and thus fiscal revenues. Budget surpluses were then returned to the private sector via tax cuts. These economic forces reallocated financial resources to the faster-growing firms and industries via the banking system and the government budget. As high-growth industries and firms gained comparative advantage relative to slow-growing industries and firms, there was an upgrading of the industrial structure and a consolidation of industries, particularly in

TABLE 3. Ratio of Japanese Industrial Production
to Manufactured Exports, Selected Years
and Projection for 1975

| | Manufacturing | | |
Year	Total	Heavy	Light
1928	1.00	0.2	1.3
1935	1.00	0.3	1.5
1950	1.00	0.7	1.3
1960	1.00	0.8	1.5
1969	1.00	1.0	1.0
1975 (projected)	1.00	1.1	0.8

Sources: Japan. Ministry of International Trade and Industry, *New Economic Plan;* Bank of Japan, *100 Year Statistics of Japan;* Rapp, "Theory of Changing Trade Patterns"; Japan Economic Research Center, *Japan's Economy in 1980 in the Global Context.*

the capital-intensive sectors. The cost of this growth was underinvestment in public facilities and high rates of industrial investment instead of personal consumption.

The government's policies in effect accelerated the impact of internal competition and market forces on Japan's development. As already noted, economic growth increases incomes, labor skills, capital stock, and technical sophistication, thus raising consumer expectations while facilitating production of more advanced products. Japan's high-growth policies accelerated these demand and supply shifts. But, while Japan upgraded her industrial structure, more advanced countries such as the United States were also upgrading theirs and becoming less competitive in Japan's new high-growth industries. Because Japan was following the United States and Europe, its high-growth industries were the maturing U.S. and European industries. Therefore, by redirecting

47

substantial resources toward high-growth firms in high-growth industries (Japan's investment and savings rate averaged 24 percent between 1955 and 1968 and is currently over 30 percent of GNP), the government's policies and the economic system accelerated Japan's evolving comparative advantage. The long-term international and domestic effects of this dynamic policy were profound.

Other elements of the Japanese economic system also foster the rapid reallocation of resources for growth, efficiency, and competitiveness. Japanese labor practices are a particularly interesting example. Workers in major Japanese companies are hired directly from school for life. They are promoted and paid according to seniority. Thus, faster-growing firms have a younger work force and lower average wage costs. The employee's livelihood is intimately involved with the firm's success; thus, strikes are few and high debt levels are less risky than they are in the West.[5] Because employment is for life, employees can only gain from innovations that improve the firm's competitive performance.

High debt levels and little proprietary technology also foster competition. Japanese managers are accustomed to rapid growth and realize the adverse consequences of failing to grow with the market. They invest heavily in anticipation of demand. As investments are uneven, temporary excess capacity is common, but fixed costs are high (fixed labor and high interest charges). Therefore, operation at capacity is efficient even if products are sold at slightly above variable costs (in fact, slightly above raw-material costs). Further, most technology is imported and is available to all producers (often a MITI requirement), so there is no patent protection to hold up prices. Prices are very flexible downward, leading to extreme price competitiveness and rapid industry shake-outs both domestically and overseas. Again, this situation favors the high-growth, low-cost firm.

This competitive process, often called *excessive competition,* is only really excessive when demand slows, the industry matures, and excess capacity is long term. At this point, the government (MITI) usually helps establish a depression cartel and encourages mergers. But because production allocations are based on existing market shares, the desire of firms to add capacity and to compete for market share in a new product remains unchanged.

In effect, Japan has developed a self-reinforcing business system, encouraged by government policies, that promotes rapid growth by favoring a rapid reallocation of resources to high-growth firms in high-growth sectors. Industry structure is rationalized when growth slows. As these growth industries have been the more modern, more sophisticated industries, this process has increased Japan's comparative advantage in higher value-added products. Because the same competitive pressures exist internationally as in the domestic market, Japanese firms have been very aggressive in exploiting changes in their comparative advantage to expand volume and to increase competitiveness relative to domestic and foreign competitors. The net result is a large trade-account surplus.

Evaluation of the System

In the operation of the Japanese system, business and government are cooperative and mutually supportive. The measures such as quotas, tariffs, and tax concessions used to protect and encourage particular industries are also found in Europe, the United States, and the LDCs. The number of regulations and the degree of market interference are currently about the same as in other advanced countries. Previously, there was substantial protection, and MITI controlled many raw-material imports as well as technology imports; but the economic situation at that time was quite difficult. Until 1964, the Organization for Economic Cooperation and Development still classified Japan as a semi-developed country, and Japan had a chronic balance-of-payments deficit. Economic success, however, has brought increased business independence and a sharp reduction in both direct and indirect controls, even if growth-oriented management and competitive pressures remain.

Still, import controls and encouragement of new industries imply interference with free international market forces and have been achieved at some cost to the Japanese economy. But it is not government interference with market forces that differs so much from the United States or Europe as direction and emphasis. Japan has defended high-growth rather than low-growth sectors. The United States protects textiles and shoes; Japan protects computers. United States antitrust regulations hinder mergers; Japan encourages mergers in order to create larger, more efficient, more viable firms. The U.S. tax system favors consumers at the expense of corporate investors and a higher savings rate; Japan emphasizes capital accumulation and higher growth rates. Japan thus favors growth, an upgrading of its economic structure, and increased real wages. The United States tries to cushion change and dislocation by keeping resources in low-wage, low-productivity industries and by short-circuiting some of the rationalization created by competition and merger. The trade-offs in trade discussions between the two countries clearly indicate these priorities.

In either case, it is ultimately a politicoeconomic decision whether interference, control, or distortion of free-market forces and business decisions is justifiable. This is true if the goal is stabilization of the existing economic situation or if it is upgrading of the economic structure as quickly as possible.

Japan has pursued as "infant-industry" strategy on a massive scale. This approach assumes a dynamic world view; yet without rapid growth and industrialization Japan was committed to a permanent poverty gap vis-à-vis the West, a situation that was politically and emotionally unacceptable. Because Japan is a follower, its perspective is naturally different from that of the United States. Japanese leaders followed Western economic development in product sequencing but not always in implementation. In targeting future industries, they observed foreign economies in terms of Japan's needs and discussed the results. Good communications, the country's small size, and its common heritage facilitated this consensus process and actual follow on. But initially they could not leave implementation strictly to the market because in the development stages follower industries need protection. This argument is the accepted infant-industry plan.

The plan has cost foreign producers markets and Japanese consumers temporarily higher prices. But U.S. protection policies have also been partially responsible for the trend. By propping up declining industries through tariffs and quotas, the United States has denied Japanese exporters potentially large markets and has used up negotiating leverage. At some point, therefore, these Japanese industries could no longer grow and ceased to attract resources. Continued growth then required moving faster into the next stage of development. In the short run, protection was needed to get things started and could be justified by U.S. policies. But as industries grew and became competitive, prices dropped and there was a large economic payoff in higher wages, profits, and export earnings. If the additional cost to the consumer is considered part of the total country investment in the industry, the calculated payout appears large (e.g., textiles, steel, shipbuilding, and autos).

Both demand volume in the early stages of product development and total incremental cost are small. Because in Japan prices fall as volume expands, cost continues to be small and eventually disappears. On the other hand, protecting a declining or mature industry is very expensive because demand volume is large and international price differentials are widening. Similarly, forcing six firms to exist when the market only efficiently justifies three is also costly. By fostering interfirm competition and rationalization except when it becomes excessive and counterproductive, the Japanese have minimized their catch-up costs, have increased their international competition, and have promoted their overall economic development. In addition, this policy has created many new and independent (non-zaikai) entrepreneurial firms like Mitsushita, Sony, Toyota, and Honda. Business has benefited greatly from their aggressive management, and this spirit has in turn benefited from the competitive postwar climate. The government has not managed Japanese corporations. Instead, this corporate success has been the collective result of Japan's managerial initiative and capability in response to a dynamic industrial system.

However, Japan's growth-oriented managers are confronting a new environment. Japan's important export industries are now mature, and the number of new leading industries available for development is few. Managers must consider the difficulties of managing a mix of high- and low-growth products and take into account the shifting comparative advantage toward the LDCs in several traditional industries. Revaluations have accentuated this changing competitive context. At the same time, Japan is committed to increasing these imports to decrease both its overall surplus and the bilateral surplus with these countries. Japan's economic structure has encouraged raw-material imports and manufactured exports, but in the future it will import large quantities of inexpensive consumer goods as well. It will export capital, capital equipment, and technically sophisticated products. Indeed, overseas investment is essential if manufactured imports are to be widely distributed by Japanese firms and if some currently exported value added is to be transferred to production abroad. These actions would imply a major revision in both government policy and business attitudes.

Japan's Evolving Industrial Policy

To meet Japan's internal and external problems, government officials, business leaders, academics, and others have been discussing alternatives since 1970. The consensus policy[6] that has emerged has both a domestic and an international component.

Internal policy—government budget. Japan is currently in a recession, and reinflation of the economy requires substantial increases in government expenditures. On a long-term basis, too, major expenditure increases are needed to meet long overdue social-overhead requirements, to reallocate resources to housing, to improve social security benefits, to improve pollution control, to reduce population pressures, and to do many other things required to improve the quality of life. These expenditures must be supported by a new set of incentives to business. Past recessions have usually been the result of tight money policies aimed at slowing the economy and reducing imports. Increased exports compensated for declining domestic demand while correcting the balance-of-payments deficit. However, currently liquidity is high, world demand is depressed, and Japanese exports are less price competitive. Thus, the government plans to increase substantially government expenditures, already up 18 percent over 1972.

In the long term, MITI anticipates that new social-overhead-investment expenditures over the decade will total $60 billion in 1965 prices. To finance this growth in expenditures, the government will issue bonds (mostly to banks) and will raise taxes. Because many firms are cash rich and are not investing at previous rates, they are repaying loans, and their depreciation allowances will shrink. Funds will be reallocated through the banking and tax systems to the new high-growth sector, government expenditures. This resource reallocation is not expected to decrease Japan's growth rate, at least in the short run, as many improvements are long overdue and have created economic bottlenecks. Through 1980, the government anticipates about a 9 percent per annum increase in real GNP. After 1980, the higher capital output ratio of public investments may have some diminishing effect on growth if such investment grows to 7 percent of GNP or about 25 percent of total investment. But if investment rates remain high, growth will continue to be substantial.

The impact of the new expenditures and taxes will be directed at the structural issues noted above. Most important (reflecting the Tanaka Plan) will be the government's attempt to redirect industry and population away from the Pacific megalopolis between Tokyo and Hiroshima. Inland transportation networks will be expanded, particularly in northern Japan (Tōhoku and Hokkaido). New high-speed trains and a tunnel to Hokkaido will be completed, reducing the travel time between Tokyo and Sapporo from seventeen to five hours. The government also plans to build industrial parks, an academic research city, and new nuclear cities (each of about 200,000 people) in the less populated, less industrialized parts of Japan (Kyushu, Hokkaido, and northern Honshu). In its 1973 budget, the Ministry of Construction asked for $30 million to assume construction of the academic city. It also plans to survey approximately 100 nuclear cities.

To encourage industry to move, the government has proposed an *oidashizeikin,* literally translated as "driving-out tax." This tax will be based on factory or office floor area and will be levied according to metropolitan location. It could cost the steel companies alone ¥4 billion ($13 million) in the first year. Also, the government is considering a head tax on the urban population. On the other hand, it will offer subsidies to firms and relocation allowances to workers to move to prepared sites. A major barrier to industrial and population redistribution in the past has been young people's desire to move from the country to the large cities. However, recent polls indicate that this attitude has changed.[7] In addition, academics have been relatively underpaid and have needed the *arbeito* (part-time employment) available in the cities. The new high-speed trains, increased education expenditures (plans call for $30 billion in 1980), and the new academic city will ease pressures on professors to remain near major cities, particularly Tokyo. A massive use of television communication for education, particularly adult education, will further decrease the cultural and educational disparities between the megalopolis and other parts of the country. Some people accuse the government of advocating pollution proliferation, but this program seems to represent an intelligent use of available land. In addition, the government's pollution-control regulations are becoming increasingly severe, and recent pollution court cases have uniformly favored the plaintiffs.

The other major area of increased government expenditure will be housing. For 1973, the Ministry of Construction is asking $700 million for loans for housing projects, financing about 312,000 units. It is also planning to subsidize private housing. This program will coincide with the emergence of housing, particularly prefabricated housing, as a growth sector. The total housing plan for 1973 is over 700,000 units.

A major problem, however, is that these expenditure programs, as well as the building of more parks, roads, harbor improvements, hospitals, and sewage, all use land. Further, increased incomes and more leisure (a five-day workweek is receiving special government, business, and labor attention) will increase the demand for resorts, hotels, golf courses, and ski areas. Already scarce land is in even greater demand, and current land prices are rising rapidly. The government recognizes this and is considering steps both to increase the available supply and to reduce speculation.

In addition to the *oidashizeikin,* the government plans to raise the capital gains tax on land sales by corporations to perhaps as high as 95 percent on short-term sales, and the individual gains tax on land will rise to over 20 percent from the current 15 percent. (The difference is due to the political influence and different economic situation of farmers.) These taxes will be raised incrementally over a two- to three-year period, and the rate increases will be announced in advance. The plan is to encourage land to come on the market before the tax rate rises. The government is also considering reassessing agricultural and vacant land in urban areas as if it were used as residential land. This tactic will substantially raise the holding cost of such property. The tax program will in turn be buttressed by a BOJ limit on the proportion of real estate loans a bank may make and a list of "appropriate" land prices for different areas of Japan. In effect, the new tax and expenditure programs are structurally complementary.

Internal policy—industrial structure. The government has targeted for development several new "clean" industries that it considers part of Japan's future industrial structure: for example, information industries, computers, information centers, consulting, basic research, fashion, ocean-resources development, leisure, housing, medical equipment, and pollution-control equipment. MITI's paper "Trade and Industrial Policies for the 1970s" predicts research-and-development expenditures in 1980 to be around six times the 1972 level of $2.5 billion. The government is specifically encouraging importation of pollution-control technology by speeding up the patent-approval process. In the case of computers, the government is promoting the industry in the traditional manner (accelerated depreciation, government loans, tariff protection, and quotas). Thus, the government, by pushing the reallocation of resources toward a knowledge-intensive structure, is emphasizing high-technology and professional-service industries.

While promoting new industries, the government is committed to phasing out or rationalizing declining or maturing industries. As former Vice-Minister Ojimi of MITI has said:

> While certain segments of the industrial structure are being encouraged, there must be modification of those industries where productivity is low, where technology is stagnant and where there is reliance on simplistic intensified use of labor . . . .
>
> The solution of this problem is to be found according to economic logic, in progressively giving away industries to other countries, much as a big brother gives his out-grown clothes to his younger brother. In this way, a country's own industries become more sophisticated.

Thus the government has an extensive program for rationalizing both agriculture and textiles by reducing the number of farms and firms. The commitment of government resources to these declining sectors is far larger than are the incentives offered to emerging industries because the government is trying to cushion the effects of Japan's rapid resource reallocation and recent revaluation. Also, in new industries, the government leaves more to the working of the private sector. The government has also set up industrial parks for handicrafts, toy manufacturers, and the like to facilitate specialization and rationalization. (This program coincides with the industrial-relocation scheme.)

In the case of still growing but mature industries such as steel, shipbuilding, chemicals, consumer electronics, and automobiles, the government appears to be following a flexible policy using depression cartels, export cartels, and limits on capacity expansions to buffer the effects of the current recession as the circumstances warrant. For example, in shipbuilding, Japanese yards are being allowed to allocate production in cooperation with European yards so as not to precipitate an international price war.

International policy. By de-emphasizing exports and by promoting overseas investment, government policy reflects the course of competitive forces. For instance, because its labor force is not expanding and wages are rising rapidly (about 15 percent a year), Japan's small, labor-intensive firms can no longer compete with producers in Korea and Taiwan. It is also difficult, because of the high price of land and local resistance, to find land sites for raw-material processing industries, which are often polluting. In addition, foreign governments are requiring Japanese companies to do more raw-material processing in their countries before exporting. Japan's large steel, chemical, and oil companies thus consider offshore processing attractive.

Small exporters can, however, maintain their markets in the United States and Europe by gaining access to cheaper labor in Taiwan or Korea. Large firms, too, can satisfy foreign-government pressures and can shift some problems by offshore investment. They also create markets for their heavy equipment and technical services, the current basis for Japan's comparative advantage. Increased imports from these offshore investments both lower the cost of living and decrease Japan's mounting trade surplus.

The government realizes and encourages the importance of overseas investment in several ways:

1. The ceilings on capital exports have been successively raised (and probably will be removed).
2. Tariffs on manufactured goods from the LDCs have been cut in half.
3. Aid levels will rise to about 1 percent of GNP (about $7.5 billion in 1980) on untied and soft terms.
4. The Export-Import Bank will be allowed to lend foreign exchange on concessional terms to small Japanese companies for investment.
5. Revaluation insurance is being proposed to protect investors overseas.
6. MOF is completely revising Japan's tariff schedule to favor finished imports.

Even MITI is becoming import and free-trade minded. It is presently attacking the monopolistic sole-agent system that allowed several importers to maintain yen prices and to raise dollar revenues after the revaluation. MITI feels more manufactured imports are an important force in upgrading the economy, avoiding another revaluation, controlling inflation, and keeping money wages from rising too rapidly.

Increased protectionism in Europe and in the United States will encourage Japanese firms to invest in the advanced countries to protect existing markets, to expand service capability, and to reduce the bilateral surplus. Trading companies and large consumer durable-goods manufacturers are taking the lead in this area. The government's exchange rate insurance will prevent currency hedging from aggravating the current surplus and reducing the flow of overseas investment. The other side of Japan's overseas investment will be Japan's emergence as an international source of funds. Several multinational firms and foreign governments have already received dollar financing from Japanese financial institutions. The internationalization of Japanese business is both an emerging reality and a policy objective.

Some short-term approaches to ease the balance-of-payments surplus appear less workable. For instance, stockpiling of raw materials is not being undertaken by trading companies, because they cannot sell them. Even if they receive interest-free yen loans, there is no allowance for depreciation, warehouse-space usage, or revaluation. The firms can only lose money and will resist "administrative guidance" if it is costly. But for the long run Japanese policy makers appear to be moving Japan into an appropriate direction both economically and politically.[8] Planners seem to take greater cognizance of the international impacts of domestic decisions. They now appreciate Japan's size, importance, and responsibilities in a multipolar economic world. They recognize the need for an acceptable trade surplus of not more than 1 percent of GNP. They are also asserting themselves more in world economic policy.

The latest white paper on trade takes the position that future world trade should be free, nondiscriminatory, and reciprocal, promoting harmony, cooperation, and international specialization among advanced countries. For this reason, Japan is opposed to further extensions of trading blocks like the European Economic Community, to nontariff barriers, and to "voluntary" restraints. Import injury should be solved through industrial adjustments, not controls or exchange rate changes. But the Japanese do not intend to push their view too hard, wishing to avoid major international confrontations similar to those of the 1930s. The government worries only that its long-term measures will not show results soon enough and that it will be forced to revalue again (though it may use an export tax first).

Implementation Problems and Issues

Although government and business leaders substantially agree on the overall direction of Japan's future structural development, they have many difficulties to work out in administering and implementing the new policy, particularly in the short run. Indeed, implementing certain programs has turned into a large problem, partly because of inertia in getting a new program started but mostly because there are real conflicts of interests. Although businessmen agree on the long-term logic of Japan's policy, few are willing to have their short-term interests affected. This attitude has resulted in a policy paralysis in which proposals are made but few concessions or actions are forthcoming. There is a feeling that long-term economic forces will work things out. This can be clearly seen in declining sectors such as agriculture, coal mining, and textiles where there is little consensus but rather a grudging acceptance of the inevitable combined with considerable political pressure to postpone and cushion their decline. However, external pressures and internal expectations are unlikely to wait for this long-term evolution. In addition, failure to implement near-term programs is likely to affect long-term policy. This situation, if it continues, could ultimately result in a serious confrontation of political pressures and vested self-interest similar to the Nixon shock. The hope is that there will be a concerted effort to break the concession bottleneck after the Diet election and achieve consensus on a short-term program.

Japan's policy determination has always been a reconciliation of conflicting interests. The Economic Planning Agency (EPA), in compiling the overall economic plan, only integrates the structural plans of the various ministries within an overall economic model. EPA is neutral and has no power or administrative authority, and its plan is indicative, having no legal force. Each ministry submits and is responsible for its own plan.

When industrial policy concerned a few key industries, MITI's policy was in effect Japan's industrial policy. It handled reconciliation among business interests. Now the economy and structural policy are becoming bigger and more complex. There is more to coordinate both in scope and size. Several ministries are now involved: MITI, MOF, MOT, MOA (Ministry of Agriculture and Forestry), MOH, (Ministry of Health and Welfare), Environment Agency, Ministry of Construction and so on, each representing its own interests and constituency.

Despite appreciation of current problems and a consensus on long-term policy, various economic groups and government ministries have different ideas on timing and procedure. Because Japanese ministries and agencies have little interchange except at the cabinet level, and because tasks are functionally assigned, differing viewpoints can retard coordinated action on current multifaceted problems. Only recently have interagency project groups been formed such as the Land Development Plan headed by the Environment Agency in conjunction with MOA and the Ministry of Construction. To achieve future program integration, these project teams will have to become more widespread. But first there will have to be more resolution of current conflicts.

For example, MOA recognizes that more food imports are required to reduce living costs and to increase total imports. But it is also concerned about farmers' livelihood and their ability to competitively produce beef, fruits, vegetables, and dairy products, which are considered possible replacements for traditional rice cultivation. They thus disagree with MITI regarding the speed of agricultural liberalization. In turn, MITI feels obliged to support major industries and is insisting on tied aid to the LDCs. MOF objects as increased aid flows will then not decrease Japan's surplus. MITI is also resisting MOF's proposed export tax as it discriminates against efficient export industries but does not encourage imports. On the other hand, neither MITI nor MOA wants another revaluation.

MOF is attempting to break this impasse by applying pressure on both MOA and MITI. But MOF's political influence has been reduced. The new ruling faction does not belong to the MOF bureaucratic tradition of Kishi, Ikeda, and Sato. MOF is thus applying pressure by allowing official exchange reserves to rise, threatening another revaluation. It has cut back dollar loans to city banks and has limited borrowing abroad. By so limiting banks, however, MOF has discouraged overseas lending as banks cannot hedge their foreign-exchange risk. In addition, potential borrowers of yen in the Tokyo capital market (e.g., Mexico and Australia) have withdrawn their proposals. Thus, funds will not flow abroad despite a marked decrease in restrictions. MOF's program is not credible and in fact worsens the short-term payments surplus. Similarly, the policy discourages overseas direct investment due to potential exchange losses. Business will wait until after revaluation. This frustrates the government's long-term plan to increase direct investment. More importantly, without direct investment, export earnings are not transferred abroad, and imports will not increase as rapidly.

While government programs are moving in this contradictory manner, it is apparent that the government's control and impact are less than in the past. Economic success has decreased business's responsiveness to monetary and fiscal influences. Lower growth rates in many industries and a payment surplus have increased cash flows and have made credit more available. MITI's control over raw-material and technology imports has also decreased substantially. Business leaders feel an increase in their relative power and are prepared to buck the government. MITI has already been forced to partially backtrack on its dispersion plan and to postpone the *oidashizeikin* due to business pressure. Steel firms complained they had no place to move, and subcontractors felt they could not easily establish new facilities. Workers were also not prepared to hurt their children's education by moving to the country. The program has thus been considerably restricted in terms of area and type of firm since its proposal.

Therefore, though many programs such as increased construction, improved social facilities, and housing are proceeding, programs related to industry relocation, structural change, and a reduced surplus are in trouble. The difficulties of policy implementation, however, may be best appreciated by a few industry examples that also illustrate more specifically basic policy principles.

Agriculture. Agriculture is Japan's oldest declining sector. Human and financial resources have continually been shifted into higher growth areas, primarily manufacturing, since the nineteenth century. Within agriculture there has also been a shift of production and resources, reflecting economic growth and new consumption patterns (higher protein diet). The per capita consumption of rice has declined, and dairy products, wheat, fruit, eggs, poultry, and meat have taken its place. But Japanese agriculture is still very labor intensive. The average farm is only 1.1 hectares compared to 117 for the United States, and the agricultural labor force averages 1.4 per hectare. Just since 1960, the agricultural population has declined from 12 to 8 million (from 27 to 15 percent of the working population). As most of the young people have gone to the city to work (only 3 to 4 percent of the new labor force enters agriculture), the average farmer's age is very old, and women account for 62 percent of the farm laborers. Even among farmers, more than 50 percent earn more than half their income from other employment. Still, farm families have considerable political power due to their disproportionate representation in the Diet. Therefore, despite the high cost of food in Japan (a Japanese diet in U.S. prices costs substantially less than in Japanese prices), the obvious need for increased imports, and rising consumer discontent with higher food prices, the government continues to support agriculture in the short term while attempting to cushion and induce rationalization in the long term.

The high average age of the agricultural labor force means that in the long run the above problems will solve themselves as the farming population continues to decline. The government is encouraging this trend by offering farmers pensions to retire. But in the short run, the problem is fairly intractable. Given Japan's lifetime employment system, it is very difficult to transfer the current agricultural labor force into industry, and planned construction increases will use only some farmers. The government feels obliged to support these people in the meanwhile. The primary form of this social security is the rice subsidy. The government supports the rice price in the market on the one hand and pays farmers not to produce it on the other (¥35,000 per one-tenth of an acre plus ¥5,000 if they produce something else, usually fruits and vegetables).

The government is also encouraging rationalization of farming units, but this is difficult because of high land prices. The government's approach is thus twofold: (1) the tax measures noted earlier to encourage land sales and (2) the formation of cooperative farms. MOA is also trying to encourage new crops, but there is no clear substitute for rice, and these are areas of the greatest potential import competition. Finally, farmers feel more comfortable producing rice, which is stable and secure and requires no new techniques.

It is anticipated that agricultural liberalization and rationalization will be quite slow.[9] This process will probably be completed around 1980 when the farm population is about 8 percent of the labor force and MOA has lost much of its political power. This change will be gradual in spite of substantial pressures from trading companies that have invested in overseas grain production, from manufacturing firms desiring land and moderate cost-of-living increases, and from consumer groups, foreign countries, and other ministries. A compromise may be worked out using income subsidies in combination with imports as an alternative to price supports and supply restrictions. But this is tentative and is likely to happen first with meat products. However, the distribution system from the farms to the cities will be improved, making domestic products somewhat cheaper in the marketplace.

Textiles. The government is spending about $3 billion a year to rationalize agriculture. It is also spending about $700 million to rationalize the textile industry, and the reasons are somewhat similar. Japan's oldest industry has a very large number of small firms. Rising wages, revaluation, export quotas, and slow domestic-demand growth have combined to make these producers increasingly uncompetitive. Yet, as in the case of farmers, their political power is considerable. In many cases the two interests are combined because farmers' part-time employment has often been in traditional sectors like textiles, handicrafts, and toys. The smaller and medium-size firms are resisting MITI's industry emigration policy, while the very large firms and the trading companies see rationalization and overseas investment as in their interest. It gives them a larger market and a lower-cost production source. But smaller firms will suffer.

MITI, however, seems fully committed to its policy. Japan's average textile tariff is only 8 percent, and imports have risen 114 percent p.a. between 1965 and 1970 (over $260 million imported in 1971). MITI has earmarked $250 million to purchase surplus equipment and $450 million as relief losses for the U.S. textile agreement. It is setting up industrial parks for textile producers. It is encouraging mergers. (The three largest fiber producers, Toray, Teijin, and Asahi Chemical, recently concluded a rationalization agreement.) Finally, it is promoting overseas investment even by smaller firms, giving them information and guidance. Small firms are also eligible for concessional foreign-exchange loans from the Export-Import Bank for these offshore investments. The effectiveness of all these programs is not yet apparent, but they indicate the level and degree of commitment MITI is showing in the face of powerful political opposition.

Steel, shipbuilding, chemicals, and automobiles. Older industries such as agriculture, textiles, coal mining, and handicrafts are actually declining and are receiving major government assistance in cushioning the effects of transition.[10] But many major industries are also becoming mature. This faces MITI and government policy makers with a need to prevent dumping overseas or excessive competition domestically.[11] In such cases, MITI usually arranges a depression cartel with permission of the Fair Trade Commission. It is illegal for manufacturers to do this by themselves. Thus, steelmakers have been enforcing production cutbacks of 15 percent since November 1971 and have curtailed planned capacity additions. Shipbuilders are advocating cutbacks in cooperation with European yards and are slowing operations at newly completed docks. The chemical and petrochemical companies have been particularly hard hit. Production increased only 5.4 percent in 1971 compared to 20 to 40 percent p.a. until that time. There is also excess capacity worldwide. Some petrochemical companies have had to stop plant operation altogether. In May 1971, a special law for restructuring the industry was passed allowing management guidelines, a depression cartel, and mergers. Even the auto industry, which is still growing, in 1971 for the first time faced a decline in domestic demand.[12] But attempts by MITI to rationalize production through mergers and model reduction have failed due to industry resistance. Firms have to face serious difficulties before seeking government-sponsored rationalization.

Computers, housing, medical equipment, pollution-control equipment, and other new areas. Given the economy's continued growth, new industries are merging, which MITI and other government agencies are promoting. But there seem to be conflicts of interest both within these industries and among ministries. For instance, Japan is trying to develop its space program, but has had difficulties in developing reliable rocketry. Therefore, the Communications Ministry wants to buy U.S. rockets to put up a satellite system and has MOF support, but Japan's Space Agency, space contractors, and MITI want the Ministry of Construction to wait until 1977, when Japan will be able to produce its own rocket. The problem has not yet been resolved.

Similarly, MITI is fighting with the Ministry of Health and Welfare over developing medical equipment. The Health Ministry wants to proceed cautiously because of deficits in the National Health Plan and the risks of inadequate testing. MITI sees health as a future growth field. In prefabricated housing, MITI is quarreling with the

Ministry of Construction, whom MITI feels is not properly using Japan's housing program to rapidly develop prefabricated housing or to standardize production. Since MITI views prefabricated housing as a natural follow on to steel, shipbuilding, and automobiles, it has formed its own housing section even though it has no legal control over this industry. Computers of course are under MITI guidance and have been supported as a future growth industry in the traditional fashion. But here there has also been conflict, that is, with the Postal Service, which controls telephone lines. Both MITI and the Postal Service wanted control of time-sharing services. The Postal Service retained its position but only after agreeing to a strict performance timetable. In the future growth industries, much remains to be worked out.

Conclusion

Examination of Japan's industrial policy has revealed several important points. This policy has been a positive response to the need for industrial development and the structural problems generated by economic growth. But it has guided economic forces and not tried to control them. Japan's success has been due to her intelligent and aggressive business management operating in a growth-oriented system. The government's role has been to support this system, to provide enough protection to get an industry started, and to prevent "excessive" competition. In addition, Japan's policy is symmetrical, explicitly using market forces to promote high-growth sectors and discourage low-growth sectors. It is also symmetrical in its domestic and foreign aspects, not fostering policies domestically that are at odds with long-run international objectives.

Japan's industrial policy has been the result of the interaction of opposing and conflicting viewpoints among ministries and various segments of society. For a long time, this policy was growth, export, and industrial-investment oriented and was formulated and implemented by MITI through its interaction with the business community. It appeared quite consistent and homogeneous to outside observers. Conflicts and difficulties, though apparent, were kept to a minimum.

Economic and business success, however, has resulted in decreased government controls, a relatively more independent business community, and a wider range of structural goals. Under the new economic conditions, policy objectives, formulation, and responsibility is more dispersed while the government's influence, particularly MITI's, is weaker. This situation combined with vested pressures to continue the old system has led to serious short-term implementation problems despite overall agreement on the economy's long-term evolution. These implementation difficulties have been especially apparent in the international sector. Exports and the surplus have continued to grow, but only limited concrete actions have been taken, increasing the frustrations of Japan's trading partners, particularly the United States. Japan agrees that something must be done and has indicated the direction of her structural reforms. But nothing seems to happen due to the conflict of internal political and economic interests. Unfortunately, the United States and Europe are unlikely to wait the four or five years it may take for economic forces to move Japan in the new direction she logically anticipates, that is, raising of her economic structure, encouragement of food and less sophisticated manufactured imports, and expansion of overseas investment.

It is this conflict between the logic of her new long-term industrial policy and the difficulty of taking specific short-term actions which will create problems for Japanese policy makers domestically and internationally over the next two to three years. Even more importantly, some positive steps have to be taken to ensure that short-term implementation failures do not obviate Japan's new and appropriate long-term goals. However, in a democratic society and a mixed economy, major changes in economic policy and in business orientation do not take place easily or immediately. This is Japan's current dilemma.

Notes

1/ Given a lack of domestic raw materials or a technological base, Japanese import requirements are high. Japan imports 100 percent of its oil, 84 percent of its coking coal, 98 percent of its iron ore, and 100 percent of its cotton. In fact, about 84 percent of its imports are industrial raw materials, food, or fuel. In addition, since World War II Japan has paid around $3 billion for foreign technology, and licensing continues on a large scale despite increasing domestic research and development expenditures. (Payments are about ten times revenue.) Japan must import to sustain its economy.

2/ These are results of the annual opinion polls conducted by the government since 1957 concerning people's views on their quality of life. The sample was stratified to include about 20,000 men and women over twenty years old. Sixty percent felt the growth policy was no longer appropriate.

3/ This situation is clearly indicated in a report entitled "Trade and Industrial Policies for the 1970s" and prepared in May 1971 by the Sangyoo Koozoo Shingikai (MITI's Advisory Committee for Industrial Structure). The effect of the Nixon shock was to accelerate the policy-planning process that was already under way. It forced Japanese government and business leaders to recognize that Japan's economy and industry were now of sufficient size to have an impact on the United States and Europe.

4/ Prior to his election in 1972, the new Prime Minister, Kakuei Tanaka, wrote *A Proposal for Remodeling the Japanese Archipelago,* which is now a part of the new policy. Its central theme is to relocate industry and population away from the Pacific megalopolis. The new council consists of top government officials, politicians, and academics. An interesting demonstration of the consensus process is that the group includes K. Ishikawa, a labor leader and outspoken critic of Tanaka's program.

5/ Japanese firms' high debt usage is a function of high investment rates. As high investment rates are fundamental to Japan's growth, high debt levels of major Japanese firms are implicitly backed by the Bank of Japan. Debt levels have been reduced as firms have lowered their investment levels. High debt levels have also disguised the profitability of Japanese firms, which are as profitable as American firms in terms of return on shareholders' equity.

6/ This policy is most clearly laid out in two reports by MITI's Advisory Committee for Industrial Structure: "Trade and Industrial Policies for the 1970s" (May 1971) and "An External Policy in the 1970s" (June 1972).

7/ Conducted by *Nihon Keizai Shimbun* [Japan economic journal].

8/ The rate of increase in imports recently crossed the rate for exports. This indicates a reduction in the surplus in about 1.5 years. This view is supported by an examination of trading companies' orders for future delivery. But short-term dollar exports remain high, and reserves are growing.

9/ About twenty agricultural items are currently subject to quotas.

10/ Small and medium-size firms who serve mostly the domestic market (e.g., not textiles or handicrafts) were not badly affected by revaluation except as major firms lowered prices to avoid dumping charges.

11/ Depression cartels are not used to keep prices high domestically while lower prices are charged overseas. Rather, they are combined with export cartels to set minimum prices in both markets. Dumping at home or abroad is seen by MITI as a counterproductive result of excessive competition.

12/ For a good discussion of the history of government-business relations in steel and automobiles as well as computers, see Eugene J. Kaplan, *Japan: The Government-Business Relationship* (Washington, D.C.: U.S. Government Printing Office, 1972).

3.

STRUCTURE IS BEHAVIOR:
An Appraisal of Japanese Economic Policy,
1960 to 1972

Kozo Yamamura

DURING THE 1960s, the relative and absolute size of the largest firms in Japan (measured in terms of capital, total assets, and bank loans) increased rapidly; concentration ratios that had fallen during the 1950–1958 period rose steadily in many markets; mergers, especially those between the largest firms, increased; the holding of shares of other firms by the largest firms rose, and consequently the control exercised by the largest firms was accelerated; and legal and illegal collusive activities increased in scope and in number. These developments are no less significant in characterizing the Japanese economy of the decade and in analyzing the Japanese economy in the international market of the 1970s than is the rapid growth of Japanese exports and of the gross national product.

As is widely known, such trends toward the concentration of financial and market power and toward the increasingly collusive behavior of firms continued to the extent they did because the government policies actively promoted such trends. The justification for these policies changed during the 1960s from making the necessary preparations for trade liberalization to mitigating the undesirable effects of the recessions of 1965–66 and 1967–68, and then to strengthening Japanese firms that were expected to face an inflow of foreign capital. Nevertheless,

67

the basic rationale of the policies has remained unchanged since the end of the Korean War. Namely, Japanese economic growth depends on increasing exports; and exports can be increased only if Japanese industries can benefit from the most advanced technology, can reap all the gains of economies of scale, and can continue to invest in stable, that is, not excessively competitive, markets. Any resulting increase in the market power of the largest firms and in collusive activities is, however undersirable it might seem in a short run, an unavoidable fact of economic life that Japan must live with for the sake of economic growth.

The basic rationale is found in the following typical views expressed by high-ranking officials of the Ministry of International Trade and Industry (MITI), the *Japan Economic Journal,* and an industry executive:

> When an excessive number of firms, for a given market size, is reduced by means of mergers and unification, it will lead to economies of scale and the ability to expand into a new technological frontier. This will not limit the entry of new firms, but it will demand that entrants possess a high level of technology and productivity.[1]

> Our industries are now faced with the need to improve their current structure with all the powers at our command. Such efforts may lead to the possibility of creating an oligopolistic structure in some sectors of industry. However, even if such a structure results, one can maintain effective competition. . . . Our logic is straightforward, i.e., if we eliminate excessive competition, we may create an oligopolistic structure. But all this means is that the structure will be effectively competitive.[2]

> The pressure of the [1965–66] depression [sic] has set off a series of corporate mergers at a tempo as yet unmatched. Such moves are eventually headed toward an oligopoly, admittedly a desirable industrial structure for enabling effective competition with major foreign manufacturers.[3]

> To realize this goal [of increasing productivity], the prime need is to eliminate all hurdles now hindering the efforts of industry. That is, the present Anti-Monopoly Act must be changed and all types of cartels necessary for the purpose of achieving rationalization, joint ventures, and capital accumulation must be permitted.[4]

Results of Japanese Economic Policies of the 1960s

Some of the results of the Japanese policies of the 1960s may be viewed in recent data on a few aspects of the increasing market and financial power of the largest firms and on legal collusive activities.

TABLE 4. Distribution of Nonfinancial Firms, by Capital, 1969

Capital (yen)	Number of Firms	Percent of Total Capital
Largest 100 firms	100	33.0
Over 1 billion[a]	999	27.5
1 billion	5,671	14.1
50–100 million	5,951	3.8
10–50 million	47,694	9.0
5–10 million	60,823	3.8
Under 5 million	704,367	8.9

[a]Excluding the largest 100 firms.
Source: Fair Trade Commission, *Nihon no Kigyō Shūchū* [The concentration of enterprise structure in Japan] (Tokyo, 1971), p. 12.

Accelerated concentration of capital. Beginning with the concentration of firm size (measured in terms of capital) as a general indicator of the results of various pro-concentration policies, one finds that the accelerated pace of concentration during the 1960s yielded, by 1969, a highly skewed pattern of distribution (see Table 4), a pattern that the Fair Trade Commission (FTC) noted was "more concentrated than in the U.S."[5]

In contrast to the 1950s, concentration in the distribution of capital proceeded even within the largest 100 firms. Between 1958 and 1969, the proportion of the capital of the 10 largest firms rose from 27.5 percent of the total capital of the largest 100 firms to 37.5 percent, and that of those firms ranked from eleventh to twentieth rose from 14.6 to 17.4 percent. That is, in 1969, the largest 20 firms accounted for 54.9 percent of the total capital of the largest 100 firms as opposed to 42.1 percent in 1958.[6]

Perhaps more significantly, the ownership of shares of other firms by the largest 100 firms rose rapidly during the 1960s. While the total capital of the largest 100 firms increased by a factor of 3.4 from 1960 to 1970 (both as of December 1), the book values of shares held by the largest 100 firms rose during the same period by a factor of 5.9 to reach a total of ¥1.9163 trillion or an amount roughly equivalent to the total capital of the 812,884 firms capitalized at less than ¥50 million (¥2.1483 trillion). Such an increase in shareholding by the largest 100 firms meant that the number of firms effectively controlled by the 100 firms also rose. If only those firms are counted in which the largest 100 firms owned at least 10 percent of the shares—the amount that is sufficiently large to enable these shareholders to have significant and dominant influence— then the number of such firms rose from 3,475 in 1960 to 7,612 in 1970; that is, they more than doubled.[7] A further breakdown of the shareholding of the largest 100 firms by the proportion of the shares they owned in each of these firms in 1960 and 1970 yields the results shown in Table 5. Although most of the largest 100 firms owned at least 10 percent of the capital in 11 to 200 firms, Matsushita Electric Appliances led the other 99 firms by owning at least 10 percent of the shares in 536 firms.[8]

Turning to the shareholders of the largest 100 firms, we also discover that there has been a significant trend toward concentration in ownership since the days of the "stockholding revolution" undertaken by the Allied Powers during the 1947–1949 period. In 1970, large shareholders, defined to mean those who owned at least 1 percent of shares in one or more of these largest 100 firms, numbered only 270 legal and natural persons. Focusing on the top 30 of the 270, for whom FTC has compiled data, we find that these largest shareholders owned nearly one-third (31.9 percent) of all the shares owned by the 270 large shareholders. All 30 were legal persons, consisting of 11 insurance companies, 18 banks, and 1 industrial firm (the New Japan Iron and Steel Corporation), which was ranked twenty-eighth. The firm heading the list of the 30 shareholders was Nihon Insurance, which owned at least one percent in 75 of the 100 largest firms, and the thirtieth on the list was the Kobe Bank, which was a large shareholder in 15 of these largest firms.[9]

In assessing the degree of concentration of financial power in postwar Japan, share capital of the largest firms is less significant than the total capital at the disposal of these largest firms. Thus, the true magnitude of concentration in financial power can be assessed only when it is realized that share capital has been a declining proportion of total capital and that bank loans have played a significant role in causing

TABLE 5. Number of Firms Whose Shares Are Owned by Largest 100 Firms, by Proportion of Shareholding, 1960 and 1970

Percent Owned by One of 100 Largest Firms	Number of Firms	
	1960	1970
10–25	1,042	1,731
25–50	875	3,063
Over 50	1,576	2,818
Total	3,493	7,612

Source: FTC, *The Concentration of Enterprise Structure in Japan*, pp. 42–43.

TABLE 6. Proportions of Share Capital and Borrowed Capital as Percent of Total Capital of Largest 1,099 Nonfinancial Firms, 1958 and 1963 to 1969

	1958	1963	1964	1965	1966	1967	1968	1969
Share capital	13.9	15.4	15.0	14.5	13.8	12.3	11.4	10.2
Borrowed capital	67.2	74.0	75.2	76.2	76.7	78.3	79.2	80.4

Source: FTC, *The Concentration of Enterprise Structure in Japan*, p. 18.

an increased disparity in the financial power of the largest firms vis-à-vis that of other firms. Table 6 provides the proportions of share capital and "borrowed capital" (bank loans) of the firms whose share capital was in excess of ¥1 billion for the period between 1958 and 1969. Owners' equity consisted of the remainder, that is, 100 minus those proportions accounted for by share capital and borrowed capital. Here it is important to remember that the total share capital of these firms more than tripled during the 1960s.

Nearly all the borrowed capital or what Japanese call "others' capital" was supplied by what are known as the Big Five banks and the dozen largest city banks. Because the largest banks increased their importance as suppliers of the ever-rising demand for capital by the largest firms and because these banks were major shareholders in these firms, the 1960s saw the formation of increasingly identifiable and distinct alliances of economic interests—"the community of interests"—between the largest firms and the largest banks. Although these communities of interests should not be equated with the prewar *Zaibatsu* that the Allied Powers once called "the cancer of Japan,"[10] it has become difficult to deny that the mutual interests and the close personal relationships fostered through joint planning of new ventures, breakfast and dinner clubs of presidents, and exchanges of officers (if mostly from the banks to the firms) closely resembled, by the end of the decade, the *Zaibatsu* of the prewar years.

In this connection, another noteworthy development of the 1960s was the rapidly increasing ownership of shares by the Big Ten trading companies. Although none of the ten is large enough in terms of share capital to be classified in the largest 100 firms, their financial power, based on their ability to borrow from the largest banks, enabled them to increase or take full financial control in many firms in the retail, wholesale, and manufacturing industries. Their successful drive to create chain stores and franchises on the basis of part or total ownership has been called by journalists "a revolution in the distribution channels."[11] As of September 1970, the number of firms in which one of the Big Ten owned at least 10 percent of the shares totaled 1,683, with the total book value of shares reaching ¥337,975 million or about 2.3 times the total capital of these ten trading companies. A breakdown of their shareholding patterns shows that the Big Ten owned 10 to 25 percent of the shares in 561 firms, 25 to 50 percent in 710 firms, and over 50 percent in 412 firms.[12]

Increase in number of mergers. Along with the increasing financial power of the largest firms, the 1960s saw a steadily rising number of mergers, especially between the largest firms. This was an important contributing factor in raising the market shares of the largest firms. Table 7 tells the story clearly.

The number of mergers rose in each class of share capital. How-

TABLE 7. Mergers, by Size of Postmerger Share Capital, 1960 to 1970

Capital (yen)	1960	1961	1962	1963	1964	1965	1966	1967	1968	1969	1970
Under 5 million	154	155	161	199	190	277	217	227	213	203	185
5–10 million	100	125	131	187	160	169	142	181	177	195	161
10–50 million	94	176	221	320	313	318	341	367	383	456	460
50–100 million	33	63	72	115	67	57	63	77	103	111	119
100–500 million	41	45	91	116	90	93	67	94	100	142	142
500 million–1 billion	8	9	10	15	14	16	11	9	16	20	37
1–5 billion	9	13	23	28	17	8	23	29	19	29	34
5–10 billion	0	3	3	5	4	3	2	4	2	5	3
Over 10 billion	1	2	3	12	9	3	5	7	7	2	6
Total	440	591	715	997	864	944	871	995	1,020	1,163	1,147

Source: Fair Trade Commission, *Annual Reports*, 1960–1970.

ever, the striking facts are that the annual number of mergers creating firms with postmerger capital in excess of ¥1 billion rose from 10 in 1960 to 43 in 1970 and that a total of 57 mergers that resulted in firms with postmerger capital exceeding ¥10 billion took place during the eleven-year period. Though it is not revealed in Table 7, among the 100 largest firms in terms of share capital as of 1970, 30 absorbed 50 firms with a total capital of ¥247.7 billion during the 1960s.[13]

When merger data for 1970 is analyzed in order to examine the types of mergers that have been taking place most recently, one discovers that of the 1,147 mergers, 574 (44.1 percent) were conglomerate mergers; 472 (36.2 percent) can be classified as horizontal, that is, mergers between firms that were within the same or closely related product markets; 47 (3.6 percent) were backward and 60 (4.6 percent) were forward integrations; and 150 (11.5 percent) mergers were to absorb failing firms or to reorganize because of changes in the values of shares or in the organization of firms. Conglomerate mergers have become increasingly important whereas backward and forward integrations gradually declined in number because such integrations were being accomplished through increased shareholding rather than through outright mergers. Also, by examining the 1970 mergers by industry and by type, one learns that the largest number of mergers, 479 out of the 1,147, took place in the wholesale and retail industries, and this figure was more than all the mergers, 395, in the manufacturing industries. To give credence to the so-called revolution in the distribution channels, of the 479 mergers, horizontal and conglomerate mergers accounted for 123 and 276, respectively, while vertical integration was limited to 35.[14] The fact that the firms in food and related industries led all other industries with 55 mergers out of the 395 also suggests that consideration for the rapidly changing pattern of distribution in Japan is playing a significant role in the recent merger activities.[15]

Mergers in such numbers and especially among the largest firms inevitably increased concentration ratios in markets during the 1960s. Though we must rely on the data for the period between 1960 and 1966 in analyzing recent changes,[16] this may not be a serious weakness because one can be reasonably confident that the same trend continues. Generally speaking, during the seven-year period, concentration ratios at the ten largest firm levels declined in 59 markets, remained stable in 32 markets, and rose in 107 markets among the 198 markets for which

TABLE 8. Structures of 198 Markets, 1966

Classification	Number of Markets	Market Structure and Distinctive Behavioral Characteristics
Monopolistic	9	Total number of firms is less than 7; market share of largest firm exceeds 50 percent and is distinctively larger than that of second largest firm. Because of dominant position of market leader, price competition is virtually absent.
Oligopolistic (1)	19	Total number of firms is less than 7; market share of each firm is relatively evenly distributed.
Oligopolistic (2)	25	There are 8 to 30 firms in market; market share of largest firm exceeds 30 percent. Price competition is limited.
Oligopolistic (3)	28	There are 8 to 30 firms in market; combined market share of four largest firms exceeds 75 percent.
Oligopolistic (4)	22	At least 40 firms are in market; combined market share of four largest firms exceeds 75 percent.
Competitive (1)	55	Less than 30 firms are in market; market share of each firm is relatively evenly distributed. Legal and illegal cartels are occasionally disrupted by spurts of price competition.
Competitive (2)	23	More than 40 firms are in market; largest 10 have at least 50 percent of market share.
Competitive (3)	17	More than 40 firms are in market; 10 largest firms have less than 50 percent of market share.

Source: Based on the data and information contained in FTC, *Kanri kakaku* [Administered prices] (Tokyo: 1970), pp. 292–294.

the ratios are available.[17] In the words of the FTC, "the concentration ratios are continuing to rise if one is to speak of the trend in general . . . because of the increasingly large scale of production, advertisement, and sales and because, as the supply leads the demand, the largest firms, all with ample capital at their disposal, have the advantage in adopting larger production units and new technology, and in strengthening their sales network by nationwide advertising."[18] Rather than examine the ratios by market over the period, Table 8 presents the 198 markets as of 1966 in eight structural groups.

Because more will be said shortly on the recent market structure and especially on the interrelationships between the structure and behavior, here is a comparison of the market structure in the United States (1963) and in Japan (1966) for those markets for which we have data. At the four largest firm levels, Japanese concentration ratios were higher than in the United States by six or more percentage points in 50 markets, similar (plus or minus six points) in 19 markets, and lower in 25 markets. At the eight largest firm levels, the numbers change to 48 higher, 23 similar, and 20 lower. Although such a comparison is at best hazardous because of a variety of factors that help determine market structure in each country, it nevertheless serves for American readers as an indicator of the degree of concentration of Japanese markets by the middle of the 1960s.[19]

Legal collusive activities. As the concentration in financial and market structures continued throughout the 1960s, legal cartels rose in number during the decade. As of March 1971, the cooperative activities sanctioned under eleven different laws stood at 836, in contrast to 448 as of March 1960.[20] The laws and the number of cartels authorized under each of these laws are summarized in Table 9.

Leaving aside cartels authorized under laws 5, 7, 8, and 9, for which the effects are regional within Japan (and of little significance in international perspective), let us briefly describe each of the remaining seven laws and the collusive activities sanctioned by them. The rationalization cartels were authorized under Article XXIV(4) of the Anti-Monopoly Act, which authorizes such cartels when "it is particularly necessary for effecting technological improvements, cost reduction, increases in efficiency and any other enterprise rationalization," provided that such cartels do not "endanger the interests of the customers,"

TABLE 9. Laws Authorizing Cartels and Number of Cartels Authorized under Each, March 1971

Law	Number of Cartels
1. Rationalization cartels, authorized under Anti-Monopoly Act	13
2. Emergency Act for the Promotion of the Machine-Tool Industry	17
3. Emergency Act for the Promotion of the Electronics Industry	2
4. Emergency Act for Price Stabilization in the Fertilizer Industry	4
5. Law Concerning Tax Collection and Trade Organization in the Sake and Related Industries	7
6. Law Concerning the Promotion of Exports by the Marine Products Industries	8
7. Trade Association Act for the Adjustment of Marine Products	7
8. Law Concerning the Optimization of Activities in the Service Industries Relating to Sanitation	123
9. Trade Association Act Pertaining to Domestic Sea Transportation	21
10. Export-Import Trading Act	195
11. Law Concerning the Organization of Trade Associations of Small-Medium Enterprises	439

Source: FTC, *Annual Report of 1970*, p. 96. (Publication of this report was delayed to September 1971.)

and do not "unjustly limit competition." Of these 13 cartels, 9 were within the iron and steel industry (to set conditions, quantities, and prices of scrap), and 4 were in the textile industry for the purpose of "controlling the quality of products."[21]

The two emergency acts for the promotion of the machine-tool and the electronics industries (laws 2 and 3 in Table 9) were two of the forty-one such emergency laws enacted since the end of the Korean War for the promotion (usually the promotion of exports) of specific industries. These two acts were combined in 1971 into the Emergency Act to Promote Specified Products in the Electronics and Machine-Tool Industries to extend the life of the original laws. Like the two superseded laws, the new law permits cartels for the purpose of maintaining agreements on types and specifications of products, on methods of buying raw materials and parts, on limitation of productive capacities, and also on areas of product specialization by cartel members in those instances in which the absence of these cartels would "materially hamper national economic progress."[22] Under the law, MITI has the power to enforce cartel agreements, and the cartels now in effect under the law cover machinery for the textile industry and specialized machine-tool products including bearings.[23]

The emergency act for the fertilizer industry is a second emergency act that was put into effect in 1964 to replace the initial act of 1954. The two cartels authorized under the act regard ammonium sulfate and urea, and they permit the fixing of prices and quantities exported. The law pertaining to the exporting of marine products (law 6 in Table 9) authorizes eight cartels to agree upon prices, quantities exported, productive capacity, and/or the time and methods of sale. The products covered by these cartels include most of the major marine products exported, that is, pearls and a variety of canned and frozen fish.

Because of the number of cartels authorized under the Export-Import Trading Act, a summary of the nature of the cartel activities and the industries involved is presented in the Appendix. During 1970, MITI invoked in twenty-six instances its power to force firms that were not members of cartels to observe agreements made by the members of cartels.

The cartels authorized under the Law Concerning the Organization of Trade Associations of Small-Medium Enterprises (the last act listed in Table 9) are numerous (439) because they include many cartels organized at regional levels within a market. Thus, if we count the number of cartels in terms of product markets, we find only 42 markets involved. Of these markets, 31 product cartels were organized for domestic purposes and 14 for exporting. The total is larger than 42 because 3 markets have cartels for both domestic and export purposes. For 11 out of the 14 exporting cartels, MITI has invoked its power to make the cartel agreement binding on noncartel members within these markets. The 11 markets involved were canned tangerines, five textile products, binoculars, binocular cases, chinaware, eating utensils, and knives. The cartel agreements cover two or more of the following: quantity, methods of sale, capacity, and price. In addition to these cartels among producers, the law authorizes 6 cartels on methods of purchase and sale in the domestic retail and wholesale industries. The cartelized products include a dozen textile products, petroleum and related products, automobile tires and tubes, and medicines.

Criticism of Policies of the 1960s

The policies fostering the trends of increasing concentration of financial and market powers and of cartelization were subjected to increasingly vocal criticism during the 1960s. Although economists of the Marxist persuasion continue to decry "the ever increasing control by monopoly capital" and "the revival of the Zaibatsu," many economists, journalists specializing in economic policy, and consumer groups challenged the policies, broadly speaking, on two levels. At one level, criticism was directed toward the unchanging rationale of the policy that to achieve increases in exports and per capita income, the degree of concentration in economic power and cartelization arising during the 1960s was necessary. At another level, opposition was expressed against specific mergers, cartels, or market behavior encouraged by or resulting from the government policy. Although academic economists tended to place more emphasis on questions relating to the first level, journalists and consumer groups reacted strongly on issues relating to the second.

Cartels. One of the most frequently and strongly voiced criticisms was leveled against the proliferation of cartels during the 1960s.

In a nutshell, the argument ran as follows: In most cases, cartels are effective in fixing prices and current output but not in limiting investment. Given large profits gained because of the cartels and the fact that market share (output for each firm during the next period of cartelization) is determined either by the cartel or by MITI according to capacity, investments are made continually and well ahead of the amounts justified by demand. As each firm is motivated by the same desire, a fallacy of composition results, and an even larger excess capacity results, thus requiring "more effective" cartels. As long as medium-sized and small firms are being eliminated because of their increasing relative inefficiency, the difficulties created by such strategies adopted by the largest firms surface only slowly. However, during the 1960s, especially after the mid-decade, progressively larger (lumpier) investments on the part of the largest firms, along with the decreasing market share of smaller firms to absorb made cartels a constant necessity. Even in a recession, as was the case for the steel industry, investment for increased capacity continued while multifaceted cartel agreements on price and output were maintained.[24]

Because MITI and FTC could be counted upon to grant recession cartels[25] and rationalization cartels as well as others authorized under various laws, and also administrative cartels sanctioned extralegally by MITI, industry came to depend on cartels to maintain profit levels and to relieve any difficulties caused by excess investment. As long as Japanese firms were relatively smaller and thus less efficient vis-à-vis their competitors abroad, some degree of short-run excess capacity might have been justified for the sake of increasing the international competitiveness of these firms and of achieving rapid economic growth. However, as the decade progressed and as Japanese firms became more efficient than many of their international competitors, as was evidenced in an increasingly larger surplus in the trade balance, there was little reason to continue "cartel capitalism."

Labor leaders and consumer groups argued that the existence of cartels meant that domestic prices, including those of the goods produced by small to medium firms that participated in international trade, were artificially maintained at a higher level than was justified, with the consequence of profiting cartel members and consumers abroad. Many economists continued to criticize cartels on grounds ranging from their undesirable effects on income distribution and resource allocation to price rigidity and increased difficulties of entry. Some economists, who had been willing to accept the undesirable effects of cartels during the 1950s and even during the first half of the 1960s for the sake of adopting advanced technology and economic growth, began to lose patience because cartels, rather than being a temporary policy to help the Japanese economy "catch up with the West," kept on increasing in number. By April 1969, when the steel industry was permitted a boom cartel by MITI—over the objections of FTC—in order to limit output and to fix prices for the purpose of "stabilizing prices on a long-run basis," few economists found it possible to support the policy.[26]

Mergers. While the criticisms against cartels came in a relatively steady stream, criticisms against mergers among the largest firms seemed to accelerate during the 1960s, reaching a veritable torrent by the end of 1969 when the two largest steel producers merged. Although it is possible to outline the nature of the criticisms directed against mergers between large firms during the 1960s using any one of scores of examples, the case of the steel merger is one of the latest and most dramatic examples with which one can contrast the basic views of the policy makers and their critics.[27]

When the intent to seek permission to merge was announced by Yawata and Fuji on April 17, 1968, pandemonium broke out in the daily papers, economic journals, television interview shows, and the Diet. Facts relating the merger thus became widely known. The merger would create a new supergiant company with a capital of ¥229,400 million, gross sales exceeding ¥800,000 million, over 80,000 employees, and the capacity to produce 22.34 million tons of crude steel, thus ranking the new company second only to U.S. Steel. The merged company's market share would reach (with its closest competitor's share in parentheses): 44.5 percent in pig iron (16.6), 35.4 in crude steel (12.4), 34.2 in hot-rolled bars (11.5), 93.3 in heavy rails (2.7), 55.1 in large shapes (10.5), 45.4 in steel wires (16.9), 34.9 in cold-rolled sheet (9.8), and 55.4 in tinplate (23.0).[28]

The firms announced that the merger was to "take full advantage of economies of scale and to acquire sufficient size to be able to replace large obsolete capacities by yet larger and more advanced capacities" as well as to "make research efforts more efficient."[29] However, MITI's role as a promoter of the merger was not an easy one because its usual argument—"to increase the international competitiveness of Japanese firms" —was not applicable in this case because of the widely known fact that Japanese steel producers were already more efficient than their international competitors.[30] The cost per ton of steel in Japan was about $85 whereas American steel was priced around $136; even allowing for the tariff and transportation, Japanese steel had a competitive edge of about $25. Although this fact did not prevent some high-ranking MITI officers from enlisting the "necessity of strengthening the international competitiveness of Japanese steel firms" in making public statements,[31] MITI's endorsement came primarily on the grounds that the reduction in costs achieved by rationalization following the merger would be beneficial to the consumer and to the economy and that the increased market share of the merged firm would be unlikely to limit "effective competition" within various markets of the industry because four other large firms would still remain to challenge the merged firm.

The first defense—that increased efficiency could result (assuming it would indeed result as claimed by the two steel firms)—was rudely shaken by a blunt statement made by the president of Yawata Steel. He candidly stated:

> Though some have included the strengthening of our competitive ability in the reasons for the merger, as far as I am concerned, I believe we already have sufficient competitive ability. . . . It is undeniable that we can secure a larger profit as a result of the merger, and there is some discussion on how such profits may be distributed. As one of the leading promoters of this merger, if I say that such profits would be returned to the consumer, it would be an easier way out, and the path to merger could be smoother. But, as an executive of a corporation, I fail to understand the argument that the profits should be returned to the consumer. I think those who wish to share in the profits are in the wrong. If the newly merged firm reduces costs and increases profits, the competitors will be forced to do the same. As the result, the price can be reduced and the consumers would gain. This I can accept. But the argument that any gain resulting from the merger should be redistributed to the consumer could cause us to lose our incentive for making the efforts we do.[32]

This statement focused the whole issue on one question: Would it be possible for the various markets of the steel industry to remain as competitive after the merger? MITI maintained they could because four large competitors had been known for successfully increasing their market shares against the largest, Yawata. The opponents challenged this on the grounds that price competition in the buying of raw materials and selling of numerous products had already been seriously restricted in the industry because of the effects of "MITI guidance," *Jishu-chōsei* ("self-regulated extralegal price agreements"), legal cartels, and price leadership exerted by Yawata. The effect of the merger, they argued, would be to create a truly dominant firm within the industry and thus make the industry even less competitive. A strongly worded "Opinion on the Big Merger," issued jointly by ninety leading academic economists, advanced the above line of opposition[33] to the merger. So also did I. Takenaka, a respected director of the National Economic Research Institute, in an article entitled "A Merger to Create Market Controlling Power Should Be Disallowed."[34] Opinions against the merger were expressed, as was expected, by union leaders, representatives of consumer groups, and unexpectedly, even a few leading executives of large firms such as the presidents of Nisshin Textile Company and Sony.[35]

During the course of the year, a supposedly objective committee formed by MITI on the merger issued its findings that the merger should be permitted.[36] Although the findings failed to surprise anyone because of the composition of its members, this constituted another pressure on FTC (which was deliberating the case), in addition to the frequent public comments made by MITI officials in support of the merger. Thus, when FTC finally announced a decision in favor of the merger nearly a year after the request for permission was made, few were surprised by the decision. For many economists who had worked on a full-time basis to oppose the merger, the decision was extremely disappointing because of the importance of the case but was far from unexpected. Since the first big merger between Yukijirushi and Clover in 1958, which created a firm having 57.7 percent of the butter market and 75 percent of the cheese market, the opponents of these big mergers had learned to accept defeat through a score of past disappointments. The fact that FTC attached four conditions for the merger received only scant reaction, because in the eyes of the opponents these conditions either were minor or missed the whole point of their opposition.[37]

Price rigidity and price-fixing. While academic critics concentrated on attacking cartels and mergers, the initiative on another major area of criticism—seemingly increasing rigidity in prices and illegal price-fixing—came from consumer groups, leftist political parties, and public media, mostly in reaction to the inflationary wave of the mid-1960s. Soon, price rigidity and price-fixing became a burning public issue. Both FTC, which had long chosen to ignore apparently illegal price-fixing, and academic economists, who despite their constant references to the relationships between the structure and the behavior of markets had been slow in undertaking empirical research, began to involve themselves with the new public issue.

At a more general level of increasing price rigidity in relation to the market structure, an FTC study found that, when the frequencies of changes in prices and amplitudes of price changes between 1963 and 1966 were examined vis-à-vis the types of market structure as of 1966, the results were as shown in Table 10. The frequency of price change is the frequency of changes in price divided by the total number of changes observed through the monthly data available for the four-year period. The amplitude of price change is obtained by dividing two times the difference between the highest price and the lowest price by the sum of the highest and lowest prices. The number of markets included in this study was smaller than that included in Table 8 because of the limited availability of price data and the exclusion of four markets in which price changes were dictated by the international market.

Both price fluctuations and amplitudes are lowest for monopolistic markets and highest for the competitive-III markets; that is, price fluctuation in competitive-III markets took place nearly five times as often as in the monopolistic markets, and the amplitude of price changes in the competitive-III market was almost six times as wide as it was in the monopolistic markets. Even without an analysis of the relationships between specific structures of the markets and their price behaviors, little doubt exists that structure is significant in determining pricing behavior. Another revealing result of this study is that, when trends in the price level are examined vis-à-vis trends in the change of the market structure, in 44 markets in which concentration ratios declined at the ten largest firm levels, the price index declined from 100 at the beginning of 1963 to 95.3 by the end of 1966, while in all other markets the price trend was either virtually nil or rising, that is, the 1966 price indices were between 99.1 and 107.2.[38]

In another study, relating concentration ratios at the largest and second largest firm levels to the frequency of price changes for the

TABLE 10. Frequency and Amplitude of Price Changes in Relation to Market Structures

Market Structure[a]		Frequency of Price Change	Amplitude of Price Change	Number of Markets
Monopolistic		15.80	0.0226	7
Oligopolistic	(1)	23.10	0.0576	10
	(2)	24.36	0.0491	20
	(3)	30.09	0.0697	20
	(4)	22.28	0.0957	17
Competitive	(1)	44.53	0.0957	41
	(2)	33.27	0.0630	15
	(3)	81.87	0.1267	11
Average, all markets		35.70	0.0739	
Total no. of markets				141

*As defined in Table 8.
Source: FTC, *Administered Prices*, p. 320.

period between 1960 and 1966 for eleven major markets, an economist found that the frequency of price change F (measured in the same fashion as the FTC study) can be explained to a significant degree in terms of the market share of the largest firm (X_1) and the two largest firm (X_2) levels. That is: $F = 112.28 - 1.65X_1$ with $r = -0.08$; $F = 128.40 - 1.37X_2$ with $r = -0.85$. And, when the difference in the market share of the largest firm and the second largest firm (X_{1-2}) was regressed against F, $F = 128.40 - 1.37X_{1-2}$ with $R = 0.64$. All numbers are expressed in terms of the price index in which the base year is January 1960.[39]

Although such studies are still limited, studies on the price-setting and price-fixing behaviors in specific industries are more numerous. Administered pricing, conscious parallelism in pricing, illegal retail price maintenance, and price-fixing have been closely examined by FTC and some economists. The major industries studied to date include iron and steel, electric appliances, film, detergents, cosmetic products, and medicine. In order to illustrate, within a limited space, the whole range of price-setting behaviors and their relationships to the market structure in general and to the recently increasing concentration in distributive channels, one can examine the problems encountered in the electric-appliances industry.[40]

Perhaps because of a charge of dumping television sets (an important product line exported by the industry to the United States) by American competitors and because of increasing public criticism, FTC decided in December 1966 to prosecute the six largest firms in the industry for illegal price-fixing. Though this industry has been known to publish a joint notice of price changes in newspapers, the action taken by FTC had the effect of bringing to the attention of the public that a black-and-white, 19-inch television set that retailed at ¥190,000 in Japan was exported to the Unied States at ¥65,000.[41] The public also learned that the six producers met monthly beginning in 1964 to fix wholesale and retail prices and the amount of rebate to be given for quantity sales, and that these meetings were conducted at two levels— sales-personnel level, which made proposals, and the executive level, which decided upon these proposals. Such public information incensed consumers to the point of organizing a nationwide boycott of television sets.

The case involved more than price-fixing at the retail level. Unlike the U.S. electric-appliance markets in which a few major independents can challenge the largest firms in some product lines, the largest Japanese firms that produced the full range of products were able to and did set profit margins for wholesalers according to the quantity that they sold. They also set rebate schedules for retail stores according to the quantity of sales of each product line and the proportion of the product of a specific firm that they sold. As the industry record of the decade clearly indicates, such practices made the entry of any other firm to any product line virtually impossible. Or, in the words of Komiya et al., "the present *keiretsu* system of each of the makers of home electric appliances is highly exclusive in nature. The distribution channel of each maker is built by each maker and made rigidly exclusive. This means that if a new independent maker happened to develop an excellent product, he could not find retail outlets to sell his product widely. The fact that retail stores in each *keiretsu* system would be hesitant to sell the products of other firms constitutes a high barrier to entry in the home electric appliances industry."[42]

The electric-appliances case, however, is only an introduction to the increasingly serious problems of illegal price-fixing—which, as the FTC study groups have admitted, is extremely difficult to prove[43]—and to an increasing amount of legal retail price maintenance. Although few believed that the legalization of retail price maintenance under article XXIV (2) of the amended Anti-Monopoly Act of 1953 would create any serious problems because of the fragmented and competitive nature of the retail and wholesale industries, the applications for retail price maintenance under the article began to rise rapidly from the early 1960s. By 1966, thanks to the readily granted permissions by FTC, the total number of items—counting toothbrushes, headache medicines, face creams, and so forth, as one item—rose to 4,412. By 1969, as many as 5,557 items produced by the pharmaceutical, cosmetic, and camera industries were involved.[44]

As with cartels, legal retail price maintenance tends to encourage illegal retail price maintenance. As an FTC study indicated and as occasional newspaper articles suggested, in an increasing number of products in the textile, food, and automobile-accessories markets retail prices have become sufficiently rigid to suggest possible illegal collusion.[45] Many now expect that the current revolution in the distribution channels will only make matters even worse by creating market structures that are conducive to such collusion activities and by making entries increasingly difficult. Komiya et al., observing such trends, recommended recently that FTC should: (1) prosecute much more vigorously all suspected cases of illegal price-fixing and retail price maintenance; (2) prohibit ex-factory prices and differentials between export and domestic markets; (3) eliminate exclusive distribution channels; (4) limit advertising expenditures in order to reduce barriers to entry; and (5) increase consumer education.[46]

As seems evident on the basis of the limited observations and evidence presented so far, the Japanese policies of the 1960s increased, directly and indirectly, the concentration in the economic (market and financial) power of the largest firms. This power, appearing as a highly oligopolistic market structure and increased financial control of a larger number of firms, was exercised to restrict competitive behavior on many fronts. Legal cartels and price maintenance further justified and encouraged some of this collusive behavior. Despite the mounting evidence, the policy makers have shown little sign of altering their policy. As late as spring 1971, the report of the MITI committee on industrial structure argued that:

> When the past data on changes in the number of enterprises, in concentration ratios *vis-à-vis* price changes, and in productivity against price changes are examined, it is not proper to consider that competition was unduly restricted because of the increases in concentration ratios. Rather, one should correctly see that our national economy has continued to be competitive in structure, aided by such factors as increased demand and progress in technological innovation.[47]

Changes and Revisions in Official Policies

The Nixon shock of August 1971 was followed by the revaluation of the yen in December. The government could no longer minimize the significance of a huge trade surplus as it had been fond of doing even during the latter half of the 1960s. Would the shock and the revaluation, accompanied by strong U.S. pressure, cause the Japanese government to modify or even to discontinue its direct and indirect export-promoting policies? The answer, a negative one, came quickly.

Recession cartels. In November 1971, the producers of stainless steel were allowed to form a recession cartel in order to limit their total output, excluding the amount that each producer exported. The steel industry followed in December, and its recession cartel began to limit the output of steel sheets, wires, and pipes. By the beginning of May 1972, nine more recession cartels had been authorized. The industries and the cartel agreements involved were: polyvinyl chloride (output and investment); steel bars and plates for construction (output, excluding exports); liner boards (investment) and corrugated sheets (investment)—both products of the paper industry, used in making containers; five specialized steel products including small and medium-sized steel bars (outputs); polypropylene (output); polyethylene (output); ethylene (output); and synthetic graphite (output, excluding exports and that for each firm's own use).[48]

As before, these cartels were authorized by interpreting Article XXIV (3) of the Anti-Monopoly Act "realistically" and "flexibly." One of the two major conditions that firms must meet before permission to form a recession cartel can be granted is that their products are being sold below average cost. It has always been extremely difficult for FTC to establish the existence of this condition because much of the decision must be based on the data and claims presented by the firms themselves. Such a difficulty provided grounds for giving the benefit of the doubt and for a flexible assessment of the data involved. Thus, even for the firms in the steel industry that were declaring dividends "because it is necessary if the steel firms are to be able to borrow more from the banks,"[49] FTC chose to rule that this condition was being met.

Even if one is prepared to give the benefit of the doubt on the first condition,[50] there seems little reason to believe that the second condition is being met by firms just been granted a recession cartel. The condition states that, before a recession cartel can be authorized, a substantial number of firms in an industry must face the distinct possibility of being forced to discontinue operation, that is, face the threat of bankruptcy, if such a cartel is not permitted. Can anyone in MITI or FTC seriously maintain that the [giant] firms in the chemical and steel industries, which account for most of the newest recession cartels, even remotely satisfy this condition?

There exist several other fundamental questions that are more economic than legal in nature concerning the recession cartels: Why shouldn't the profits of good years and the claimed loss of recession years be averaged? Why should certain industries continue to benefit from a policy that seems to strive to guarantee profits even in a recession? Don't recession cartels, especially those for the steel products that are inputs of other industries, aggravate the recession in a macroeconomic sense because prices of these products usually rise (as have the prices for steel products in this recession) as a result of the cartels? And, isn't the degree of the excess capacity suffered by each industry its and MITI's own making? Won't the current recession cartel create only more problems to be solved again in another recession?

Lack of policy changes. Along with the above recession cartels, another indication that the policy remains unchanged came in the extremely limited application of one of the eight programs that the government announced during the summer of 1971 for the purpose of reducing the increasing trade surplus. One program that could have affected much of what has been observed in this essay read: "to eliminate measures which were specifically designed to aid exporting industries." However, the only action taken under this program has been, as of May 1972, to eliminate preferential interest rates for loans granted to exporting firms. That is, as a result of the postrevaluation monetary market in which interest rates have fallen visibly because of the excess supply of loanable funds, no meaningful action has been taken to eliminate measures promoting exports.

When added to the legacies of the policies of the 1960s, these unchanging policies are expected not only to prolong but also to compound numerous economic problems that Japan faces and will continue to face domestically as well as in the international economy. Just as the multifaceted domestic problems are obvious from our earlier descriptions, the problems and criticisms that Japan faces in the international market are equally evident. Because the policies of the 1960s continue, the most recent data still show a trade surplus, one larger than that being accumulated by any European nation.[51] Although officials maintain that the effects of the revaluation will appear after eighteen months to two years, reports are numerous to the effect that Japanese firms are "increasing their export drive even though they have to lower the prices to adjust for the revaluation."[52] The export drives are more ardent in those industries in which the pains of the excess capacity are severer now because of reduced domestic demand. This fact applies to both the large and the small to medium firms that have been encouraged to build capacities on the assumption that both domestic and international demands would continue to increase and that any short-run problems arising out of rapidly increasing capacity could be eased by various types of cartels.

The most recent reactions of the policy makers and the exporting industries to the continuing complaints of aggressive exporting lodged by the U.S. and European nations have been to suggest and to put partially in effect what has come to be known as orderly marketing.[53] However, even if the practice could be adopted widely across industries (and this is extremely doubtful), it should result in no more than a temporary and symptomatic relief of increasingly vocal complaints expressed by Japan's trade partners. Worse still, this symptomatic relief can be had only by violating or risking violation of the antimonopoly laws of various nations.[54]

When it is realized that the policies of the past decade are responsible, to a significant degree, for the current export drive and the attendant problems created by it, changes in these policies are clearly called for if Japan sincerely hopes to reduce its large trade surplus. When it is clearly seen that the direct and indirect effects of the policies have been to increase the concentration of market and financial powers and to encourage legal and illegal collusive behavior at the costs of increasingly obvious undesirable effects within Japan, the policies should be revised.

Suggestions for change. Changes and revisions in the official policies could only benefit the Japanese economy, as well as ensure continuing international trade for the benefit of all the trading partners. Although such changes and revisions could take many possible courses, the author suggests within the context of this paper two important avenues of change that should be carried out as soon as practicable.

The first is that FTC realizes that the structure of each market is the most important determinant of the behavior of the firms in that market. Thus, to increase competitive behavior, FTC must not only cease to encourage directly or indirectly any further action by the largest firms to make the market structure more concentrated but also to take measures, where possible, to reduce concentration in the structure of some markets. From the time of its earliest decisions on mergers among the market-leading firms, FTC has maintained that structural changes do not necessarily lead to collusive or restrictive behavior and that it can make each decision only on a case-by-case basis. This view has not changed, as is evidenced by recent remarks made by the commissioner of FTC and by the mergers permitted.[55] Although the decisions are made on a case-by-case basis "realistically" and "flexibly," the consequent structural changes continue to invite, encourage, and result in collusive and restrictive behavior, more and more of which is extremely difficult to prosecute because it is based on tacit communications among a limited number of market leaders. It seems evident, at least to the author, that any further pretense that structural changes do not result in restrictive market behavior is wholly unjustified.

What are clearly and urgently needed are specific guidelines on the degree of concentration of market structure to be permitted and the determination to abide by these guidelines. If not at the relatively stringent level applied to the Bethlehem Steel case of 1958 in the United States, guidelines at least disallowing the most recent merger between Yawata and Fuji should be evolved. The author strongly believes that such guidelines are especially necessary in Japan where the relative political power of FTC vis-à-vis the combined political power of MITI and industry is such that the case-by-case approach is no other than an open invitation to an increasingly concentrated market structure and consequent behavior.

Such guidelines are desirable not only in limiting the undesirable behavior of highly oligopolistic firms within domestic markets but also in alleviating the current problems that Japan faces in the international market, that is, the increase in the trade surplus because of the export drive that is effectively mounted by those firms relieved from the necessity of competing in domestic markets. Noncompetitive structure and behavior also impose a significant deterrent, despite government efforts, to increase imports, because the highly and increasingly concentrated market structure of wholesale and retail industries can impose a de facto tariff on foreign goods by their ability to claim large profit margins and to maintain effectively fixed prices at the retail level.[56]

No less urgent than such guidelines is the second avenue of change —the effort to eliminate a clearly excessive number of cartels and to constrict MITI from issuing extralegal "guidance" that restricts competitive behavior both in the domestic and in the international markets. Not only do these cartels create immediate and long-run problems for the economy, but they are also clearly counterproductive to efforts of the government to reduce the international trade surplus. Cartels, as applied to export industries, have been and continue to be an effective, but no longer necessary, "crutch" on which Japanese firms depend. As for any long-accustomed supports, the sudden removal may be more harmful than desirable. But what the author wishes to see is a nonequivocal expression of intent on the part of Japanese policy makers to eliminate such crutches as soon as possible rather than their recent actions and announcements to the contrary. A stricter standard in granting legal retail price maintenance (assuming total abolition is not practicable) is needed as is a much more vigorous prosecution of illegal collusive activities.[57]

The policies that once proved effective in aiding recovery and achieving rapid growth are no easier to discard than is an ideology that one once held with conviction. However, in 1972, when Japan's international trade continued to show a surplus even after revaluation with the consequence of further increasing an already large reserve, the justifications have definitely ceased to exist for tolerating the socially and economically costly domestic effects of past policies promoting exports. The postwar years ended at the Smithsonian Institute, and so should the postwar policies. As the MITI committee explains:

> The decade of new conditions and new problems has come. The '70's are different from the '50's, and the '60's. . . . Thus what is needed is an international trade and industry policy for the '70's. When the new decade differs from the old, different ideas, actions, policies, and organizations are demanded. Those who still have the mentality of a person climbing a hill even after he has conquered the tallest mountain will find no place for themselves in the new age. Ideas and actions which merely follow inertia must be eliminated. . . . Obsolete ideas, structure, and power bases must be reduced to ashes and we must work towards creating new ideals.[58]

APPENDIX

Cartels Authorized under the Export-Import Trading Act, March 1970

1. Cartels among exporters: 124[a]
   a. Cartel agreements are: price, 42; quantity, 61; market share, 4; sales method, 49; quality (design), 40; other,[b] 79.
   b. Number of cartels, by industry, is: textile, 51; heavy industries, 27; sundry,[c] 25; chemical, 6; nonferrous metal, 1; agricultural and marine products, 3; other,[d] 1.

2. Exporters' cartels in domestic markets: 60[a]
   a. Cartel agreements are: price, 43; quantity, 34; market share, 32; quality (design), 7; adjustment fund[e] 7; other,[b] 7.
   b. Number of cartels, by industry, is: textile, 10; heavy industries, 30; sundry, 2; chemical, 14; agricultural and marine products, 4.

3. Import cartels: 3
   a. Cartel agreements are: price, 3; quantity, 2; quality, 2.

b. All cartels in this category are in agricultural products (corn, onions, and bananas).

4. Export-import trade associations: 8
   a. Cartel agreements among small- and medium-scale exporters and importers are: price, quantity exported, and various other aspects of exporting and importing.
   b. All cartels in this category are exporters and importers of textiles (cotton and chemical fibers).

---

[a]Because one cartel agrees upon one or more of the items in categories 1a and 2a, the total number of agreements exceeds 124 and 60, respectively.
[b]This includes methods of receiving payments, observance of brand names, "after-care," methods of bidding, resgistration of customers, receiving of joint orders, and so forth.
[c]This (*zakka* in Japanese) covers all goods produced by industries not included in 1b. Typically, these are goods produced by small- and medium-sized firms.
[d]This includes products of any industry, provided quantities exported are extremely small and limited to a specified region. When these provisos are met, a firm is designated "a champion," and it acts on behalf of cartel members.
[e]This type of agreement covers two types of adjustments. One is called *calculation pools*, which are organized to share the export market and profits when an export market is "unusually" profitable and faces the danger of extremely competitive behavior among Japanese exporters. The other type, called *adjustment fund*, is established among member firms in an exporting industry in order to compensate exporting "losses" suffered on the part of some member firms by using profits made by those member firms that have sold their goods domestically. (FTC informed the author that as of June 1972, no adjustment fund is in effect while two calculation pools exist in the chemical industry.)
Source: See note 21.

Notes

---

*The author wishes to thank Hiroshi Iyori of the International Section of the Fair Trade Commission, Japan, for providing me with the most recent FTC publications and for answering numerous questions. Thanks are also due to Professor Teiichi Wada of Waseda University and the office of the Vice-Minister of International Trade and Industry for sending me the publications that the author requested. The author alone, however, is responsible for the views expressed in this paper.

1/ Y. Morozumi, "A Proposal by MITI," in T. Chigusa, ed., *Sangyō taikei no sai-hensei* [A reorganization of industrial structure] (Tokyo: Shunju Publishing Co., 1963), p. 65. Morozumi is the Vice-Minister of MITI.

2/ Y. Komatsu, "The Urgent Need to Eliminate Excessive Competition in Order to Face Foreign Competition," a special issue of *Tōyō Keizai Shimpo* (an economic weekly) on oligopolistic structure (December 1966), p. 77.

3/ *Nihon Keizai Shimbun* [Japan economic journal] (Nov. 30, 1965).

4/ R. Kodō, "A Proposal from the Industry," in T. Chigusa, cited in note 1, p. 134.

5/ FTC, *Nihon no kigyō shūchū* [The concentration of enterprise structure in Japan] (Tokyo: FTC, 1971), p. 31. For comparative data for the 1945–1962 period on distribution of capital by size and on other data cited in this essay, see K. Yamamura, *Economic Policy in Postwar Japan* (Berkeley: University of California Press, 1967).

6/ The total operating profit of the 100 largest firms in 1969 accounted for 25.8 percent of the total earned by all firms, excluding the financial. The data by industry are as follows:

(1) Industry	(2) No. of 100 Largest Firms in Each Industry	(3) Percentage of Industry Earned by the Firms (2)	(4) Total No. of Firms in Each Industry
Marine	2	45.0	1,924
Mining	2	27.7	2,227
Construction	3	10.3	49,071
Manufacturing	63	29.0	183,376
Wholesale and retail	7	8.1	249,863
Real estate	1	6.9	21,561
Transportation	7	24.3	19,615
Shipping	4	26.4	2,667
Electricity	9	97.5	28
Gas	2	74.4	122

Among the manufacturing industries, the steel industry led with 65.6 percent for 8 firms. Y. Higuchi and K. Watanabe, "Concentration and Current Changes in Japan," *Kōsei Torihiki*, no. 231 (January 1970), p. 10.

7/ FTC, *Concentration of Enterprise Structure*, pp. 42–43.

8/ Because of what is usually referred to as *keiretsu* ("lineage relationships"), the extent of the financial control exerted by the largest firms does not end with these firms. For further discussion of *keiretsu*, see Yamamura, *Economic Policy*, chap. 7.

9/ FTC, *Concentration of Enterprise Structure*, pp. 44–45.

10/ K. Yamamura, "Zaibatsu Prewar and Zaibatsu Postwar," *Journal of Asian Studies*, vol. 23, no. 4 (August 1966).

11/ For a description of the recent integration of distributive channels by the trading companies, see I. Katō, *70-nendai ni idomu sōgō-shōsha* [The general trading companies challenge the 1970s] (Tokyo: Seikei Tsushin-sha, 1970).

12/ FTC, *Concentration of Enterprise Structure*, pp. 142–143.

13/ Calculated from ibid., pp. 153–162.

14/ The remainder is "other" mergers including "reorganizations."

15/ The data contained in this paragraph on mergers are taken from FTC, *Concentration of Enterprise Structure*, pp. 62–85 and pp. 158–172. These pages contain much more information on recent mergers than is presented here. The pattern of mergers during the few years preceding 1970 is similar to that observed for 1970 as can be confirmed in *The FTC Annual Report* for these years.

16/ Concentration ratios are published only at irregular intervals, and the latest data now available are for 1966.

17/ FTC, *Kanri kakaku* [Administered prices] (Tokyo: FTC, 1970), pp. 276–279.

18/ Ibid., p. 278.

19/ Ibid., p. 282.

20/ For a table presenting the same information contained in Table 6 for 1960 and 1961, see Yamamura, *Economic Policy*, p. 78.

21/ The data on and explanations of cartels in the remainder of this section are based on the FTC *Annual Report of 1970*, pp. 94–115 and pp. 286–347, and the information produced by Mr. H. Iyori. For the entire text of the Anti-Monopoly Act in English, see Yamamura, *Economic Policy*, pp. 196–216.

22/ *The FTC Annual Report of 1970*, p. 9.

23/ Ibid., p. 348.

24/ For the author's and several Japanese economists' criticisms on cartels of the late 1950s and the early 1960s, the readers are referred to Yamamura, *Economic Policy*, pp. 87–107.

25/ Recession cartels are discussed in the last section of this essay.

26/ One of the best analyses and criticisms of cartels is found in Kenichi Imai, "Iron and Industry," in a special issue of *Chuō Kōron* on economic problems, published in summer 1972, pp. 364–408. Although Imai focuses on the iron and steel industry, his analyses cover numerous problems relating to the postwar Japanese cartels.

27/ Among many recent articles on the mergers between the largest market-leading firms, seven articles by leading economists found in a special issue of *Tōyō Keizai Shimpo* (July 1968) are excellent. The authors and articles were (with titles translated into English): Masao Baba, "The Meaning of Opposition against the Big Mergers in Economics"; Hirobumi Uzawa, "A Theoretical Approach to Competition and Growth of Firms"; Akio Mori, "The Economics of Mergers and the Growth of Firms"; Yoshirō Kobayashi, "Apparent Dangers of Collusive Oligopolists in the Big Mergers"; Yuichi Shionoya, "The Big Mergers Seen from the Perspective of the Theory of a New Industrial Nation"; Tadao Konishi, "The Atheoretical Nature of Theories Supporting the Big Mergers"; and Akira Shōda, "The Recent Big Mergers in Defiance of the Anti-Monopoly Act."

28/ These data are as of 1968 and were supplied by Hiroshi Iyori.

29/ As quoted in the article by Baba, cited in note 27, p. 51.

30/ Ibid., p. 51.

31/ In *Nihon Keizai Shimbun* [Japan economic journal] (Apr. 10, 1968) and in *Mainichi Shimbun*, (May 23, 1968). Both are leading newspapers.

32/ *Nihon Keizai Shimbun* (May 8, 1968).

33/ Issued on June 15, 1968. The leaders of the group were Professor Ryuichirō Tachi and Tadao Uchida (Tokyo University), Shigeto Tsuru (Hitotsubashi), Hideo Aoyama (Kyoto University), and Hisao Kumagai (Osaka University).

34/ *Tōyō Keizai Shimpo* (May 4, 1968).

35/ *Asahi Shimbun* (Apr. 30, 1968) and *Mainichi Shimbun* (June 4, 1968). Many other statements against the merger, issued by labor unions, the Socialist and Communist parties, and consumer groups during the same period, are too numerous to be cited fully.

36/ Of the eighteen members, eleven were from industry and banking. For the text of the committee report, an interesting description on the committee deliberations, and a strongly worded criticism of the report by Professor R. Komiya, see *Ekonomisuto* (a weekly) (Sept. 3, 1968).

37/ The conditions attached by FTC were that: (1) the Fuji Iron and Steel Company "transfer the equipment relating to the production of rails" to Nippon Kōkan Company along with "the knowledge of the technology"; (2) Yawata sell shares in Tōyō Kōkan, a tinplate producer, to Nippon Kōkan; (3) Yawata "transfer" one blast furnace to Kobe Steel; and (4) both Yawata and Fuji provide technical assistance to Kawasaki Steel and Nippon Kōkan in relation to the production of steel-sheet piles. Presumably, the method of "transfer" is left to the parties involved. For a strong view criticizing the FTC consent decree, see T. Uchida, *Asahi Shimbun* (Oct. 31, 1969).

38/ FTC, *Administered Prices*, p. 322.

39/ From the article by Kobayashi, cited in note 27. He also obtained statistically significant results by regressing the concentration ratios at the largest and the two largest firm levels on returns on capital. However, the findings need to be disaggregated to be useful because both his concentration ratios and profits are averages for eleven industries and not for specific markets. A few more empirical studies of interests could not be incorporated here. The two most appropriate ones in the context of this essay are: (1) Y. Tsuji, "The Current Conditions of Industrial Concentration in Japan," *Tōyō Keizai Shimpo* (June 1969), a special issue on the Anti-Monopoly Act, which contains data on the increasing rigidity of changes in market shares by market and by industry and (2) the Editorial Department, "Changes in the Power of Big Business in Japan," *Tōyō Keizai Shimpo* (December 1966), a special issue on oligopolistic firms. This article, which studied the changes in market shares within a market and in ranking in terms of the absolute volume of sales among the largest 200 firms across industry, found, for example, that both market shares and the ranking by volume of sales had become increasingly rigid; that is, the annual means of the coefficients of variation for both declined as follows: The averages of the means of coefficients of variation of the ranking for the 1956–1958, 1959–1961, and 1962–1965 periods were 0.1842, 0.1500, and 0.1239, and the averages of the means of the coefficients of variation of market shares for the same three periods were 0.1027, 0.0798, and 0.0670. On the bases of these findings and others, the editors concluded that rigidities in both the ranking and market shares increased visibly from the beginning of the 1960s.

40/ Although FTC's *Administered Prices* contains many valuable observations and data, the most thorough analysis of price-setting and price-fixing behaviors is in R. Komiya et al., "Home Electric Appliances," in a special issue of *Chūō Kōron* on economic problems which was published in summer 1971, pp. 360–412.

41/ The author has vivid recollections of being surprised during the early 1960s by these joint announcements.

42/ R. Komiya et al., "Home Electric Appliances," pp. 405–406.

43/ FTC, *Administered Prices*, pp. 3–4.

44/ FTC, *Saihan seido* [The resale system] (Tokyo: FTC, 1971), p. 50.

45/ Ibid., p. 1.

46/ Komiya et al., "Home Electric Appliances," pp. 403–412.

47/ The Committee on Industrial Structure, *70-nendai no tsūshō sangyō seisaku* [The international trade and industry policy of the 1970s] (Tokyo: Japanese government, 1971), p. 70. This is an interim report of a committee created by MITI.

48/ Based on the information supplied to the author by FTC. These recession cartels are usually granted for a specific time period, often six months as was the case with these cartels. The cartels for stainless and for other steel products, however, were granted an extension of another six months (*Asahi Shimbun*, July 1, 1972). FTC, in granting the extension to the steel cartel, attached the condition that a reduction in the amount of output from the level agreed upon by FTC and the cartel members as base output should not exceed 10 percent because the excess stock of the product covered by the cartel has declined and the prices of these products have risen since the beginning of the recession cartel. The cartel members requested a reduction up to 20 percent. The above is based on an FTC announcement issued on July 1, 1972, supplied to the author by FTC.

49/ H. Misonou, "Dangerous Recession Cartels Are Rampant," *Ekonomisuto*, (Dec. 14, 1971), p. 26. On the same page, Misonou went on to argue that "as long as a total dividend of ¥18.4 billion is distributed for the year, a recession cartel simply does not make sense." Among a score of recent articles that criticize the recent recession cartels, the most informative ones are A. Shōda, "Dangerous Recession Cartels," *Asahi Shimbun* (a weekly) (Dec. 12, 1971); and K. Niino, "Recession Cartels Cannot Be Anti-Recession Measures," *Tōyō Keizai Shimpo* (Dec. 4, 1971).

50/ Although the details are not available, the difference (losses) between the prices and costs of cartelized steel products are contained in *Tekkō-Kai* [The steel world], a trade journal (Dec. 1971), p. 15. In this issue, an executive of New Japan Steel stated in defense of the recession cartel in his industry that "we hear complaints of 'an excessively friendly relationship' between the government and the industry. That is, some are complaining that the steel industry competes vigorously in creating more capacity and, when a recession comes, the industry cries for help from the government. Such a view must be reconsidered within a perspective of the interests of the national economy. . . . Our economy is now facing a big stock which was not anticipated; thus, our dependence on recession cartels should not be criticized under the current circumstances" (p. 17).

51/ "Japan's exports continue to increase even following the revaluation. The monthly dollar volume of exports for January, February, and March exceeded those of the past year by 24.4, 23.8, and 19.0 per cent respectively." *Tōyō Keizai Shimpo* (May 6, 1972), p. 33.

52/ Ibid., p. 33. For a description of "export drives" currently practiced by various industries, see ibid., pp. 35–37.

53/ Many industries are for the orderly marketing "in principle, but not on specifics." One steel firm executive is quoted as saying: "The yen has been revalued. This means that we are going to make, with our utmost ability, a renewed effort to export. My guess is that exports will increase rather than decline." *Tōyō Keizai Shimpo* (Feb. 12, 1972), p. 17.

54/ As of May 1972, ten Japanese products were under investigation for possible violation of the U.S. antidumping law. In Canada, five products are being investigated. *Tōyō Keizai Shimpo* (May 6, 1972), p. 34.

55/ The commissioner of FTC, Seiichi Yamada, stated in a recent interview that: "If we are to follow guidelines, there will be a risk of applying it too rigidly. At present, we cannot adopt them. We could have guidelines on the adoption of foreign technology and on fair competition, and these guidelines are desirable. However, on mergers, guidelines are difficult and not proper." *Nikkei Center Kaihō* (a monthly review issued by an economic research organization sponsored by the *Nihon Keizai Shimbun*), no. 91 (October 1971), p. 16.

56/ Most illustrative of this is the case involving whiskey for which imports have been "liberalized." Despite the liberalization, the quantity imported fails to increase at a rate anywhere near the demand because of the extremely limited and tightly controlled distribution channels that at least quadruple the import price by the time the product reaches the consumer. For example, the most popular brand, Johnny Walker, is imported exclusively by the Mitsubishi Trading Company and the Tomen Trading Company, and they in turn distribute to thirteen distributors. As any price-cutting by a retailer means the end of the privilege to market the whiskey, the retail price is collectively set, and price-cutting is extremely rare. Providing strong legal support for this arrangement is Article 21 of the Tariff Act, which considers the importation by any person—other than a few trading companies that currently hold exclusive marketing rights and have registered the brand name with the patent office—of any foreign good enjoying an established brand name in violation of the exclusive rights to the brand name. Since the liberalization of imports began during the early 1960s, those who attempted to import seventy-four products, including Johnny Walker, Ronson lighters, Twining tea, and Lipton tea, outside of the established channels have been successfully prosecuted. FTC is now considering investigation of these exclusive arrangements, and the Ministry of Finance announced that it is considering enforcing Article 21 "more flexibly" in the future. For a future discussion concerning this problem, see *Tōyō Keizai Shimpo* (June 10, 1972), pp. 76–78.

57/ However, the most recent indication is that the realization of the hope expressed in the text may be slow in coming. After this paper was drafted, the author learned that MITI recommended to the members of the stainless-steel cartel that a new firm, financed by the cartel members and banks, be formed to buy nearly 50 percent of the current capacity for the purpose of continuing effective output limitations after the current recession cartel expires at the end of 1972. If such a recommendation is adopted, the effect will be to create yet a new type of cartel without a time limit. The recommendation is being considered by the association of the presidents of the member firms in the stainless-steel cartel. *Nihon Keizai Shimbun* (July 5, 1972).

58/ Taken from the preface of *The International Trade and Industry Policy of the 1970s*, p. 10. See note 47.

4.

APPROACHES TO DISTRIBUTION IN JAPAN

C. Tait Ratcliffe

ASIDE FROM THE FORTUNATE U.S. EXPORTER who can leave all the details of marketing and distribution in Japan up to an intermediary, almost any producer in the United States who is interested either in exporting to Japan or setting up manufacturing facilities there will face the problems of understanding and coping with the Japanese distribution system. Although the modes are diverse, distribution of most consumer goods and many industrial parts and products is still characterized by a high degree of fragmentation and specialization in production and end sales, and by multiple layers of wholesalers servicing the producers and outlets.

It should be stressed at the outset that the idea that the distribution system in Japan is a kind of nontariff barrier must be rejected, for it is clearly a self-defeating attitude. The U.S. marketing system was an obstacle to Sony and other Japanese manufacturers who now have strong positions in the United States, but they overcame it by investing the needed time and money to cope with the problems of selling in the U.S. market. A similar investment is warranted on the part of any U.S. producer who has a product that can be sold competitively in Japan. With incomes still rising in Japan at rates near 10 percent and with the likelihood of further revaluations of the yen—or equivalently a drive on the part of the Japanese to encourage imports before this happens —the Japanese market is now and will continue to be an extremely attractive one for U.S. producers. Both Japanese and U.S. producers face the distribution problem in many industries to exactly the same degree. For both it is a problem to be solved but not a nontariff barrier in the sense this term is usually used.

The problem of market entry by a non-Japanese firm requires an understanding of the structure of production; the structure of final sales; who the intermediaries are and what functions they perform; and who the intermediaries and end sellers easiest to reach are and how they can be motivated to handle the product. Despite the complaints of "complexity" and "nontariff barrier," a number of non-Japanese producers have already been very successful in either remolding the distribution system or working effectively through the present system with a minimum of changes.

Implications of Fragmentation in Production and Final-Sales Units

Production, on the one side, and end-sales outlets, on the other, tend to be highly fragmented in Japan. Eighty percent of retail sales still go through neighborhood outlets. As a result, the small producer and small retailer are dependent upon wholesalers for transport, storage, sales promotion, the provision of credit, and the absorption of risk through the sale of goods on a consignment basis. Often, the small producer or retailer cannot provide the same functions for himself as cheaply or does not have the borrowing power to provide them for himself.

As Table 11 shows, the number of wholesalers and retailers of various products in Japan is exceptionally large. International comparisons of the number of retail outlets per 1,000 population shows this clearly. For example, in 1970 Japan had 18.9 retailers per 1,000 population, the United States had 9.1, and the United Kingdom had 10.9. To service such a large number of retailers requires a large number of wholesalers. In distribution of any particular good—for example, canned goods—this translates directly into an expanded sales force compared to distribution in other nations. Because retailing for many

TABLE 11. Number of Wholesalers and Retailers,
by Selected Products, 1968

	Number of Outlets
Wholesalers	
Foodstuffs	63,358
Apparel	20,515
Household products	11,007
Retailers	
Foodstuffs	711,136
Apparel	198,997
Household products	51,468
Total wholesalers	281,081
Total retailers	1,389,222
Total end-sales outlets	281,081

Source: Japan. Ministry of International Trade and Industry, *Waga Kuni no Shōgyō* [Commerce of Japan] (Tokyo, 1968).

products is not highly concentrated, as it is in the United States, where supermarkets handle about 70 percent of total food sales and often purchase through a central procurement unit, the need in Japan for smaller wholesalers to service small retail outlets is greatly increased, as is the need for people to pay sales calls, both for the purpose of selling the product and for gathering information on how the product is being received by the consumer. This information can be particularly valuable in Japan because the retailer normally buys from the wholesaler, and the wholesaler from the producer on consignment. Sales ex-factory in January are absolutely no guarantee of performance until goods returned in June are taken into account.

The reasons for the large number of wholesalers and retailers are economic, historical, and cultural. Production of many consumer goods is fragmented for a wide variety of reasons. For example, until very recently most cattle were raised on very small farms with only a few head of cattle because capital needed to concentrate the industry was being diverted into other uses, such as investment in manufacturing. Another reason for fragmentation is that the optimal scale for some processes tends to be very small. The textile industry is a good example of a series of processes that have a widely varying optimal scale. Spinning is most economical in large factories—Japan moved from cottage-industry and small-factory spinning at the end of the nineteenth century. However, weaving presents another problem. Because many fabrics are made only in small lots, production on a small scale or cottage-industry production may be the least expensive. Thus, even today weaving in Japan is largely concentrated in very small firms located in rural areas. The suiting fabric in a tailor's window may have moved from the most modern petroleum combinate as a raw material to the highly mechanized operations of one of Japan's major companies; then to the countryside via one or more intermediaries; to a factory employing five people where it was woven into a fabric according to the latest design provided by the design department of a major trading company; then via one or more intermediaries who attended to storage, transportation, financing of both the weaver and tailor, and sales promotion; and finally to the tailor's shop. Despite the complex journey of the piece of men's suiting, it may still be cheaper than that turned out by integrated processes in the United States.

Another reason for fragmentation in production is that labor, originally at least, was less expensive in smaller establishments than it was in larger factories. Although this fact is less applicable today, it is still true that very small-scale production, particularly when it is located in rural areas, is generally less costly than production in highly mechanized urban factories—for some products and processes.

Many small factories need some kind of intermediary for a number of reasons, for instance: (1) Because of the tightness of capital during most of the postwar period, small-scale producers have experienced difficulty in raising operating funds. In many cases, the wholesaler acts as financier to the small producer, either providing him with the raw material on credit or prepaying for part of the orders. If the raw material is imported, the role of financing and the other services of a wholesaler are provided by a trading company. Trading companies were originally responsible for importing the raw material. (2) The small producer finds that economies of scale can be realized by relying on the wholesaler for such specialized functions as storage, transportation,

TABLE 12. Scale of Retail Operations, 1968

Number of Employees	Number of Stores	Percent of All Stores	Percent of Retail Stores
1–2	932,951	67.1	1.9
3–4	295,481	21.3	4.4
5–9	116,148	8.4	13.0
10–19	30,829	2.2	17.2
20–29	7,080	0.5	9.8
30–49	4,163	0.3	12.2
50–99	1,801	0.1	15.3
100 or more	769	0.1	26.2
Total	1,389,222	100.0	

Source: Japan. Ministry of International Trade and Industry, *Waga Kuni no Shōgyō* [Commerce of Japan] (Tokyo, 1968).

and sales promotion. For example, the individual maker does not maintain his own sales force; instead, the wholesaler represents a number of the smaller producers to the secondary wholesalers or end users.

Fragmentation at the retail level is another factor creating dependence on the wholesaler. As Table 12 indicates, clearly the average retail store in Japan is very small, both in area and in level of sales. The inventory of these stores is found on the shelves, stocked in one corner, or piled out in front of the store. For the most part, the retailer must depend on the wholesaler to store goods for him. Similarly, the average small retail store is not in a position to own a truck to pick up goods, as it would often be idle; it is much more economical for the wholesaler to provide this function. The small size of most retailers also makes it convenient for the retailer to pay for the goods he receives after they have been sold. If he cannot sell them, then the understanding is that the wholesaler will take them back. Lastly, although retailers may undertake a kind of sales promotion through the design and arrangement of their stores or design and printing of point-of-purchase materials, such as posters advertising new products, preparation of advertisements for radio and television is much more efficiently performed by the maker or the wholesaler.

The functions performed by the wholesaler are certainly not unique to Japan. The difference in their importance in Japan compared to that in the United States lies in the degree of concentration at the two extremes of the distribution chain. As production concentrates, the maker tends to move closer to his retail outlets. The degree to which this tendency is present depends on the type of product, but for most consumer products for which brand is important, the maker's desire to eliminate the middleman may be very strong—for good economic reasons. As the maker takes a larger share of the total market and begins to use a number of wholesalers to distribute his product, he begins to seek stability in distribution and often aligns himself closely with the largest of his wholesalers and merges the rest into one operation. This move results in increased economies in storage, transport, and sales promotion. Whether the producer moves all the way to the retail level and begins to organize a chain will depend upon his product line. The determining factor is the width of the producer's product line compared to the product line of the retail outlet. If a producer makes nothing but instant noodles, it becomes very difficult for him to convince a retailer to become an exclusive dealer for his noodles, because customers demand more variety in processed foods. Although the large producer may be able to rationalize distribution down to the wholesaler level, he probably will not be able to eliminate the wholesaler. The function that the maker cannot perform, and that the wholesaler can, is to assemble a wide line of goods for the store that handles more than a few products.

At the other extreme, suppose that a producer has a full line of electrical appliances and that there is a type of store in Japan that specializes in electrical products. If the producer can supply all of these, a close tie-up with the retail outlet is advantageous. No wholesaler is needed to perform the function of assembly of goods from various producers. The wide-line producer may either distribute directly or distribute from a sales company that it has set up as an autonomous entity. The sales company is responsible for stocking the inventory in strategic locations, for transporting it on short notice, for financing credit sales to the retailers, and for promoting sales to retail outlets. Many sales companies were originally major wholesalers for the producers when the latter had a smaller share of the product or did not produce as wide a line of products. Major wholesalers were merged into one sales company to realize economies of scale in distribution.

Other economies are realized by organizing a chain of this type because a brand image can be established simultaneously for the products themselves and for the chain of retailers. The best example is Matsushita, which has exactly this type of relationship with its end retailers. Other electrical-appliance makers either do not have a sufficiently wide product line or have not been as aggressive as Matsushita in setting up a chain. Sony, for example, has specialized in a narrower group of products than has Matsushita, which limits the number of outlets Sony can bring into its chains. An interesting outcome of the Sony offer to import U.S. products into Japan should be that Sony will be able to fill out its product line and enlarge its chain of shops. One of the questions that Sony's move poses is: Will Sony's tie-up with the most efficient U.S. producers result in its being more competitive than Matsushita across its product line? Sony will be providing the same service that a trading company or wholesaler provides in Japan—it will assemble a wider line of goods and offer U.S. producers access to a group of retailers that Sony has assisted and cultivated in the past. Surely, if a U.S. producer already has connections with retailers, he might be better off going direct, but in fact U.S. producers do not. In addition, the small retailer might be unwilling to deal directly with a foreign company. Who would be responsible for stocking and transportation services? Even if the U.S. producer were to invest in setting up all these functions onshore in Japan, he might find that his cost is not so low as the margin charged by Sony because of the economies Sony will realize by handling a large volume of products. In addition, the retailer may still need someone to perform the function of putting together a wider line of goods to supply him.

In general, the more highly concentrated the production and retail ends of the distribution channel, the fewer the number of entities needed for distribution. For instance, a large producer of processed foods would require only a primary wholesaler in order to reach a larger retailer. The same producer, however, would need two levels of wholesalers—the primary and the secondary—to reach a small retailer.

Trends toward Concentration in Wholesaling

As the product mix in Japan has evolved, concentration in production has taken place. This change has put the producer in a much stronger position with respect to the wholesaler in some industries. As a result, producers have concentrated sales through a limited number of strong wholesalers. As these wholesalers realized economies of scale, wholesaling has concentrated.

In point of fact, as Table 13 shows, processing for many products and wholesaling is concentrating. Some of the reasons for concentration at the processing level include: (1) The introduction of new products. For example, the introduction of chemical seasonings such as Aji-no-moto, which was a completely new product that could be mass-produced, allowed one company to capture more than 90 percent of the market for that particular product. In traditional products such as sake and soy sauce, monopoly is more difficult to accomplish because the market is no longer growing to any significant degree and substantial investment is needed to undersell competitors and bring about concentration. Even if concentration can be brought about in traditional products, often local products are preferred to mass-produced national brands. (2) The introduction of products that can be standardized and mass-produced. Unlike local products that are often unique, products such as beer, catsup, and mayonnaise or integrated circuits can generally be produced more cheaply in quantity. Thus, the producer who invests first in the latest cost-reducing innovations can undersell his competitors and concentrate the market. (3) The increased need for information and financing in order to compete effectively. For example, in the textiles industry fashion is becoming an increasingly important factor. In the past, conservative dark suits had always found a market, but with the emergence of a youth market in recent years fashions have begun to change more rapidly. Small producers of jackets and other garments have found it advantageous to move closer to larger producers that supply them with information on new designs and finance them, when necessary. In some cases, groups of small producers have been integrated into larger producer operations or groups organized by major trading companies.

Although one of the major changes behind concentration in production has been evolution of the product mix in Japan, the reasons for

TABLE 13. Concentration in Wholesaling, 1966 to 1968

	Decrease in number (percent)
All wholesaling	2.1
Apparel	1.4
Textiles (fabric)	9.0
Processed foods	7.1
Construction materials	10.5
Pharmaceuticals, cosmetics	1.8

Source: Japan. Ministry of International Trade and Industry, *Waga Kuni no Shōgyō* [Commerce of Japan] (Tokyo, 1968).

concentration at the wholesale level are much more diverse. First, as industrial concentration has taken place in manufacturing industries and stronger producers have emerged who have a substantial share of the market, these producers have found it advantageous to organize a group of wholesalers into one sales unit. This assures the producer of a steady outlet for his products and may also allow him to distribute more directly to retail outlets.

Second, as manufacturers have moved to gain control of distribution by concentration of product flow through a few wholesalers, other wholesalers who have had their sales positions jeopardized have organized or merged into larger, more competitive operations.

Third, in addition to merging or cooperating to strengthen their position vis-à-vis the producers, some wholesalers have organized voluntary chains of retail outlets. In return for a contractual obligation to purchase a certain minimum of products from the central office of the voluntary chain, the retailer can generally purchase his goods at a lower price than he could from independent wholesalers. The voluntary-chain headquarters purchases in larger quantity, realizes economies of scale in storage, transport, sales promotion, and in addition provides goods on credit. Voluntary chains are most common in foodstuffs, textiles, bedding, and pharmaceutical products, but the number of retail outlets who are members of these chains is still a very small portion of the total number of retailers.

The fourth force acting to concentrate wholesaling has been the movement of major trading companies to rationalize and to shorten distribution chains for the products in which they have a particular interest. Some of the products are foodstuffs and textiles, for which the trading company is originally responsible for raw-material imports. To maintain their position as importers of raw materials, the trading companies have worked to strengthen their relationships with producers, wholesalers, and retailers by providing goods on credit, by loaning additional funds when needed, and by providing information on overseas markets and trends which producers and wholesalers would have difficulty obtaining for themselves. One of the policies adopted by trading companies has been to merge wholesalers and, where necessary, to force mergers by relying on the larger wholesalers who can distribute at lower cost than can smaller companies and who are aggressive in seeking new customers.

A fifth factor responsible for concentration in wholesaling has been the growth of supermarkets and volume outlets for some products. Large supermarket chains such as Daiei and Seiyu have adopted a policy of selling high volumes at low prices. This practice has led them to cut out all but one layer of wholesalers or to go directly to producers to obtain their products. As these supermarket chains have grown, wholesalers have found it necessary to expand their operations at the same rate to maintain the business of the supermarket chains. This situation in turn has led to a substantial demand for funds to finance the investment in new distribution facilities. In many cases, the wholesaler has become more and more dependent upon the supermarket chain in order to finance its growth.

Table 14 points out a sixth reason for concentration in wholesaling, namely the economies of scale realized by larger wholesaling operations. The level of sales per employee is substantially greater in larger wholesaling operations than in smaller ones.

Other factors, such as the movement of population and production to urban areas, have played a role in the concentration of wholesaling. The rural population in Japan has declined from 60 percent just after World War II to less than 20 percent at present. The position of wholesalers serving rural areas has diminished significantly, just as the role of wholesalers responsible for transporting rural products to urban areas has diminished with movement of production to the cities and the shift

TABLE 14. Index of Sales per Employee, by Size of Store, 1966 to 1968

Number of Employees	Wholesaling	Retailing
1–2	100	100
3–4	156	162
5–9	197	219
10–19	231	221
20–29	272	201
30–49	309	205
50–99	370	260
100 or more	714	375

Note: Sales per employee for stores with 1 to 2 employees are set at 100.
Source: Japan. Ministry of International Trade and Industry, *Waga Kuni no Shōgyō* [Commerce of Japan] (Tokyo, 1968).

in product mix away from labor-intensive, cottage-industry products. Another major factor accounting for concentration has been increase in wages. Rising labor costs have forced producers to maintain productivity increase at the same rate as the industry or suffer a loss in margin. Wholesalers unable to meet the investment requirements that growth in productivity has required have had to face extinction or merger.

Slower Concentration in Retailing

An important feature of the Japanese retail market is the prevalence and tenacity of the small retailer. Although supermarket chains and other mass-retail outlets are developing, the position of the small retailer is eroding only slowly for reasons such as the difficulty of obtaining urban land at prices that will justify setting up a volume-sales store; the fact that the sheer size and number of retail outlets and the number of people they employ would present social problems if change were too rapid; and the preference of the Japanese consumer for neighborhood shopping for everyday items.

Despite a clear trend toward concentration for wholesaling and manufacturing, the same cannot be said for retailing. One explanation for the lower rate of concentration in retailing can be found in Table 14, which shows the level of sales per employee by size of store. Although larger stores generally realize a higher level of sales, the spread is not nearly as great as in wholesaling; thus, the economic pressures for concentration are not as great.

But there are a great many other factors that account for the strength of smaller retail outlets:

Daily neighborhood shopping is the cultural pattern in Japan. For example, a preference for fresh foods results in the need to purchase vegetables and meat every day. Although over 80 percent of households have a refrigerator, these units tend to be about one-fourth the size of the typical unit in the United States. Until recently, freezing compartments were either not included or were very small. In addition, the Japanese household often has little storage space for canned goods or other items that are often purchased in quantity in the United States and stored at home. Despite the fact that supermarkets have experienced substantial growth and currently account for slightly more than 10 percent of total food sales, the problems of storage place limitations on how much the average household can purchase at one time.

Small stores are usually conveniently located. Within walking distance of virtually any home in an urban area, there is usually a cluster of small stores which offer nearly all the daily needs of the Japanese household. Unlike the United States, the rate of automobile ownership is still only slightly above 20 percent in Japan. In addition, the narrow streets common in urban residential areas make driving to the shopping center less convenient than walking.

Smaller retail stores have not been subjected to the strong pressures from government policy that retail stores in the United States have. For example, the land-tax valuations for many urban areas are based on early postwar figures. Land values have increased by more than ten times in many urban areas over the last twelve years. This increase has worked to the advantage of the small retailer in two ways: His costs are lower than they would be otherwise, and it is more diffi-

TABLE 15. Percent of Total Income Derived from Sources Other than Retail Enterprises

Type of Store	Percent of Stores					
	20 or less	20–40	40–60	60–80	80 or more	No Reply
Food	57.6	9.0	10.2	10.4	9.6	3.2
Apparel	61.3	8.8	9.6	9.9	6.0	4.4
Consumer durables	74.8	4.8	6.4	4.1	8.2	2.7

Source: Japan. Ministry of International Trade and Industry, *Shōgyō Ryūtsū Kōzō Chōsa* [Survey of distribution structures in the commerce sector], cited in idem *70-nen ni okeru Ryūtsū* [Distribution in the 1970s] (Tokyo), p. 122.

cult for a supermarket to enter closely settled urban areas. Whereas supermarkets must be concerned with earning a certain minimum return on their investments, the small retailer probably does not take this into account. His home is often located on the second story above his shop, and at least part of his income typically comes from sources other than the family store. As Table 15 shows, 40 percent of small retail enterprises derive 20 percent of their income from sources other than the retail store itself. Although the average owner of a small retail store in Japan is usually not affluent, he is able to make a reasonably good living.

For a number of reasons, supermarkets have not taken the share of the market that was originally forecast for them. For example, (1) much of the growth in the 1960s has been due to increase in the product line rather than increase in the sales of particular items, and (2) until fairly recently, supermarket chains have not been sufficiently aggressive in moving closer to manufacturers. However, the current trend is for companies such as Daiei to tie up with manufacturers of appliances, apparel, and other items for production under their private label and to adopt direct distribution. The typical independent supermarket and even a few of the chain stores still depend upon the same chain of wholesalers as do the smaller retail outlets for supply. Thus, in some areas small retail stores compete pricewise with the nearby supermarket and provide higher quality as well. Although supermarkets surely will not remain with only about 10 percent of retail sales, their continued growth will depend upon the solution of the above problems. However, given the patterns of shopping in Japan, neighborhood shopping centers will probably continue to play a major role in retail sales for the next ten years. Not only is the small retailer in a position of relative strength, but also smaller retailers are beginning to cooperate with one another to increase their competitive strength vis-à-vis the volume-sales stores.

There are several methods of cooperation among smaller outlets. Neighborhood shopping areas, for instance, are being rebuilt and modernized. This movement has been going on for many years and was first evident at the more important suburban commuter railway shops in major cities. Stores formed an association and paid for designs to transform their heterogeneous collection of stores into a modern shopping street. Often these shopping streets are covered with an arched roof, and efforts have been made to unify and to improve the appearance of all the stores. Although this type of cooperation improves the desirability of the shopping area from the point of view of the consumer, of course it does nothing to affect distribution to the heterogeneous group of stores.

The formation of voluntary chains, however, is indeed important for its effect upon distribution. The motivation for organizing voluntary chains has come both from wholesalers and from retailers themselves. Voluntary chains have as their purpose the strengthening of retail outlets vis-à-vis large volume-sales outlets. Moreover, the influence of small retailers over the type of products the manufacturer turns out may be increased, because planning for new products is usually done jointly with the chain headquarters, considering the needs and desires of the retailers, who are in close contact with the consumer.

Another movement arising in part because of the lack of concentration in retailing is the formation of regular chains by major manufacturers. For example, Onward Kashiyama—the largest maker of ready-to-wear apparel—is currently setting up a chain of retail stores. In some cases, Kashiyama will buy out an existing retailer, and in others Kashiyama will make a contract with the current owner. Kashiyama will then supply its full line of goods to the stores in the chain. Although this company also sells a major portion of the apparel that is sold through

TABLE 16. Share of Retail Sales, by Type of Store

Type of Store	Percent of Retail Sales			
	1964	1966	1968	1970
Single-line stores	85.9	85.5	83.0	81.1
Self-service stores (supermarkets)	4.7	5.4	7.6	9.0
Department stores	9.4	9.1	9.4	9.9

Source: Japan. Ministry of International Trade and Industry, *Waga Kuni no Shōgyō* [Commerce of Japan] (Tokyo, 1968).

department stores and other types of larger retail outlets, because much of the market is still in the suburban shopping centers and neighborhood areas they have had to expand into a chain of small stores as well in order to widen the company's share of the market.

On a more limited scale, franchise stores have also developed. Dry-cleaning establishments, for example, have been organized by several large companies, with the organizing company providing some of the technology and its name and reputation. In cosmetics, Shiseido has a large chain of franchise stores that handle its complete line of cosmetics for women and men. In electrical appliances, Matsushita has one of the largest franchise chain systems and even supplies the small electrical retailer with products on credit and money for remodeling stores.

All the above movements toward cooperation in retailing should strengthen the position of the small retailer in regard to the volume outlets. Given cooperation in procurement of products and in storage, transportation, and sales promotion that the voluntary, regular, and franchise chains provide, the position of the small retailer should remain strong, resulting in development of retailing in Japan according to a pattern more reminiscent of Europe than of the United States.

Judging from past trends, retailing will not concentrate at a rapid pace as many observers once believed. As Table 16 indicates, the share of self-service stores, which includes supermarkets, has grown, but from a rather small base. Much of the growth has been accounted for by growth in the sales of chain supermarkets, which rose at the rate of 20 percent or more during the latter half of the 1960s. The growth in sales of supermarkets has had little effect on the share of department stores —only the single-line retail stores have lost their share. Nevertheless, these smaller neighborhood stores still handle about 80 percent of all retail sales. If the foregoing factors are taken into consideration, the small retail store will probably continue to hold a substantial share of retail sales, perhaps as much as 70 percent during most of the 1970s. This naturally places limitations on the degree of rationalization which is possible in distribution. For many products, the role of the wholesaler will continue to be a necessary one, and it will not be practical for the manufacturer to attempt to tie up directly with end retailers. Although distribution may not be as direct as it is in the United States for many products, the distribution problem that potential exporters to Japan will face will be similar to the problem their Japanese competitors face. The originality and effectiveness of finding a solution within the given framework of a multitude of retail outlets will ultimately play a large role in determining the competitive strength of the U.S. exporter.

Concentration and Functions of Intermediaries

The main factors that account for the length of the distribution channels and therefore make the intervention of an intermediary wholesaler economically justifiable are:

1. The type of product. For example, perishable products like bread and milk must have direct or near direct distribution. Although it might make economic sense for a major producer of bread to rely on wholesalers to distribute its product to small low-volume retail outlets, by the time the product reaches the shelves it will have turned stale. The producer's additional economic cost of a fleet of trucks that are not as fully utilized as are those of a wholesaler who handles a wider line of products is simply reflected in the price of the bread.

2. Shopping patterns. As long as the Japanese consumer prefers to do most of his shopping in the neighborhood, particularly for everyday goods, the position of the neighborhood retailer and the wholesaler remains strong.

3. Concentration in production. Industries that have grown very rapidly and manufactured goods that can be mass-produced and standardized generally have a dominant producer and a few other producers with smaller market shares. Although these producers may be restricted in their ability to shorten distribution channels by factors such as retailer or end-user concentration, if other factors are favorable these industries generally have shorter distribution channels than do industries in which production is highly fragmented.

4. The width of the product line of the manufacturer in relation to the width of the product line handled by the retail store. Because they must rely on wholesalers to assemble the product line, manufacturers producing items that compose only a small percentage of the product lines handled by a certain category of retail outlets are in a much weaker position in relation to wholesalers than are firms that can supply a major portion of the product line.

5. The degree of concentration in retailing or end users. With the development of large supermarket chains or voluntary chains that purchase goods in large quantities, manufacturers can economically justify direct distribution to these outlets because the total volume will justify the manufacturer setting up the functions of storage, transport, and a sales force, rather than relying on the wholesaler to perform the same function.

The last three factors are the most significant for the majority of products. Concentration in production is difficult to achieve for products that are traditional and show little growth. However, the products that most U.S. exporters would be interested in are new to the market or are still growing—for example, citrus fruits, frozen foods, and certain types of household appliances. Thus, concentration in production is a limiting factor on the distribution channels for domestic goods but is less so for imported goods. Concentration in retailers or end users is and will remain a problem for importers because of the slow rate of concentration in retailing; that is, distributors of some products may find it more economical to make use of existing wholesalers rather than try to establish their own distribution channels. Several examples of producers who have been successful include Nestlé in instant coffee, Sunkist in lemons and more recently grapefruit, and United Fruit in bananas. The number of outlets through which the goods of these companies are sold is extremely large: 100,000 or more stores sell instant coffee, 66,000 stores sell lemons and bananas. The investment needed to establish and to maintain a distribution relationship with so many outlets would have been prohibitive. Careful choice of wholesalers and a study of their needs and the way in which competitor producers motivated them through rebates and other forms of direct and indirect financial assistance were major factors in the success of the distribution policies of these companies.

The limiting factor of the width of the product line is a hindrance both to U.S. producers and Japanese, but it is a problem with a solution. The formation of a U.S. trading group consisting of producers who can supply a complete line of products to one type of retail outlet, for example, would greatly strengthen the position of smaller U.S. producers in their efforts to sell into Japan. The formation of trading groups or a trading company to handle the functions of assembling a product line, providing transport, arranging for storage, and perhaps undertaking promotion under a single label would also have the important additional advantage of greatly reducing the cost of entering the market to the individual firm. The combination of a trading group in the United States and the major retail supermarket chains and voluntary chains in Japan would provide much better market access at a far lower cost per company than if each company attempted to enter the market on its own.

Role of the Japanese Trading Company

The roles of the trading company are so diverse that the top ten Japanese trading companies can probably claim to be unique in world business. No other nation has similar organizations. Their basic functions are three in number: (1) selling—performing many of the functions of a wholesaler; (2) providing finance and risk absorption; and (3) organizing such projects as overseas raw-material resource development using their financial ability and connections with producers and buyers.

These trading companies are often not fully understood and too often appear to be regarded as historical or cultural relics that are of little usefulness to the potential U.S. exporter to Japan. For many products, this view of trading companies is inaccurate. In fact, one of the strengths of Japan in export competitiveness is the trading company, and the United States surely could benefit from either making use of Japanese trading companies or having similar organizations for certain types of products.

Selling. The basic function of the trading company has been to perform some or all of the functions of a wholesaler, but a substantial portion of its revenues comes either directly from import and export transactions or indirectly from the handling of intermediate and finished products made from imported raw materials. Over 50 percent of Japan's imports and exports go through the top ten trading companies. In the case of textile goods, virtually all wool fiber, for example, is imported by trading companies. Trading companies sell the wool fiber to spinning companies and then in many cases buy back the thread and supply it to the weaving industry on liberal credit terms. Because weaving in Japan is a highly fragmented industry, the trading companies then buy back the finished fabric and supply it to suitmakers, again on liberal credit terms. Although their control over distribution beyond weaving is very weak, overseeing of distribution by the trading companies has two desirable effects from their point of view: (1) By providing credit and sales services, the trading company facilitates product flow and thereby increases the imports of raw materials over what they might be otherwise; and (2) the trading companies can maintain their position as importers of raw materials through their connections with spinners and weavers in the industry.

As the textile industry has begun to move offshore, trading companies have taken the initiative in setting up joint ventures with Japanese and overseas textile producers, again preserving their position as importers, now of the finished products rather than the raw materials. Thus, the trading company is motivated to maintain its position, but at the same time it contributes to the reallocation of domestic resources from noncompetitive industries.

As part of the basic function of selling goods, the trading company either provides or arranges for such functions as transportation, storage, sales promotion, and so forth. For some industries and products—such as those that require extensive marketing or after-service by the producer—the role of trading company is often simply that of handling the paperwork and arranging for physical distribution. In providing these functions, the trading companies often realize substantial economies of scale because of the large volume of transactions that they handle. For other products, the function of the trading company extends to the actual marketing and sale of the product. This is true in particular of commodities that are sold in bulk, steel products, and other goods that require little after-service. These generalizations are not hard and fast because some small specialized trading companies provide nearly all the distribution functions for a limited number of products.

As part of their sales function, the major trading companies maintain a network of overseas and domestic offices that are responsible for handling local transactions and providing information on overseas markets to companies affiliated with the trading company. Although no economic studies have been made of the value of this network, the economies of scale realized in basic information gathering by these trading-company offices is clearly substantial.

Finance and risk absorption. The banking system in Japan is largely set up to deal with major firms. Evaluating the credit worthiness of small customers is difficult. Banks instead have preferred to allow the trading companies to play the role of financier to smaller companies. As a result, the larger trading companies have an advantage because of the large number of products that they handle. First, a substantial portion of their revenues, aside from dividends and interest, are related to imports of raw materials. These sums provide a steady source of income for the major trading firms. In addition to raw materials, trading companies may handle between seven and ten thousand different products. The combination of a steady source of income plus a highly diversified product line makes lending to these companies relatively risk-free for major banks. The trading companies in turn finance many of the processors of the raw materials they import by providing the raw material on liberal credit terms, by giving direct loans in some cases, and by guaranteeing purchase of the finished product from the processor.

Organization. Trading companies have a basic interest in maintaining their position as importers, either of the raw materials or—if the domestic industry becomes noncompetitive—of the finished product. This basic aim leads trading companies to undertake a wide variety of projects in which they provide some finance and act as the project organizer. The best example is the procurement of overseas raw-material resources. With the exception of petroleum, which is largely provided by the "majors," the trading companies have played a major role in organizing nearly all of Japan's overseas resource-procurement projects. As Japan's industrial structure has changed and noncompetitive industries have been moved offshore, the trading companies have also played a role here. One of the most significant developments in recent years has been the loss of competitiveness of Japanese producers in several consumer-product areas, due to both changing comparative advantage and lowering of tariffs and other barriers. These factors have created a need not only to invest offshore to maintain trading-company positions but also to establish closer relationships with retail outlets. If left completely alone, major supermarket chains might invest in their own projects overseas. Again, if the trading company maintains its position, the beneficial effects may outweigh the disadvantages. To make its margin, the trading company needs to pass the goods over its books at only one point. It therefore has no interest in maintaining multiple layers of wholesalers if these are unnecessary. Trading companies are also one of the few institutions with the financial resources to invest in substantial concentration of the physical-distribution functions.

Thus, far from being relics of the period when Japanese firms were incapable of doing their own overseas marketing, the trading companies have very specific tasks to perform and justify their existence fully in the majority of instances. Like many concentrations of financial power, however, trading companies also have their disadvantages. As their behavior after the recent yen revaluation has indicated, the trading companies apparently have made the decision to share the 17 percent windfall gain between themselves and their distributors for many products. This choice naturally works to the detriment of U.S. attempts to expand sales in the Japanese market and exacerbates the balance-of-payments problem. A government study is currently under way to determine the causes of the failure to lower prices after the revaluation. However, the decision not to pass the windfall gain on to the consumer in some cases was the decision of the U.S. suppliers and their distributors in Japan, not a unilateral decision by the trading companies.

Another disadvantage from the point of view of the United States is that the trading companies make their overseas investments to supply the Japanese market in areas where they believe production will be most economical in the future, or in some cases to achieve a trade balance with a smaller nation. A major trading company, for example, invested in a beef-cattle farm in Madagascar instead of in the United States. Thus the trading companies cannot be counted on to make investments in the United States solely for the purpose of achieving a balance in U.S.-Japanese trade, particularly if they do not view the investment as being in their long-run interest.

Some Case Studies

As the recently published white paper on international trade by the Japanese Ministry of International Trade and Industry (MITI) points out, compared to other nations at similar stages of development, the level of imports of processed commodities is substantially lower in Japan than the level in other countries when their per capita incomes were the same as Japan's current level. The same white paper suggests the need for Japan to utilize its accumulated foreign exchange to control the rapid increase in the domestic price level for many consumer goods, by increasing the emphasis on imports of processed goods. The import structure of the Japanese economy should begin to reflect, even more strongly than it has in the past, a shifting of resources from industries that have become noncompetitive and an increase in imports of these products either from Japanese offshore investments or from producers in other nations. Although a number of product areas should be of particular interest to U.S. producers, the following discussion covers products in three industries which appear to have significant prospects for future development: processed foods, focusing on instant coffee; electrical appliances; and cosmetics.

Processed foods. A typical pattern of distribution for processed foods might involve primary, secondary, and tertiary wholesalers between the manufacturer and the retailer. As noted previously, in general the larger the retailer and producer, the fewer the number of wholesaler intermediaries in the distribution chain. Instant coffee offers an interesting example of a distribution system that has altered as an industry has expanded and concentrated. Figure 1 shows the current distribution channels for the two major makers of instant coffee in Japan. Both firms are foreign-owned companies and between them had 91 percent of the market in 1970.

Distribution channels originally were similar to those illustrated above, with several layers of intermediaries. When the product first came into general use in Japan, about 1959, the position of the whole-

TABLE 17. Index of Domestic Consumption of Instant Coffee (1960 = 100)

Year	Index
1960	100
1961	1,469
1962	2,160
1965	2,816
1968	5,235
1970	7,415

Source: Japan. Ministry of International Trade and Industry, *Torihiki Jōken nō Jittai* [The existing situation of transaction conditions] (Tokyo), pt. 2, pp. 4–5.

saler and his responsibilities were substantially greater than they are now because of the small volume of the product and the large number of producers. Between 1961 and 1963, about forty domestic companies entered the market, and there were thirteen imported brands. After 1961, a substantial increase in demand was experienced, as Table 17 suggests.

Behind this substantial increase has been the gradual shift of Japanese tastes to a pattern similar to that in the West. Although overall this shift has been a gradual one—rice, for example, still maintains its position as the main dish—some items such as coffee and soft drinks, which form a relatively small proportion of total food purchases but nonetheless add an element of variety, have grown very rapidly. By 1967, about 80 percent of households interviewed by the Asahi newspapers brand-research organization indicated that they used instant coffee at home.

In 1962–63, when demand growth slowed somewhat, many of the forty producers found themselves with excess capacity. The major producers began lowering prices, and by 1965 only five producers remained in the market: Nestlé, Maxwell House, Morinaga, Meiji, and MJB. Production since then has continued to concentrate as Nestlé takes a larger and larger share of the market.

Unlike many products, the market for instant coffee is found largely in supermarkets and in volume outlets; these stores handle about 60 percent of total volume. The product is particularly suited to volume-sales stores because: (1) it is easy to standardize and mass-produce; (2) production, which is fairly capital intensive, leads to industrial concentration and greater ease of tie-ups between makers and mass-sales outlets on a near direct basis; (3) as it is a relatively new product with no association with a particular district, it can be mass-advertised and can use national brands; and (4) it is relatively low priced and can be employed as a loss leader by volume stores to attract customers.

As the production side concentrated, the major producers selected a limited number of the wholesalers with the widest connections and motivated them with various types of rebates, including progressive payments based on the level of sales. This encouraged strong competition among wholesalers and led to cooperation and mergers in many instances. One of the trends that has been particularly noticeable is that the functions of the wholesaler have progressively passed to the manufacturer. When the industry was small, the wholesaler performed most of the functions of transport, and so on. At present, however, the maker delivers directly to large-volume outlets and often uses the wholesaler only for the purpose of maintaining a personal relationship with the retailer. The wholesaler's margin is consequently reduced. Manufacturers, for example, are responsible for all mass-media promotion and in addition send salesmen to the larger retail outlets to take orders and assist in maintaining personal relationships.

Although most of the market is in the larger retail outlets, about 40 percent still goes through smaller outlets. To service these outlets, the selected contract or primary wholesalers distribute to secondary wholesalers who in turn distribute to the smaller retail outlets. The strategy of the two major companies in the industry appears to have been to utilize the volume-sales outlets to the fullest extent in expanding sales, then gradually to extend distribution to the smaller outlets.

The major difference between the distribution of the two major producers is that Nestlé is closely affiliated with four major trading companies. The reason for this is that Nestlé began domestic production only in the mid-1960s and before that relied on trading companies to import and distribute its product. According to the distribution survey of MITI (see source for Figure 1), the main function of the trading

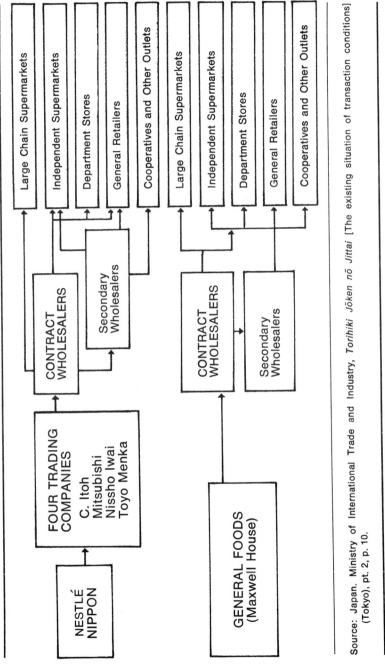

FIGURE 1. Distribution Channels for Instant Coffee

Source: Japan. Ministry of International Trade and Industry, *Torihiki Jōken nō Jittai* [The existing situation of transaction conditions] (Tokyo), pt. 2, p. 10.

company has been to provide financial support to Nestlé. Undoubtedly, the trading companies have also provided assistance to Nestlé in setting up connections with wholesalers and retailers. While trading-company connections with small retailers are weak and indirect (i.e., through wholesaler affiliates), their connections with chain supermarkets are becoming stronger. Another benefit that association with major trading companies provides is to alleviate some of the anxiety on the part of wholesalers and retailers about the behavior of a non-Japanese business entity. The "brand image" of the four trading companies may have played a very important role in Nestlé's success.

Electrical appliances. Although not as concentrated as the production of instant coffee, the appliance industry in Japan is dominated by a small number of fairly large firms. One of the characteristics of demand in the industry has been concentration on a limited number of products, until these have reached a high rate of ownership among households, then movement to other products. From the mid-fifties to the mid-sixties, over half of production in electrical appliances was accounted for by washing machines, black-and-white television, and refrigerators. As Tables 18 and 19 show, washing machines accounted for a substantial portion of the production of the industry in the latter half of the 1950s. Black-and-white television dovetailed with the demand for washing machines, and later production of refrigerators took the place of demand for washing machines. By 1965, as Table 19 shows, television sets were owned by over 90 percent of households, washing machines by about 70 percent, and refrigerators by about 50 percent of households.

The next wave of consumer-durable purchases was the so-called three Cs—color television, room coolers, and cars. Of these three, however, only color-television ownership has exceeded 20 percent, with diffusion currently at 42 percent. Room coolers are owned by less than 8 percent of households, and automobiles by slightly more than 20 percent. This pattern of concentration in demand on a relatively small number of products has been partially responsible for the development of a number of wide-line manufacturers whose appliance lines consist primarily of the major demand items, but who produce in addition a subsidiary line of appliances.

Figures 2 and 3 show the basic distribution patterns in the in-

TABLE 18. Production of Selected Electrical Appliances
(percent of total)

	1955	1959	1963
Refrigerators	21.5	7.2	6.6
Black-and-white television sets	25.7	43.7	29.1
Washing machines	5.7	8.8	21.0

Source: Japan. Ministry of International Trade and Industry, *Henbō suru Kaden Ryūtsū Kikō* [Evolving distribution of electrical appliances] (Tokyo), p. 3.

dustry. There are a number of producers whose sales are either primarily or substantially concentrated in heavy electrical equipment. Examining the shares for each product, the specialized appliance makers, such as National (Matsushita), tend to be much stronger, partly because they have much more control over their distribution.

TABLE 19. Percent of Households
Owning Selected Electrical Appliances

	1965	1971
Refrigerators	51.4	91.2
Black-and-white television sets	96.6	82.3
Washing machines	68.5	93.6
Color television sets	0.0	42.3
Room coolers	—	7.7

Source: Japan. Economic Planning Agency, *Shōhi to Chochiku no Doko* [Trends in consumption and saving] (Tokyo, 1971), pp. 132–134.

FIGURE 2. Distribution Channels for Appliance Makers
Who Also Produce Heavy Electrical Equipment (Toshiba, Hitachi)

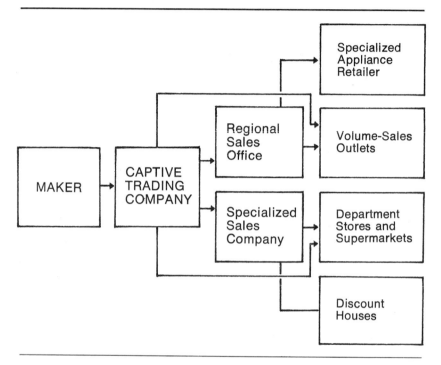

Source: Japan. Ministry of International Trade and Industry, *Henbō suru Kaden Ryūtsū Kikō* [Evolving distribution for electrical appliances] (Tokyo), pp. 22–23.

According to a pattern similar to that employed by the major producers of instant coffee, as Matsushita's share of the market increased, the company became more selective in its wholesalers and then began to incorporate former wholesalers into their sales system. The former primary wholesalers became regional sales offices, and the smaller wholesalers were merged or eliminated. At the same time, Matsushita moved to set up a franchising system. Under this system, members of the chain are provided certain benefits such as higher rebates, store signs to improve the appearance of the retailer's shop and to advertise Matsushita products, and the opportunity to purchase goods at a lower price than from wholesalers. In total, Matsushita was able to recruit

FIGURE 3. Distribution Channels
for Specialized Appliance Makers (Matsushita)

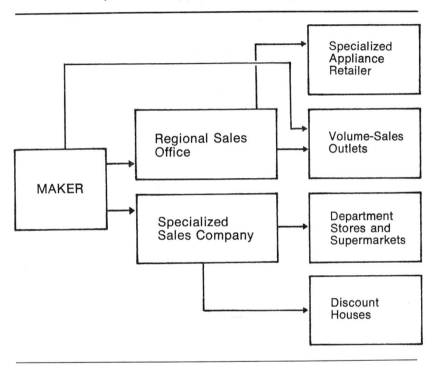

Source: Japan. Ministry of International Trade and Industry, *Henbō suru Kaden Ryūtsū Kikō* [Evolving distribution for electrical appliances] (Tokyo), pp. 22–23.

about half the small retailers in Japan, about 30,000 stores, into its chain. There are several types of contracts, under which the retail store agrees to take varying percentages of Matsushita's products.

Other makers have been unable to duplicate Matsushita's highly successful franchise network because Matsushita is able to provide a full line of products for the small retail appliance stores, the Matsushita brand is well known and advertised, and Matsushita is a specialist in the area of appliances and has not dispersed its resources into many fields as have companies such as Toshiba.

As with many products, electrical appliances are still handled primarily by small retailers. The MITI report on distribution in this industry shows that 85 percent of sales are through specialized outlets, 10 percent through volume-sales stores, and the remainder through department stores and other outlets. Volume stores are the fastest-growing retail segment, but their growth has been limited to some extent by the problem of providing service. For less sophisticated appliances, the neighborhood retailer provides service. For other products requiring specialized repairs, the small retailer will generally call the maker service unit for his customer. Volume stores, on the other hand, until recently did not provide this type of service. The customer had to contact the maker for himself to obtain service and perhaps had to wait for several days. This appears to be one of the main reasons why sales through small outlets still account for more than 80 percent of the total.

Cosmetics. The cosmetics industry presents many of the classical problems of distribution in Japan:

> —A large number of wholesalers and retailers are involved. There are 4,000 wholesalers and 62,500 stores selling cosmetics.
> —Much of the market is still in smaller, neighborhood stores. Stores specializing only in cosmetics total 20,400 and account for 60 percent of national sales.
> —Within the category of cosmetics specialty stores there is a wide range of quality of goods handled by different stores. There are stores employing only one or two persons, which handle only average or lower-quality items, but at the other extreme there are also stores located in residential suburban shopping centers that handle only relatively high-quality items.
> —Aside from stores specializing in cosmetics, there is also a class of store that handles cosmetics, medicines, and other types of everyday goods.

In addition to the above characteristics, the retail outlets are characterized by fairly distinct segments. Department stores handle products of higher cost and quality. The producer often rents space in the store to set up his own display area and sends his own sales personnel to the department stores. Generally, the more expensive the cosmetic items, the more distinctive the display of the maker. At the other extreme, supermarkets specialize in low-priced items. Producers such as Shiseido who have adopted a policy of maintaining their market share by selling into the growing supermarket segment often rent space to distinguish their products from the run-of-the-mill items. Smaller retail stores have a very wide range of quality, but there is a trend toward upgrading of product line by most stores. Several foreign brands, including Revlon and Max Factor, have adopted the practice of renting space and setting up small displays.

Shiseido, the most successful firm in the industry, has adopted a policy similar to that of Matsushita in electronics. As Shiseido's volume increased, the company moved closer to its wholesalers and retailers. A limited number of wholesalers were selected for regional distribution, and a franchise system for retail outlets was set up. Sales to franchise stores are generally direct from the regional distributor. Sales to other small outlets are made either through the regional distributor or by relying on secondary wholesalers. Sales to volume outlets are made through the regional distributor. As in other products where a wide-line maker has enough products and a strong enough brand image to set up a franchise chain, the functions of the wholesaler have increasingly come to be performed by the maker, and the wholesaler has essentially become a captive distributor.

Market Entry of U.S. Producers

Given the above considerations on the nature of distribution in Japan, a number of suggestions can be made for solving the wide range of problems which arise as U.S. producers begin to plan to export to Japan. But it would be very presumptuous indeed to suppose that any of these suggestions could be applied without further thought and modification. The "solutions" presented below should be regarded only as indications of the general direction that U.S. producers might take in planning for distribution in Japan.

There are at least two reasons why adequate resources may not be available for full penetration of the Japanese market. One is simply the fact that, given the number of outlets and wholesalers which a U.S. producer must contact in order to assure full market development, the firm's resources are simply inadequate. Another reason is that firms do not wish to commit the necessary resources to the development of the Japanese market. It is becoming increasingly apparent that U.S. firms in many industries have not been exposed to sufficient competition to maintain the level of innovation and investment which is necessary to preserve international competitiveness. This is only natural for a nation where exports and imports form a very minor portion of the gross national product. With no particular need to import, there are few pressures to export. The Japanese firm finds itself in a totally different environment. To live, Japan must import. To import, it must export. To export, Japan must innovate and invest. Very simply, U.S. businessmen often do not have what the Japanese call an "export mind"; consequently, they hesitate to devote resources to market development overseas.

As noted elsewhere, one possible solution to the problem of market entry for firms with inadequate resources to invest in market development is to organize groups of exporters manufacturing similar products. Setting up a trading headquarters for such a group along the lines of a Japanese trading company would greatly increase the effectiveness of market-penetration efforts. Economies of scale would be realized in physical distribution and in sales promotion, and firms would be able to share the risk of market entry. One of the most notable successes in market entry is that of Sunkist, which is of course just such an organization of producers.

The sheer number of retail outlets which handle many types of products is another major problem in market entry. A group of exporters working together or a U.S. trading organization would be much more effective in approaching this problem. While direct distribution may be out of the question, it seems that U.S. exports could approach the problem for some products in two stages. The first would be to select the most economical outlets to approach, that is the outlets which handle the largest volumes, such as major supermarket chains and department stores. This might be followed by approaches to major wholesalers who supply the smaller retail outlets. A method which would probably be more effective in the long run would be to work through larger wholesalers or retailers to set up voluntary or franchise chains. The position of the small retailer is still a strong one, and for many products full market penetration cannot be achieved by distributing only to volume-sales outlets.

While some of the difficulties encountered by U.S. firms in selling in Japan have centered around a failure to provide adequate promotion within the distribution channel (that is, to provide competitive rebates and adequate detailing of wholesalers and retailers), there have also been problems of inadequate promotion through media for the end consumer. Perhaps the real problem has been a belated awareness of the cost of a product introduction and attempting to stretch inadequate resources over too many uses.

Communications in Japan can perhaps best be described as dense. When a foreign producer makes his entry, it is reported extensively in the press, competitors are usually fully apprised of every detail, and the consumer often hears details that the public relations department would prefer not to have released. One detail of particular interest is whether the foreign firm has taken full account of the fact that the Japanese people have tastes that differ subtly but substantially from those of Americans. For this reason one of the best forms of public relations can be publicity about companies' seriousness in pleasing the Japanese consumer.

The proper price is one of the most perilous decisions a U.S. exporter has to make. The temptation is to sell in the outlets that are easiest to reach, such as department stores and more expensive supermarkets, at high prices and take a high margin. The result is often that the product remains in the luxury segment, and a less expensive Japanese substitute appears for mass distribution.

5.

THE JAPANESE FARMER AND POLITICS

Haruhiro Fukui

THE JAPANESE FARMER is beset with many and difficult problems. Like all other members of society, he is caught in the social and economic turmoil that has descended on this once tranquil land of rice-growing people. The urban salaried worker faces basically the same problem of adjustment and survival in his rapidly changing environment. In some ways, his lot is probably even worse than the farmer's. Pollution hazards are no doubt greater in cities than in villages. In at least one important respect, however, the farmer's problems are qualitatively different. The urban dweller belongs to an ever-growing majority in a fast-industrializing nation. The numbers make a difference not only in psychological terms but also in more mundane and material ways. In a system in which the majority rules both in law and in practice, numbers constitute a formidable political force. The bureaucracy, which is often impervious to demands of social and political minorities, is obviously susceptible to pressures from the ruling party and the majority among the electorate and in the national legislature.

The farmer is a member of a diminishing minority in a nation undergoing industrialization and urbanization at a frantic pace. Whereas his urban counterpart may feel secure with the belief that "when he goes down, the whole boat will go down," the farmer lives with the gnawing apprehension that "he may fall off the boat any moment, and the captain will not hear his cries for help." As he contemplates the future, he may well see only loneliness and confusion. His neighbors, who until recently had sipped tea and chatted with him around the fireplace, who used to sing and dance with him on festival nights, are no longer there. They may still live next door, but they now work in town and often are too tired to spend time with him as they used to. Commuting to town by crowded bus or train is far different from walking to the nearby rice fields. Perhaps they no longer enjoy talking about the crops and rain, and the farmer does not understand the problems they may have in a town factory or sweatshop. Because some of his neighbors are away for weeks or months, he does not even see them very much.

Worse yet, his own children do not work on his farm and leave for town as soon as they have finished school. Perhaps they write to him three or four times a year or come home for New Year's Day, but even then they are often like strangers. They enjoy alcohol—even his daughters—but they seldom join him in the conviviality of *sake* drinking. Instead of taking part in a family talk, they watch television the whole evening. There is no longer the warmth of family life.

To the farmer, the village agricultural cooperative is still handy and helpful. He keeps his savings in the cooperative account; he buys fertilizers, insecticides, packing materials, and even such luxuries as a television set or a washing machine from the cooperative store. When in need, he can get small short-term loans from its loans department. In fact, many of the officials at the cooperative headquarters are his personal acquaintances from the village, and the younger employees have just left the village secondary school. He hears, however, that the cooperative is in trouble, too. During a time when many people are quitting farming, when rice growing (and rice warehousing and marketing) is being held down by government order, and when the government is less receptive to farmers' demands, many cooperatives are in as deep financial trouble and moral crisis as the farmer himself. In any event, the farmer does not feel as certain as he did several years ago that his cooperative will protect him and his interests against arbitrary government actions and the encroachment of urban power.

Neither is he sure that the Liberal-Democratic party (LDP) and the conservative government really understand his problems. After the last few years of annual price setting for rice purchased by the government, limited rice production, and increased foreign agricultural imports, the farmer often feels slighted by his representatives in the Diet and by the LDP cabinet. If he believes some of the television newscasters and newspaper editors, perhaps it is true, as his children have been saying, that the Socialists and the Communists take his problems far more seriously. He is not sure. However, he has been told since he was a young boy that the Communists are interested in overthrowing not only the government but also the foundations of the entire Japanese nation, including the emperor system. He does not really care for a revolution. Although today's conditions are bad, a revolution must be worse. He understands that the Communists want to nationalize land. That they would take away his property would be terrible, for his house and his land are his only personal possessions. The Socialists do not seem to be very different from the Communists in this respect. Again he feels obligated to vote for the LDP man.

The Japanese farmer of today faces multiple crises—the crises of material survival, of loneliness and old age, of communal and political loyalty, of individual and class identity. In some areas, he retains lingering hopes for a better future, but these areas are rapidly diminishing. What the future holds for him and his kind, the farmer does not know. It cannot be very good. Yet, because he has a stake in this life and in this world, he keeps going. His efforts are reflected in the organized groups with which he is associated and in the political arena where he and his organization turn protagonist in the game of pressure group politics.

Changing Environment of the Farmer's Life

The simplest yet most impressive indicator of the farmer's plight in today's Japan is the rapid and continuous outflow of farming population. This exit has been taking place for the last two decades, but since about 1960, when the Ikeda cabinet began to trumpet the call for accelerated economic growth with heavy emphasis on industrial development, the flow has become torrential. Between 1960 and 1965, farming population diminished at the annual rate of 4.6 percent. The pace somewhat slowed down in the following year, but it soared to 6.3 percent in 1970, 8.9 percent in 1971, and 8.4 percent in 1972.[1] As a result, the total Japanese farming population dwindled over twelve years (1960–1972) from 14.5 million to slightly less than 6.9 million. In 1960, farmers still accounted for 27 percent of the nation's gainfully occupied population, but by 1970 their numbers diminished to no more than 16 percent.

All who have quit farming have not moved to urban employment. Some have left because of old age, illness, or, perhaps, death. It is significant, however, that they have not been replaced by younger farmers. Many who have quit farms have not even moved their place of residence, but have, in fact, remained in their native village and begun to commute to their new jobs in nearby towns by bus, train, or car. Statistics show that the decline in the number of people living with at least partially farming families has been much slower than the decline in farming population. Between 1960 and 1972, for example, those residing in full-time or part-time farmer family households dropped from 34.4 million to 24.9 million.[2] Even in the latter year, they accounted for nearly a quarter of the total Japanese population.

Statistics show that nearly 85 percent of the slightly over 5.2 million farming families in January 1971 were engaged only partially in actual farming. In most cases, some of the family members were practicing farmers, while others had nonfarming jobs. In far less common cases, a farmer was employed for a nonfarming job on a part-time basis. In 48 percent of the "farming families," not a single member engaged in full-time farming and in 15 percent of the families the only full-time farmer was the wife.[3] To summarize, by 1960 nearly two-thirds of Japanese farmer families were deriving part of their incomes from nonfarming occupations, but among these partial farmer families about one-half were still deriving more income from farming than from nonagricultural employment. By 1972, however, not only had the percentage of partial farmer families increased to 85 percent of all farmer families, but among the partial farmer families almost two-thirds were dependent primarily on income from nonfarming sources. This trend is likely to continue, perhaps at a somewhat reduced pace.[4]

If nonfarming jobs are readily available in nearby towns and cities, off-farm employment does not necessitate physical removal from one's native village or family. If jobs are not available within commutable distances, however, both the individual seeking an off-farm job and his or her family face a problem. Acute personal strains and social problems especially occur when the man of the family goes to faraway places and returns home only infrequently. In early 1970, the government decided to enforce rice production curtailment by ordering rice farmers to leave part of their paddy fields fallow for the forthcoming planting season. It was the task of village officials to announce the government decision to farmers and to set up quotas for individual rice growers. In the northern prefecture of Akita, village officials had a great deal of trouble locating those who could speak for their families. Some 60,000 of the 118,000 rice-growing families in the prefecture had lost their men to Tokyo and other large cities along the southwestern seacoast. Most of them were gone for months.[5] To their annoyance, the officials had to go to the distant cities themselves, rather than recall the exiled farmers back to their native villages, in order to deliver the messages from the government. To the men and their families, the problem was obviously far more serious and painful. This state of affairs certainly has far-reaching effects on the basic fabric of family life and community structure. It also affects norms of political behavior and allegiance and may in the long run influence the general alignment of political power in the entire society.

The social and political consequences of the dramatic increases in the outflow of farming population and in the number of rural residents who are nonfarmers are accentuated by the fact that the majority of those who leave farming are young males. In 1970, for example, only about 20 percent of the farming population were thirty-four years old or younger, as compared with nearly 55 percent in the manufacturing industry.[6] On the other hand, those over fifty-five years old were less than 10 percent in the manufacturing industry but nearly 30 percent in agriculture. Thus, not only are young farmers moving out of farming, but even more important, new village or provincial town secondary school graduates never enter the ranks of farmers. In 1972, those sons and daughters of farmers who finished lower or upper secondary schools (equivalent to the ninth and the twelfth grades in the United States), 39 percent went to work upon graduation. However, only 5.5 percent of these young workers, or 2.2 percent of the entire population of new secondary school graduates, went into farming.[7] If one considers the fact that as recently as 1967 nearly 10 percent of the new secondary school graduates became farmers, at least temporarily, and that the percentage point has since been steadily falling each year, the implications become unmistakable. In a few years, new blood may completely stop flowing into Japanese agriculture, and in a few decades the entire farmer population may well disappear either by attrition or by the continuing city-bound migrations.

Changes in agricultural production. With the decrease in farming population, the volume of agricultural production has begun to decline, too. After steady growth up to 1968 (between 1965 and 1968, gross agricultural production grew by 5.3 percent per year),[8] it fell for the first time in 1969 by 1.4 percent, then slipped further by 2.4 percent in 1970, and 5.5 percent in 1971. This has happened while mining and manufacturing output continues to increase, though at a substantially reduced rate: 17.7 percent in 1969, 13.5 percent in 1970, and 4.4 percent in 1971.[9] The decrease in overall agricultural production may be explained to a large extent by the policy-induced curtailment of rice cultivation. Rice output in 1969 was 9.4 percent less in tonnage than in 1968, and in 1970 it was 14.5 percent less than in 1969.[10] After all, rice is still the mainstay of Japanese agriculture, accounting for nearly 40 percent of the nation's total farm production. However, some other important produce, notably wheat, beans, and potatoes, fell sharply too. Increases in new or expanding areas, such as poultry, eggs, and meats, made up for the decline of staple-food production to some degree but not to the extent of allaying the alarm widely spreading among the rapidly diminishing rice and grain farmers.

The general decline of production in the key sectors of Japanese agriculture was reflected also in the falling level of capital investment in farmhouses and machines. Overall fixed capital investment fell 3.7 percent in 1971.[11] This sort of thing had not happened in the last fifteen years, except in 1957 when rice farmers suffered a particularly poor crop. The diminution of capital investment in equipment and facilities aggravates the severe shortage of labor caused by the process of depopulation. Rapid mechanization and increased use of new and efficient equipment could conceivably make up to a certain extent for the population loss, but the fact is that farmers are neither able nor willing to invest in such substitutes for human labor on a sufficiently large scale. This is another poignant indicator of the general malaise that appears to be permeating the major segments of the nation's agricultural class.

The above remarks do not necessarily apply to all Japanese farmers. In a few areas of agriculture—particularly in large-scale garden farming and livestock raising—production has expanded. The typical up-and-coming garden farmer makes substantial investment in modern equipment, especially greenhouses of plastic, manmade fiber, or glass materials, as well as in chemical fertilizers and selected seeds. His kind has increased nearly twofold in the five years between 1965 and 1970, from about 70,000 families to over 130,000 families.[12] With the help of the greenhouses, the farmer manipulates the growth of cucumbers, eggplants, tomatoes, and so forth, almost at will, so that he may harvest and sell them at peak prices. Livestock farming is still limited in Japan. As late as 1972, the entire country held only 1.8 million head of milking cows, 1.8 million head of beef cattle, 7 million hogs, and 232 million chickens. However, over the last twenty years the combined total of livestock has increased ten times and is likely to become the single most important sector of Japanese agriculture by the end of the present decade. In fact, several mass-producing livestock firms of substantial scale have already emerged, a fact that could not have been imagined two decades ago. Sonogaya Hog Raising Company in Kanagawa prefecture holds more than 25,000 hogs, the C. I. Firm in Iwate raises 600,000 broiler chickens, Morinaga Company's Nasu Ranch has 250 head of cattle, and the Hidaka Ranch Feeding Lot in Aichi is capable of supporting 1,000 cows.[13] The "plant" facilities of these large-scale livestock and chicken firms are almost completely automated.

The phenomenal growth in these two expanding areas is certainly a bright spot on the otherwise bleak landscape of today's Japanese agriculture. Their share of the nation's agricultural production and marketing no doubt will expand steadily in the years to come. However, the plight of the masses of Japanese farmers will remain unchanged. In fact, in some ways these two advances further the deprivations of ordinary small farmers. In view of the heavy financial outlays involved, it is virtually impossible for the average rice or grain farmer to quit his traditional line and join the ranks of the few wealthy garden and livestock farmers. Even if he somehow managed to overcome the formidable financial problems, he would find it difficult to win a niche in the highly competitive market. Competition comes not only from the fast-growing domestic livestock firms but also increasingly from foreign imports. Although breaking into garden farming may be less strenuous for the average farmer, both in terms of financing and marketing, even here risks are great. Vegetable and fruit prices fluctuate in a most unpredictable manner, and foreign imports are likely to invade the heretofore protected markets much more freely and ruthlessly in the future.

Advantages of garden and livestock farming derive partly from the large-scale operation as well as from mechanization and systematized marketing. The scale of operations depends in a large measure on the size of land available. Herein lies another constraint on the average farmer's decision to venture into these seemingly lucrative areas. Land mobility in rural Japan has never been high. In recent years, the skyrocketing land price has discouraged most small farmers from parting with their land or from acquiring neighbors' land. Between 1960 and 1971, the value of wet rice land nearly doubled, while that of dry farmland rose more than six times. The rising price makes it impossible for a small farmer to buy additional land from his neighbors. At the same time, the prospect of further price increase makes him less than enthusiastic to sell his own land at the current price level. When substantial land transactions have taken place in recent years, the buyers have been almost invariably public highway or housing builders, or commercial factory and housing developers. In other words, land has been diverted from small-scale farming use not to large-scale farming but to the growth of urban and suburban amenities and influences.

All these factors lead to the perpetuation and aggravation of the small farmer's difficulties. In 1970, farmers with ¥5 million or more annual incomes, nearly all of whom were large-scale livestock and garden farmers, accounted for only 0.3 percent of the farmer families in the entire nation.[14] More than 90 percent of Japanese farmers still earned less than ¥2 million a year. As far as the average rice and grain farmer is concerned, the spectacular successes that the few "agri-firms" seem to be making are irrelevant to his personal interests.

Current Policy Issues

All the policy issues that currently agitate and preoccupy the several groups who are interested in the present state and future of Japanese agriculture relate in one way or another to the basic changes that are taking place in its demographic and social environment. Responses to the problems are naturally diverse. Generally speaking, farmers and their pressure groups are most directly susceptible to and suffer from these changes. Their reactions tend to be strongly negative. They often appear to resist the forces of history only to be eventually overcome by those forces. Politicians, bureaucrats, and nonfarmer interest groups, on the other hand, do not have as direct and immediate a stake

in the consequences of those changes. They seem to be willing to accommodate themselves with and even ride the tidal waves of change.
The extent and nature of their involvement vary, however, from group
to group and from one member of a group to another. A politician may
need farmers' votes to win the next election and therefore may listen to
their demands with genuine personal interest. A bureaucrat in the Ministry of Agriculture (MOA) may feel professionally responsible for the
welfare of the common farmer and therefore may try to be helpful.
A businessman may be counting on farmers' cooperation in relocating
his business in a rural area as well as in recruiting young village secondary school graduates into his firms or factories. For these and other
reasons, nonfarmer groups frequently show concern for the farmer's lot.
Because they have other, often conflicting, interests and commitments,
their ideas and behaviors tend to be complex, in fact, at times contradictory. The recent debates on agricultural policy issues reflect all these
forces and tendencies.

Postwar government programs. The first comprehensive
agricultural policy plan in postwar Japan was embodied in the Agricultural Basic Law (*Nōgyō Kihon Hō*) of 1961. The law was aimed at
shifting surplus rural population from farming to industry; at promoting
large-scale, mechanized farming operations; and at bridging, through
these means, the wide gaps of income and well-being between urban
dwellers and farmers.[15] The basic assumption underlying this plan was
that a decrease in farming population would lead to consolidation of
the fragmented farms and the growth of more viable and efficient units
of farming activities and production. These changes would indirectly
facilitate the development of heavy industry and stimulate the overall
economic growth. The Ikeda cabinet that presided over the drafting
and promulgation of the law was publicly committed to a policy of
doubling Japan's gross national income in ten years.

This prediction, however, has not been fulfilled. Rural population
has indeed moved out of agriculture in massive numbers and has been
absorbed largely by secondary and tertiary industries. The units of
landholding, on the other hand, have remained virtually unaffected for
the reasons mentioned already. On the average, 69 percent of farming
families owned less than 1 hectare (2.471 acres) at the end of 1970, as
compared with 71 percent in 1960.[16] In light of the obvious failure of

the 1961 program, a new comprehensive agricultural policy was announced in 1968 by the minister of agriculture. His ideas were not well formulated at the time, but the major purpose of the new plan was to discourage the production of rice and to encourage development of livestock and garden farming. Surplus rice had been steadily piling up, and the cost of storing it was growing at an alarming rate. Because the cost was borne by the government and, therefore, ultimately by taxpayers under the existing price-support system, criticisms against government complacency were raised not only by the consumer public but even by fiscal experts in the bureaucracy and academia. Under the growing pressure, the agriculture minister also suggested a review of the rice price-support system itself.[17]

The more detailed plan formulated by MOA in response to the minister's instruction proposed various steps to hold down rice production, including control of land development for rice cultivation, shift in the use of existing rice fields to the cultivation of other crops, and partial liberalization of government control on the marketing of rice. By early 1970, the contents of the new program became more or less definitive. They included steps to balance the supply of rice with actual demand, to improve price standards and pricing practices for agricultural products, to eliminate gradually the existing barriers against agricultural imports, to promote the shift of work force from agriculture to industry, and to foster modern and efficient types of agriculture.[18] All these propositions were calculated to have depressive effects on agricultural production, especially rice. They were therefore destined to meet intense opposition from farmers and their organizations.

These ideas were promptly translated into concrete government actions, despite the fierce opposition and resistance of rice farmers. More recently, however, the tone of the debates over the long-term issue of agriculture and the farmer in Japanese society has been gradually changing. The statement of the new minister of agriculture in August 1971, for example, indicated a subtle change in the climate of opinion among politicians and, possibly, among bureaucrats. After declaring that Japanese agriculture stood at an important crossroads in its history, the agriculture minister proposed to strengthen its basic constitution so that it might effectively compete with foreign imports and overcome other difficulties.[19] The statement was much too short and abstract for one to pin down exactly what the government was proposing to do about rice price, import barriers, and other immediate issues. It nevertheless offered some faint signals that the Tokyo officialdom was having a second thought about "bulldozing" over the 9.5 million farmers as well as their paddy fields.

A report released in December of the same year by a group of agricultural-cooperative leaders, big-business representatives, and academic experts that was functioning as a semiofficial advisor for the government was just as abstract but more revealing about what may have been on the minds of the government leaders. According to the report, several basic functions had to be performed by farmers. First, staple foodstuffs (presumably rice and grains) must be supplied by domestic producers. Because feeding the nation is a matter of "national security," Japan must aim at complete self-sufficiency in staple food supply. Second, rural residents constitute a "stabilizing factor" in the society. A minimal number (unspecified) of them must be therefore maintained, even if "farming population" may inevitably decrease. Third, agriculture contributes to the protection of a wholesome environment from congestion, pollution, and other ills arising from the sophistication of the economy. It provides also a wholesome labor force. This important function of agriculture must be duly recognized.[20] The intents of the report, which may well have been endorsed by the LDP politicians and bureaucrats, are clear. Rural voters have been the most reliable supporters of the conservative government and the LDP. The enforcement of the 1970 agricultural policy program had, however, alienated large numbers of these rural voters, who had consistently voted LDP candidates to the Diet. The consequences of the policy frightened the conservative politicians and their supporters in the bureaucracy, business, and academia. Hence the subtle, seemingly inconsistent about-face within a year.

The idea that self-sufficiency in basic food supply is vital to the survival of a society, whether a small tribe or a large nation, of course is ancient and was once universal. Its appeal must be particularly strong in a group geographically isolated from the rest of the world. In an age when interdependence has become a fundamental fact of international life and in a society that is critically dependent on overseas sources of supply for practically all industrial raw materials, the idea may sound far less convincing. The fact is, however, that the government of Japan has begun to take it more seriously and to formulate it into an official policy more systematically than ever before. According to an MOA announcement in April 1972, Japan was already self-supporting 106 percent in rice, 97 percent in eggs, 88 percent in meats, and 84 percent in fruits.[21] It imported, on the other hand, 91 percent of wheat and 66 percent of barley and rye. By 1977, the ministry bureaucrats predict, the share of domestic supply will increase by 3 to 6 percent in all articles mentioned above, except rice, of which the rate of self-sufficiency will be reduced to 100 percent. Farmers surely should be happy with the assurance for their increased share of national income and contribution to national security. From the perspective of the Tokyo officials, they may thus continue to behave as an important "stabilizing" element in Japanese society and politics, just as the big-business representatives, academic agricultural specialists, and even leaders of agricultural co-operatives have suggested.

Industrial relocation and formation of agri-blocs. In addition to the long-term good tidings, the government has also proposed somewhat more practical and tangible measures to strengthen the backbone of the nation's agriculture. One such measure was to bring industry to where farmers lived, instead of urging the farmers to move to the cities where major industrial operations were currently located. This plan began to be discussed among the MOA and the Ministry of International Trade and Industry (MITI) bureaucrats in 1969. In the spring of 1970, they brought together representatives of big-business organizations, such as the Federation of Economic Organizations and the Chamber of Commerce and Industry, on one hand, and those of farmers' national organizations, such as the National Union of Agricultural Cooperatives (NUAC) and the Agriculture and Forestry Central Fund on the other, to meet with them to discuss the still rather amorphous plan.[22] The idea must have sounded attractive to all concerned. Businesses were thirsty both for the cheaper land away from the major population centers and for young workers, who were available in significant numbers only in rural villages. The leaders of the farmer groups were looking for alternative sources of income for farmers to make up for their long-term losses resulting from the reduced rice production. Besides, the arrival of major industrial plants would no doubt accelerate the rise of rural land prices. By the summer of the same year, not only the MOA and the MITI bureaucrats but also the Ministry of Labor published their own plans for industrial relocation in agricultural areas.[23] These plans were subsequently incorporated in the Law to Promote the Introduction of Industry in Agricultural Village Areas (*Nōsonchiiki Kōgyō Dōnyū Sokushin Hō*) in June 1971.[24] The law provided for substantially reduced tax rates and public loans on easy terms for industrial plants relocating in rural areas in accordance with plans to be announced by the prefecture, city, town, or village concerned. If the plan is effectively implemented, by 1975 some 15,000 hectares (37,065 acres) spread out over 2,600 cities, towns, and villages will have been diverted to industrial use and some 600,000 farmers turned into industrial workers.[25]

The coming of industry to their neighborhoods indeed may offer farmers, especially younger ones among them, better employment opportunities and therefore increased cash incomes. It will not, however, solve the basic problem the farmers face today, namely, the economic and political vulnerability of a steadily shrinking minority. By further sapping the best among the remaining members of their community, it will in fact aggravate the situation. The ministry bureaucrats were not oblivious to this implication of their industrial-relocation program. If part of their purpose was to maintain a reliable force of conservative rural voters, the plan to move industry to villages obviously had to be balanced by a measure to help the minimum sufficient number of farmers left on their farm not only survive but also expect a better deal from the government and the society. Such a measure was embodied by the plan to create agri-blocs (*Einō Danchi*), large blocks of land devoted to commercial farming on which farmers will form close-knit communities of cooperative labor and living.

The agri-bloc idea was not new. It was floating among livestock farmers around 1960. It was not until early 1972, however, that the idea was given an official blessing and began to be formulated into a general government policy. Prompted by the personal intervention of Minister Akagi, bureaucrats in MOA mapped out a strategy to turn the idea into a budgeted government program in that year. It suited well the ambitious plan to remake the entire Japanese archipelago, which the new Prime Minister Tanaka had just announced. Combined with the industrial relocation plan, which was also boosted by Tanaka's vaunted program, the emergence of tidy and efficient farming blocs would no doubt repaint the landscape of Japanese villages.

According to the ministry plan, by 1977 there will have been

formed some 10,000 agri-blocs, which will be classified into three categories: "high-efficiency production blocs," "wide-area farming blocs,"
and "model agri-blocs."[26] Most will engage in livestock, dairy, and
garden farming. By November 1972, work had been started in nearly
600 units of local government (cities, towns, and villages) to form blocs
of these kinds.[27]

Immediate issues facing farmers. These government programs and their implementation were probably welcome to most hard-
pressed farmers. There has been no overt opposition from any quarters,
at least so far. Farmers were not entirely appeased by these measures,
however, but their attention was directed to other and more immediate
issues. As of late 1972 and early 1973, the most important of these were,
from the average farmer's point of view, the continued government
policy to curtail rice production, the proposed change in the rice price-
support system, the liberalization of agricultural import restrictions,
and the increased property tax rates on agricultural land within city
districts.

In 1969, the increasing financial burden caused by piling up rice
surplus, combined with the pressure of consumers and fiscal experts in
the bureaucracy, led the government to launch a pilot policy to discourage the cultivation and production of rice. Rice farmers were paid
¥20,000 per 10 ares (0.247 acres) of rice land that they withdrew from
rice cultivation in that year.[28] The policy met fierce opposition from the
farmers, however, and only slightly over a half of 10,000 hectares
(24,710 acres) earmarked by the government were actually affected. In
the next two years, the opposition was considerably toned down, and
the targeted levels of production cuts were successfully reached. In
1970, some 340,000 hectares (84,014 acres) were kept from rice planting, a tactic that resulted in nearly a 1.4-million-ton reduction in the
year's rice production.[29] In 1971, the corresponding figures were 540,000
hectares (1,434,340 acres) and 2.26 million tons. Over half of the land
affected was simply laid off for the year, rather than being diverted to
cultivation of other crops, and could be used again for rice planting any
time except for the deterioration by disuse. Yet the quantitative achieve-
ment of the plan was quite impressive, at least in the short run.

The problem of rice price support was far more complex and far
less amenable to farmers' cooperation or acquiescence. In the early post-

war years, rice farmers were required by law to sell all their yearly rice produce to the government. Individual quotas were imposed and farmers were expected to produce no more or no less rice than would meet these government-set quotas. As a result of farmers' complaints against this rigid system and also because of the growing abundance of rice, which rendered the system anachronistic, the quotas were abolished in 1955. Since then, rice producers have contracted with the government the sale of whatever quantities of rice they expect to harvest in the fall. Normally the contract was signed at a price set by the government in July, and farmers were paid advances on their expected sale at that time. The government monopoly in the wholesale purchase of rice continued, but the new system depended much more on the farmer's voluntary contribution than did the previous quota system. Although it generally worked to the farmer's advantage and satisfaction, it was basically a dual price system that had a built-in element of instability in the period when rice was no longer scarce but was overabundant. The government bought from producers at a mutually agreeable price, a situation that meant a rather high price in terms of actual supply and demand, and sold to consumers at a price more or less reasonable from the consumer's point of view. Up until 1967, the producer rice price had risen at the rate of 9 percent per year.[30] The government inevitably incurred huge losses in this operation, losses that were ultimately passed on to taxpayers. Besides, farmers were free until 1969 to grow as much rice as they wanted, assured that they could sell all at an attractive price to the government.

The apparent contradiction in this rice price-control system became a hot political issue by the second half of the 1960s. Because the postwar government controls on the sale of all other important agricultural and industrial products had been lifted long ago—in fact, all before 1952—the peculiarity of the direct government intervention in fixing rice prices was too obvious to be left alone much longer. Under the growing pressure, the government kept the annual percentage increase of producer rice price down to 5.9 percent in 1968 and to zero during the following two years. But without a reformation of the system itself, this was but a stopgap measure. In 1971, the government yielded to farmers' pressure and raised the producer price again by 3 percent, and in 1972 by 6.12 percent. The wholesale price thus jumped nearly 37 percent between 1965 and 1972.[31]

In 1971, the government finally took a modest step toward a long-term solution of the problem. For the first time, the quantity of rice a farmer could contract to sell to the government was limited. Also, each farmer was allowed to sell part of his rice produce to nongovernmental buyers, mainly to agricultural cooperatives, which would then enter private distribution channels without government intervention. In 1971, for example, about 5.8 million tons were purchased and distributed by the government and about 2.2 million tons through nongovernmental channels.[32] This involved a significant change in the rice price-support system. Until this time, farmers were forbidden by the Food Management Law to sell rice to anybody but the government, and rice dealers and consumers to buy from anybody but the government. This provision was naturally eliminated in 1971. The change pointed to a more fundamental reform to come. Even if government control of rice price is maintained for several more years, the current practice of deciding the price in July and paying the farmers out of a special account independent from the regular annual budget is likely to be abandoned much sooner. In fact, some Finance and Agriculture Ministry bureaucrats have been calling for such a move for several years now.[33] The use of the special account has made the process of rice price decision making singularly susceptible to political pressure, but if and when it is made part of the regular budget making, farmers' organizations and politicians representing their interests will find it much more difficult to put effective pressure on the Finance Ministry's Budget Bureau offiicials. Hence the latter's desire to enforce the change as quickly as possible and the farmer-organization officials' resistance to the contemplated move.

A third issue of great importance from the farmers' point of view concerns the prospective elimination or reduction of the current barriers against agricultural imports. Since about 1968, external pressure had been building, particularly from the United States, for drastic liberalization of Japan's import restrictions. As a result, the Japanese government decided toward the end of that year to take steps for trade liberalization within a few years. In accordance with this decision, 80 of the 120 articles restricted in 1969, including 45 of the 73 agricultural items, were liberalized by the fall of 1971.[34] In April 1972, an additional 4 agricultural items, such as assorted feeds, ham, and bacon, were released from import restriction. The remaining 24 articles are, however, especially sensitive. They include such items as meats and fruits, which happen to be, as pointed out already, the products of the fastest-growing sectors of Japanese agriculture, and a few items, such as peanuts and the esoteric konjak, which have been protected primarily because of pressure from influential LDP politicians representing their local growers.[35] Only substantially increased foreign pressure or unusually strong leadership on the part of the LDP cabinet, or perhaps both, will lift the restrictions on these products.

One important factor contributing to the Japanese reluctance to part with the import restrictions is the price differential between Japanese and foreign agricultural products. Except for a few items, notably eggs, production cost is much higher in Japan than in other industrialized nations. For example, it costs more than three times as much in Japan to grow wheat as in the United States and just as much more to raise a head of beef cattle. Even rice growing costs nearly four times as much in Japan as in the United States.[36] Hence Japanese resistance to rice-flour and rice-meal imports.

Despite the desperate attempts of the Japanese government, however, the mounting international pressure is forcing Japan to lift one import barrier after another. The steadily widening trade imbalance between Japan and the United States, reaching nearly $4 billion in 1972, adds to the already formidable pressure on the Japanese government. Its decision in early 1972 to allow the import of 900 tons of fruit juice, 12,000 tons of oranges, and 5,000 head of calves from the United States was not the last concession Japan was asked to make. In September of the same year, Prime Minister Tanaka promised President Nixon in Honolulu that Japan would buy $440 million worth more of American agricultural products in 1972 than it had bought in 1971.[37] The United States has been consistently by far the most important source of Japanese agricultural imports, accounting for about 40 percent of the total value of agricultural products Japan imported in 1971. Further increases must inevitably touch some, if not all, of the politically most sensitive items that still remain protected. This change will intensify the domestic producers' and politicians' opposition. The Japanese government is thus driven to an extremely delicate and vulnerable position.

The fourth issue is the rise in property tax on agricultural land that lies within a city district. As a result of the revision of the Local Tax Law in 1971, such land is now assessed by the same standards as apply to residential land. Organized opposition to the change from the affected property owners made the ruling LDP drag its feet in an agonizing indecision for several months.[38] Ultimately, however, the party executives made up their minds to push the amendment bill through the Diet in cooperation with all opposition parties except the Communists. In March 1972, the bill was passed after several important exception and exemption provisions were written into it.

With the passage of the bill, the long-maintained privilege of the small minority group of urban and suburban "farmers" was again sacrificed by the conservative government under the pressure of far more numerous and powerful land developers and housebuilders. In view of the soaring land price and the all too apparent needs for adequate housing on the part of substantial numbers of urban dwellers, the government action was even too mild. Yet all the steps mentioned above which the government has belatedly taken in recent years—concerning rice production control, the rice price-support system, import liberalization, and tax rate change—have added to the individual farmer's plight and deepened the crisis of Japanese agriculture. Stripped of its privileges, which had become almost the sine qua non of its survival and security, the fast-disappearing class of Japanese farmers is reaching the end of the rope. Most of its individual members may emerge more prosperous and happier in the newly acquired attire of the industrial worker or office clerk, some even as managers of spacious agri-blocs and pilot farms. However, rice and grain farmers as a distinct class in the Japanese society may be becoming part of history.

The battles the farmers are fighting today are thus probably hopeless, losing battles. Although they may not last very much longer, they are nevertheless leaving indelible marks on the entire Japanese society and politics. The forms, structures, and styles of the political battles waged by the farmers and their organizations tell us a good deal about the elemental forces that drive contemporary Japanese politics and its major components.

Politics of Farmer Organizations

The structure and the style of farmers' political activities in contemporary Japan are in many ways also a function of the sweeping changes that have been under way in their living and work environment.

The significant increase in the percentage of older people among farming population tends to perpetuate the traditional identification of farm votes with the prominence of conservative political forces in agricultural communities, represented by the LDP. On the other hand, however, the strength of these forces rapidly diminishes as more and more members of rural village communities leave farms and enter the secondary and tertiary industry labor market. Those who find new jobs in nonfarm work environments often change their political loyalty. Physically and psychologically freed from old family and village ties, they join the growing ranks of floating voters or establish new identity with opposition parties through labor-union membership and association with other urban-oriented groups.

This trend has been evident not only among factory and office employees fresh from villages but also among many older people who have recently left farms.[39] Even among those left on farms, substantial diversification of political allegiance and voting behavior has been taking place, especially among women. In those instances when wives become principal providers of farm labor in the absence of their husbands, they often become coequals of men in political as well as family and social activities. This is particularly true in those agricultural communities to the west of Tokyo where women are today generally better educated than men.

In a recently published comparative study of social and political consciousness among residents of a suburban garden-farming village in Okayama prefecture and a predominantly rice-growing village in Akita prefecture, sociologist Tadashi Fukutake demonstrated a significant shift in the distribution of conservatism and progressivism.[40] He divided respondents to a set questionnaire into conservative, intermediate, and progressive groups. Questions were asked about their views of old practices and new developments in the family, hamlet (village), and national politics.[41] The tabulation of the results showed that even in the Akita village those holding conservative views fell from 64.1 percent to 20.0 percent for family-related questions, from 13.6 percent to 7.6 percent for village-related questions, and from 36.3 percent to 13.6 percent for nation-level questions. In the meantime, progressives rose in percentage from 2.7 percent to 23.9 percent, 23.2 percent to 47.5 percent, and 6.8 percent to 21.0 percent, respectively. These figures clearly reflect the drastic changes in the general idealized environment of village Japan that was described in the preceding section.

The recent government policy to force substantial acreage of rice fields out of cultivation has also affected farmers' mentality in a fundamental way. Under this policy, the rice farmers were paid for not working their fields. It no doubt added to their sense of despair in the future of rice farming. It also destroyed their traditional work ethic. Hard work and thrift were no longer virtues when the government encouraged and rewarded idleness and transience. In short, the policy taught the farmers that rice agriculture as an occupation was no longer respectable or promising. The widespread sense of disappointments and uncertainty has generated deep-running political discontents that, combined with the changes in basic social and political values mentioned above, threaten to affect the general patterns of political alignment in the entire system.

Farm organizations. Outlets for farmers' political frustrations and discontents are provided by several kinds of farm organizations— for example, local agricultural committees (*Nōgyō Iinkai*), which were originally formed to administer the postwar land reform, and their national federation, the Chamber of Agriculture (*Nōgyō Kaigisho*). These function as semipublic agencies of the government and are generally conservative. The several farmer unions, on the other hand, are associated with either the Japan Communist party (JCP) or the Japan Socialist party (JSP) and tend to be reformist and antigovernment. The most important in terms of size and range of activities are, however, the agricultural cooperatives, which operate at both national and local levels. The linkages between the different levels of organization and activity are not very complex, but a brief explanation may be helpful.

The basic local unit of agricultural-cooperative organization operates at the village and town level. Its members are local farmers. The cooperative serves their needs in a variety of ways. If its major function is to market the members' products, it is called a marketing cooperative; if it is to purchase merchandise that the members need, such as fertilizers, farm machines, and even household appliances, it is a purchasing cooperative. Likewise, there are credit cooperatives and mutual-benefit cooperatives.[42] Those that combine credit operations with other functions are generically called general cooperatives (*Sōgō Nōkyō*), while those which lack a credit department are specialized cooperatives (*Senmon Nōkyō*) in the cooperative-movement parlance. The unit cooperatives form a prefectural federation, and prefectural federations combine into a national federation. Some of the prefectural federations are marketing and purchasing federations; others are credit or mutual-benefit federations. In some prefectures, one finds also federations specialized in a particular area of agriculture, such as livestock raising, dairy farming, sericulture, and so forth, or in a particular social function, such as welfare and land development. In addition, there is in each prefecture a union of agricultural cooperatives (*Ken Nōkyō Chūōkai*), of which unit cooperatives and various prefectural federations are members. At the national level, there are again specialized federations and a national union (*Zenkoku Nōkyō Chūōkai* or NUAC) of which all the unit cooperatives, prefectural federations, prefectural unions, and national federations are members.[43] As of March 1972, there were 5,688 general unit cooperatives, 8,907 specialized unit cooperatives, 846 prefectural federations, 22 national federations, and, of course, 46 prefectural unions and 1 national union.[44]

An important fact about Japanese agricultural cooperatives is that, although their memberships are voluntary in principle, virtually all farm families are affiliated with them. When there were some 5.3 million farm families in 1971, there were 5.4 million regular and 1.4 million associate cooperative members.[45] The latter are mostly wives. Thus, the cooperatives together represent the entire community of the nation's agricultural families, and presumably also their views and interests, although not those of every individual farmer.[46] Herein lies an important reason for their collective political strength and politicians' respect for it.

The role of the agricultural cooperative in the economic and social life of a farmer is also great. In 1969, for example, nearly all rice and wheat sold by farmers (either to the government or rice dealers) was handled by cooperatives, as well as over 80 percent of potatoes, sweet potatoes, vegetables and fruits, milk, silk cocoons and rapeseeds, and between 70 and 80 percent of beans, eggs, beef, and pork.[47] During the same year, farmers bought from cooperative stores 90 percent of the rice and animal feeds they purchased in that year as well as over 70 percent of fertilizers, agricultural machines, packing materials, weedicides and insecticides, oil and gasoline, and so forth. They bought from the cooperatives more than a half of their clothes, cars, and even household appliances such as refrigerators and washing machines, and daily necessaries such as drugs and tissue paper.[48] The general and credit cooperatives handled over 70 percent of the loans extended to farmers in that year, while commercial banks contributed less than 6 percent to their total borrowings.[49] The total savings deposited in cooperative banking departments amounted to ¥5,021 billion in 1969 and ¥7,118 billion in 1971. In the latter year, nearly 40 percent of total farmer-family savings were deposited with them, as compared to 14.4 percent with regular commercial banks or 7.5 percent in postal savings accounts.[50]

The extent to which agricultural cooperatives intervene in the farmer's daily life is indeed impressive. The above statistics give an impression of almost total dependence of the average farmer on the services provided by the local cooperatives. This impression may be, however, rather superficial. So is the vaunted strength of a cooperative. If one looks more closely at the economic operation of an average unit-level cooperative as it faces the future in the first years of the 1970s, one realizes that not all has been going so well. In 1970, for example, only the credit and the mutual-benefit cooperatives and the corresponding departments of general cooperatives made profits. All others lost quite substantially. For the average general cooperative, the loss amounted to ¥3.3 million in the purchase department, ¥2.9 million in the sales department, ¥1.4 million in the processing department, ¥0.6 million in the warehousing department, and ¥4.0 million in all the other departments combined.[51] These losses are not surprising at all, considering the impact of the rice production-curtailment policy, which naturally depresses the cooperative sales and warehousing activities. In the long run, it also adversely affects the farmer's income, which in turn reflects on his purchases of goods from the cooperative stores. Thus, the cooperative management faces a creeping financial crisis, the full impact of which is not yet apparent. For the time being, the false image of the invulnerable agricultural cooperatives may stay, thanks to the apparently thriving credit operations. However, farmers' deposits do not derive so much from stable profits made on crops as, increasingly, from income from nonfarming employment and, occasionally, from the quick sale of farmland. The cooperatives invest that money in nonagricultural profit-making projects and enterprises, despite the explicit provision of the Agricultural Cooperatives Law prohibiting such operations.[52]

Political influence of farm organizations. Unit agricultural cooperatives engage in a variety of political activities in the particular localities. They put pressure on local government officials on a variety of issues in which they see a stake. They support or oppose particular candidates in local and national elections. Generally speaking, however, many of their political activities are so well integrated into the general fabric of the local social system and their political influence is so implicit that it is difficult to subject them to a brief shorthand description and analysis.

The political actions of the prefectural and national federations and, especially, NUAC, are, on the other hand, much more explicit and visible. On wide-ranging issues, from the annual budget appropriations for agriculture to tax and price policies, they actively campaign and get their messages across to the government, politicians, and bureaucrats by memorializing, petitioning, and blackmailing. They often call for massive farmers' rallies in Tokyo to demonstrate their particularly strong interest in the outcomes of such issues. As a rule, NUAC becomes the major vehicle of their concerted efforts to bring effective pressure to bear on the government.

In principle, NUAC does not identify with any particular party. It pursues what its executives call a policy of "equal distance" from all five major parties.[53] There is in fact a nonpartisan Diet members' group called an Agricultural Policy Study Association (*Nōsei Kenkyūkai*) working in close cooperation with NUAC. Half a dozen JSP members as well as about thirty-five LDP men are affiliated with this group. In practice, however, NUAC is interested in influencing the majority LDP for quite obvious reasons. And the LDP has been generally susceptible and responsive to farmers' pressure and lobbying activities.

First, an overwhelming majority, probably upward of 80 percent, of LDP Diet members come from rural election districts. Second, the LDP is a top-heavy parliamentary party with a very spotty organized-support base at the grass roots, apart from the highly idiosyncratic "support associations" (*Kōenkai*) formed by and for individual LDP Diet members and would-be Diet members. Agricultural cooperatives are a valuable keystone of the party's fragile base of organized support. Third, the present system of member apportionment in the House of Representatives elections, which is grossly skewed against urban voters, exaggerates the importance of farm votes. In the recent December 1972 election, for example, a JSP candidate was defeated in a Tokyo district with 144,415 votes, while an LDP candidate was elected in a rural Gumma district with 37,258 votes. In fact, including the JSP man mentioned above, four Democratic Socialist (DSP), two JSP, two Clean Government (CGP), and two LDP candidates lost with over 96,000 votes, seven of them with more than 100,000. On the other hand, six LDP and four independents (undeclared LDP) won with less than 47,000 votes, three of them with less than 40,000.[54] If one can be elected with 40,000 votes, the votes of 80,000 farmers represented by the cooperatives in the given election district certainly make a difference.

For these reasons, 70 to 80 LDP Diet members find it both appropriate and necessary to attend rallies for rice price raising sponsored by NUAC and other farmer organizations. In the 491-member House of Representatives, their number carries tremendous weight, especially if many others, not only from the ruling LDP but the opposition parties, are sensitive to the pressure of farm voters for precisely the same reasons. In the smaller 250-member House of Councillors, where the LDP's numerical edge over the opposition is slight (25 in March 1973), even a small farm-bloc LDP member can defend their clients' interests more effectively. For example, a group of 17 LDP members is determined to block agricultural import liberalization. They threaten to bolt the LDP should the government force a liberalization measure through the House despite their opposition. Their defection would mean a 17-man gain for the opposition parties. The LDP would then lose its majority overnight. That loss is a high risk the party's executives are most reluctant to take, especially when the LDP's dominance in the House of Representatives seems to be fast disappearing.

As the foregoing discussion suggests, NUAC and its collaborators owe their successes in driving the LDP and the government on a course of action that they prefer or restraining them from one that they oppose almost exclusively to the strength of numbers. They have not given the LDP or any other party any significant amounts of political funds. In fact, one of its executive officers claims that it has not given a cent.[55] Ever since they were first established in 1948 with substantial financial and other forms of assistance from the office of the Supreme Commander for the Allied Powers (SCAP) and the Japanese government, agricultural cooperatives have been directly subsidized by the government again and again. In the 1950s, they received a series of interest-free public loans, and in the 1960s this practice was continued through the Modernization Fund Assistance Law (1961), the Agricultural Cooperatives Amalgamation Promotion Law (1961), the Processed Milk Producer Subsidy Law (1965), the Vegetable Production and Shipping Stabilization Law (1966), and so forth.[56] The agricultural cooperatives have thus acquired a quasipublic character in practice as well as in law. They are therefore morally obligated to maintain a nonpartisan political posture. To make political contributions to a party would no doubt compromise such a posture.

Rural conservatism. The number of practicing farmers alone does not fully explain the impressive political power of the cooperatives. Just as important has been the politicians' belief that they constitute a valuable asset to be cultivated and utilized in their electioneering activities. And the politicians' judgment seems to have been generally sound, so far. It must be noted, however, that a significant time lag probably exists between a change in social environment and the resulting change in man's value judgment. In the case of the Japanese farmers, the lag has been particularly large. Of course, one reason for this is that most members of a farmer's family who get nonfarm jobs continue to reside in the same house, with other members of their families. They thus remain exposed, perhaps with greatly reduced frequency and intensity, to the conservative influence of the older members, typically their parents, who continue in farming. This must inhibit an instant shift in their political allegiance.[57]

Another factor contributing to the staying power of rural conservatism is the presence of farm and farm-related organizations, especially agricultural cooperatives themselves. Organizations acquire their own raison d'être and motivation for survival and growth after having been around for a while. Frequently, long after the initial conditions that brought them into being have disappeared or radically changed, they continue to thrive on their own acquired will to stay and expand. Both internally and externally they begin to show signs of progressive bureaucratization. Although the number of regular members of agricultural cooperatives has been slowly but steadily falling in the last several years, from about 6.2 million in 1966 to about 5.9 million in 1971, the number of cooperative employees has been growing, from about 200,000 to 247,000, during the same period.[58] This is probably true of local government bureaucracies both at the village and at the prefectural levels. Still another reason for the peculiar attraction of agricultural cooperatives to LDP politicians is that it is much easier for them to conserve old friendships with rural voters than to befriend far more independent-minded and temperamental urban voters. Farmers have been voting, until very recently, consistently for LDP tickets and may still be persuaded to support them for some more years. In view of the far-reaching changes in the social environment of rural Japan and their effects on rural voters' political perceptions and voting behavior, their allegiance can no longer be taken for granted. Yet there are some good reasons for LDP politicians to believe that farmers will not abandon them overnight.

To the average farmer, the JSP appears to be insensitive and indifferent to his needs and interests. The party is basically a Tokyo-bound spokesman for organized labor. The JCP has been far more interested in his problems and willing to help, but it is after all a party committed to the ideology of communism. An average farmer does not feel comfortable with any explicit and systematic ideology, and communism has been a stigma for a long time. The moderate DSP is also a predominantly urban- and intellectual-oriented party, as is the CGP. The latter is an adjunct of the Nichiren Shoshu Buddhist sect, which is a minority in rural Japan. By tradition, most farmers are affiliated with more conventional sects, such as Jōdo, Jōdo Shin, Shingon, Tendai, and Zen. Farmers today are far less fearful or suspicious of any of these opposition parties than they were several years ago. They are, in fact, defecting from the ranks of LDP supporters in significant numbers in many areas. From an LDP politician's view, however, where else could he turn for support than to rural villages when an election time arrives?

The results of recent national and local elections have in a way confirmed the general validity of the LDP politicians' assumption, to which many others subscribe, that the strength of the conservatives still lies in rural villages. In the 1971 prefectural and local elections, large cities elected opposition candidates as prefectural governors, mayors, and, to a less spectacular extent, prefectural and local assembly members, while the LDP managed to hold its ground in provincial towns and villages.[59] In the most recent House of Representatives election of December 1972, the LDP lost again heavily in metropolitan districts. In the most densely populated 16 of the 124 election districts, for example, the LDP share of votes fell an average of 3 percent and the number of seats 12 percent from the December 1969 election.[60] In rural and semirural districts, on the other hand, the LDP maintained its strength, and the opposition parties, except the JCP, failed to make significant inroads.

All this may change within several years. If the LDP loses its majority in either one or both of the two houses, particularly in the House of Representatives, by the second half of the present decade the whole context of the game may radically change. The LDP owes its electoral victories largely to the gross malapportionment of seats between urban and rural election districts, which has not been changed since 1947. All other parties have a good reason to force a change in the distribution of seats simply by revising Appended Table I of the Public Office Election Law. When this happens, the LDP's artificial advantages will largely disappear. An important reason for the party's preoccupation with the views and demands of rural voters will also be lost. Until this happens, however, the LDP and the conservative government will continue to keep farmers as content as possible under the hard circumstances.

For the moment, LDP politicians remain eagerly solicitous of rural voters' favor. An impressive number of them attend the public rallies called by NUAC from time to time to register with the government farmers' demand for rice price increases or opposition to import liberalization and to new property tax rates. When the cabinet cannot sponsor a bill demanded by farmers for larger political considerations, individual LDP Diet members sponsor it, often in cooperation with opposition-party members. The LDP policy board and executive council are vulnerable to the pressure of the farm bloc in the party that controls and operates from policy-board departments for agriculture and local government. The recommendations of these departments normally become policy-board decisions and are passed on to the executive council as such. The latter then proclaims them as official party decisions, which bind the hands of the top party leadership and the cabinet. Actual flow of farmers' influence within the LDP is naturally far more complex, but this statement abbreviates rather than distorts what actually happens.[61]

Government services. Generally, it is much harder for the government and LDP to satisfy farmers' demands that require new legislation than to handle those demands that require only administrative discretion. A member's bill is a rarity and usually calls for collaboration with opposition members. On most agricultural issues, opposition members are less reticent about collaborating with the LDP than on most other issues. As was mentioned earlier, agricultural cooperatives, especially NUAC, pursue a policy of "equal distance" from all parties. At election times, they often support particular JSP and DSP candidates who have especially commendable legislative records on agricultural issues. NUAC has been working on the opposition parties, including the JCP and the CGP, as well as on the LDP on the question of property tax rates on certain types of "agricultural" land lying within city limits.[62] All five parties helped in February 1973 emasculate a draft bill prepared by the Ministry of Local Government to increase the tax rates.[63] This sort of thing, however, does not happen very often. Usually differences and squabbles over other issues interfere and foul up their efforts to mount concerted nonpartisan actions to satisfy farmers' demands. As a result, LDP tends to try to appease farmers with many small favors, rather than with large legislative action. Most of these small favors involve relatively simple manipulation of existing laws and regulations, for example, by providing low-interest government loans to farm groups, subsidizing rural road construction or repair works, or just ignoring minor violations of the Agricultural Cooperatives Law by a unit cooperative or a prefectural federation.

MOA bureaucrats intervene and help the LDP politicians with this kind of administrative operation. By profession, they are defenders of farmers and their interests. Unlike many MITI and Finance Ministry officials who join their client companies almost as soon as they retire, few MOA bureaucrats join agricultural cooperatives or their national and prefectural federations. In a more general sense, however, their fate is bound with the fate of farmers and the nation's agriculture. Their powers and resources derive ultimately from actual or hypothetical services they perform on behalf of the agricultural community.

In the past, however, the relationship between ministry bureaucrats and NUAC officials was not as intimate and direct as one might have expected. In the period when rice farmers were contented with a rice price rise almost automatically each year and when agricultural cooperatives were prosperous, farm organization leaders wanted above all more independence from the bureaucrats' control and interference. They could negotiate with politicians on large policy questions from a position of strength. The bureaucrats' intervention was usually either irrelevant or superfluous. NUAC thus kept MOA officials at arms' length. More recently, however, as the signs of imminent trouble have begun to appear, cooperative leaders are having second thoughts.[64] They find it necessary now to gain the bureaucrats' sympathy and assistance to tide over the difficulties. Because the bureaucrats are also under similar pressure, a sort of camaraderie has been born between them. Members of a minority have to close their ranks against the pressure from the majority. A crisis presents all the more reason for them to unite for survival.

On the other hand, MOA does not have the kind of exclusive jurisdiction that it once had over the farmer's life and well-being. MITI is vitally interested in the industrial-relocation program. The Labor Ministry intervenes in the recruitment of rural youth by industry and in various training and retraining programs. The Local Government Ministry is extensively involved in the rehabilitation of the rural communities that are either very sick or dying from the massive outflow of population. The Construction Ministry oversees most road, bridge, and port construction projects throughout the country. The role of MOA is thus considerably less conspicuous now than it was several years ago.

All this points up the significant change in the manner in which the government relates to rural communities and their residents, a change that corresponds with the basic socioeconomic changes in the environment of Japanese agriculture. The direction of the change is clear. The diversification of employment patterns caused by rapid industrialization and urbanization leads to diversification of needs and demands of those caught in the turmoil. The latter in turn leads to diversification of government services required. Thus, more segments of the national and local bureaucracies penetrate more deeply the once tranquil world of rice farmers.

Future of Japanese Farmers

The steady decrease of full-time farmers, the encroachment on rural land and work force by urban industry, and the accelerating involvement of government bureaucracies in rural development projects all combine to destroy the basic foundations of Japanese agriculture as it has existed for thousands of years. Farmers today have little control of their own daily existence, much less of their future. An autonomous rice farmer is becoming the shadow of the past. The agricultural cooperatives which were jealous and proud of their independence only several years ago are desperately fighting for survival, as their dependence upon and control by the government inevitably increases. They are losing virtually all major battles they have been fighting over the rice production-curtailment policy, the rice price-support system, import restrictions, and the agricultural-land property tax issue. But the true dilemma of the Japanese farmer is that he really has a choice only to fight to prolong his life as a farmer or to stop fighting and cease to be a farmer.

On a positive note, even if rice farmers as a class may indeed disappear, the individual farmers will of course survive and adapt to new jobs and environment. Many of them will be much better off. The nation as a whole may not lose much by near-total urbanization and industrialization. It may be that industrialization cannot continue indefinitely to absorb all agricultural population and that, in the end, a few but prosperous groups of farmers, perhaps on livestock and garden-farming agri-blocs, will remain and grow as a vigorous force in the society. Even a substantial number of rice and grain farmers may manage to survive the present plight and supply foods to the growing urban population in the period of food scarcity that seems to be bound to come in a not so far future.

The global shortages of agricultural produce, particularly foodstuffs, may have a profound impact on the life and interest of the Japanese farmer in the long run. In the short run, however, his predicament deepens and the aggravation of his personal hardships will inevitably reflect on his political attitude and behavior. It is probably correct to equate his continued support for the LDP with the still relatively low level of his dissatisfaction, if not a high level of satisfaction. In a sense, the increase of opportunities for nonagricultural employment helped to keep farmers contented, despite the obviously negative effects on the welfare of their families and village communities. Though it may be hard for others to believe, many farmers did find the nonfarming jobs they had newly landed less onerous in terms of working conditions and more profitable in terms of wages than growing crops on farms.[65] This may simply prove how hard farming still continues to be in "advanced" Japan, but that is not the point. The point is that the majority of the farmers employed on a part-time basis by sweatshops and road gangs in towns have been sufficiently contented to help keep the conservatives in power by voting for them. Their positions as urban workers are, however, extremely precarious. As a rule, their wages are substantially lower than the average in secondary and tertiary industries. Moreover, they have no security of employment.[66] As long as the industrial sector of the economy is expanding, they will not have much difficulty retaining their jobs or finding new jobs to earn extra income to help them pay back debts to the agricultural cooperatives back home or even to purchase a few luxury items, such as television sets and motorbikes. Once a recession hits, however, they will be the first to be squeezed out of the job market. When that happens, and indications are that it is already happening, their disappointments may well turn into bitter resentments against the LDP government.[67] And that may well spell an electoral disaster for the LDP such that its members and affiliates would hate to contemplate. Even with the present election system of malapportionment intact, the LDP may lose crucial House of Councillors or even House of Representatives elections within a few short years.

This is then an interim report on the current conditions of Japanese agriculture and the social and political life of its members. It analyzes certain configurations which one observes today on the changing face of rural Japan. These trends may grow larger and more visible to a future researcher. They may soon disappear. What the author has attempted to do in this paper is therefore no more than to describe and analyze some of the current and passing phases of a very large and complex problem.

Notes

1/ Nihon Nōgyō Nenkan Kankōkai, ed., *Nihon Nōgyō Nenkan, '73*, Ie no Hikari Kyōkai, 1972, p. 163; Keizai Kikakuchō, ed., "Sankō Shiryō," *Keizai Hakusho: Shōwa 48-nen Ban*, Okurashō Insatsukyoku, 1973, p. 119, Table 7-5.

2/ Ibid., p. 161.

3/ Ibid., p. 126.

4/ *Nihon Keizai Shimbun*, July 23, 1970.

5/ *Asahi Shimbun*, Feb. 22, 1970. For a more general discussion of the predicament of the farmers away from home and their families, see Masanori Horie, *Nihon no Hinkon Chitai*, vol. 2, Shin Nihon Suppansha, 1969, esp. pp. 185–194, 212–218.

6/ Nihon Nōgyō Nenkan Kankōkai, *Nihon Nōgyō Nenkan*, p. 125.

7/ "Heri tsuzukeru Kōchi Menseki to Sakibosori no Nōgyō Shūgyōsha," *Nōgyō Kyōdō Kumiai*, July 1971, pp. 151–152; Keizai Kikakuchō, *Keizai Hakusho*, p. 119.

8/ "Kome Seisan Chōsei ka no Nōgyō Keizai," *Nōgyō Kyōdō Kumiai*, July 1971, p. 107.

9/ Nihon Nōgyō Nenkan Kankōkai, *Nihon Nōgyō Nenkan*, p. 117.

10/ Zenkoku Nōgyō Kyōdō Kumiai Chūōkai, *Nōkyō Nenkan, 1973*, 1972, p. 12.

11/ Nihon Nōgyō Nenkan Kankōkai, *Nihon Nōgyō Nenkan*, p. 126.

12/ Ibid., p. 94.

13/ Ibid., p. 91. See also Keizai Kikakuchō, *Keizai Hakusho*, pp. 180–188.

14/ Ibid., p. 85. See also Horie, *Nihon no Hinkon Chitai*, pp. 158–160, 172–175, 195.

15/ "Nōgyō Kihon Hō," Chap. 4, in Sakae Wagatsuma, ed., *Shō Roppō*, Yuhikaku, 1971, pp. 1742–1744. For critical discussions, see Otohiko Hasumi, *Nihon Nōson no Tenkai Katei*, Fukumura Shuppan, 1969, Chaps. 2–3; Tsutomu Ōuchi, "Nihon no Nōgyō wa Yomigaeru ka," *Chūōkōron*, September 1973, pp. 79–80.

16/ Zenkoku Nōgyō Kyōdō Kumiai Chūōkai, *Nōkyō Tokuhon*, rev. ed., 1972, p. 71.

17/ Ibid., 86; Ōuchi, "Nihon no Nōgyō wa Yomigaeru ka," pp. 79, 88.

18/ Zenkoku Nōgyō Kyōdō Kumiai Chūōkai, *Nōkyō Nenkan*, p. 21.

19/ *Mainichi Shimbun*, Aug. 24, 1971.

20/ Report of "Kokusai-ka ni taiō shita Nōgyō Mondai Kondankai" in Nihon Nōgyō Nenkan Kankōkai, *Nihon Nōgyō Nenkan*, p. 50.

21/ *Nihon Keizai Shimbun*, Apr. 11, June 4, 1972.

22/ *Asahi Shimbun*, Mar. 15, 1970.

23/ *Nihon Keizai Shimbun*, Aug. 28, 1970.

24/ Zenkoku Nōgyō Kyōdō Kumiai Chūōkai, *Nōkyō Tokuhon*, pp. 89–90.

25/ *Nihon Keizai Shimbun*, Jan. 25, 1972, and Nihon Nōgyō Nenkan Kankōkai, *Nihon Nōgyō Nenkan*, pp. 131–132.

26/ Ibid., pp. 132–133.

27/ *Asahi Shimbun*, Nov. 5, 1972. For negative comments, see Ōuchi, "Nihon no Nōgyō wa Yomigaeru ka," p. 85.

28/ Zenkoku Nōgyō Kyōdō Kumiai Chūōkai, *Nōkyō Tokuhon*, p. 88.

29/ Nihon Nōgyō Nenkan Kankōkai, *Nihon Nōgyō Nenkan*, p. 121.

30/ Ibid., p. 124.

31/ Ibid., p. 213.

32/ Ibid., p. 211.

33/ Zenchū Einō Nōseibu, "46-nendo Beika Kettei no Keii to Kongo no Kadai," *Nōgyō Kyōdō Kumiai*, January, 1973, p. 51.

34/ Zenkoku Nōgyō Kyōdō Kumiai Chūōkai, *Nōkyō Tokuhon*, p. 90.

35/ For a list of protected agricultural articles, see Zenkoku Nōgyō Kyōdō Kumiai Chūōkai, *Nōkyō Nenkan*, p. 84.

36/ Nihon Nōgyō Nenkan Kankōkai, *Nihon Nōgyō Nenkan*, p. 116.

37/ Ibid., p. 134.

38/ Ibid., p. 131.

39/ Many of these ideas I owe to suggestions offered by Professor Masao Soma of Kyūshū University during our informal discussion in February 1973.

40/ Tadashi Fukutake, "15-nen kan no Nōmin Ishiki no Henka," *Nōgyō Mondai*, December 1970, pp. 2–38.

41/ Questions asked were: (1) Family—"What do you think of primogeniture?"; "Should a bride be picked by parents or the son?"; "Should children obey parents' commands?"; "Should main family-branch family relation be continued?"; (2) Village—"Should village affairs be left to officials' decisions?"; Should agricultural cooperative officers be nominated by hamlets?"; "Can agriculture be collectivized?"; "If hamlet members cannot agree on something that needs to be done, should it be done despite disagreement?"; (3) Nation—"Do you think agriculture is not profitable?"; "Do you believe agriculture is the foundation of a nation?"; "Should one sacrifice one's own interests for the sake of state?"; "Do you think farmer movement is necessary?"; "Do you think workers have to go on strikes?".

42/ Zenkoku Nōgyō Kyōdō Kumiai Chūōkai, *Nōkyō Tokuhon*, pp. 8–9.

43/ Ibid., pp. 11–12.

44/ Zenkoku Nōgyō Kyōdō Kumiai Chūōkai, *Nōkyō Nenkan*, pp. 118, 120–121.

45/ Nihon Nōgyō Nenkan Kankōkai, *Nihon Nōgyō Nenkan*, p. 325.

46/ In 1971, there were 9.6 million individuals who engaged in farming either on a full-time or part-time basis.

47/ Zenkoku Nōgyō Kyōdō Kumiai Chūōkai, *Nōkyō Tokuhon*, p. 130.

48/ Ibid., p. 135.

49/ Nihon Nōgyō Nenkan Kankōkai, *Nihon Nōgyō Nenkan*, p. 273.

50/ Ibid., pp. 278, 308.

51/ Ibid., p. 233.

52/ Agricultural Cooperatives Law, Art. 10, in Wagatsuma, "Nōgyō Kihon Hō," pp. 1764–1765.

53/ Interview with Shoji Matsumura, Executive Director of NUAC, Feb. 21, 1973.

54/ *Asahi Shimbun*, Dec. 13, 1972.

55/ Matsumura. See note 53.

56/ Zenkoku Nōgyō Kyōdō Kumiai Chūōkai, *Nōkyō Tokuhon*, pp. 52, 61–67.

57/ This and other aspects of the political values and behaviors of rural youth drafted into nonfarm employment were pointed out to me by President Takekazu Ogura of the Institute of Developing Economies during an interview, Feb. 17, 1973.

58/ Nihon Nōgyō Nenkan Kankōkai, *Nihon Nōgyō Nenkan*, pp. 325, 327.

59/ Mitsunori Ōhara, "Machi to Mura no Seiji Henbō," *Nōgyō Kyōdō Kumiai*, July 1972, pp. 16–23.

60/ *Mainichi Shimbun*, Dec. 12, 1972.

61/ For a more comprehensive and detailed discussion on this subject, see my *Party in Power: The Japanese Liberal-Democrats and Policy Making*, University of California Press, Berkeley: 1970, esp. Chaps. 4, 6, 7.

62/ Matsumura. See note 53.

63/ *Asahi Shimbun*, Feb. 24, 1973.

64/ Matsumura. See note 53.

65/ Shingo Takasugi, "Shūdatsu ni kōsuru Dekasegi Nōmin," *Asahi Jānaru*, Feb. 22, 1974, pp. 36–40.

66/ See Horie, *Nihon no Hinkon Chitai*, pp. 183–184, 229.

67/ Ibid., pp. 199–201, 212–214; Takasugi, "Shūdatsu ni kōsuru Dekasegi Nōmin."

6.

FOREIGN TRADE IN JAPAN'S ECONOMIC TRANSITION

Leon Hollerman

IN LONG-TERM PERSPECTIVE, a structural transition can be seen occurring in Japan on various planes—economic, social, and political. On the economic plane, structural change is taking place in the fields of production, distribution, and finance. Each of these affects and is affected by the role of foreign trade in the Japanese economy; likewise, each is linked with the role of Japan's foreign trade in the world at large. After World War II, a shift occurred in the composition of Japanese industry—predominance passed from natural-fiber textiles and labor-intensive sundry goods to heavy and chemical products. Now a new shift is taking place in which sophisticated activities, as in computers and atomic energy, are assuming prominence and in which the tertiary sector is becoming modernized. What is the relation between this economic transition and the internal role of Japan's foreign trade? How will Japan's international comparative advantage be affected? How will Japan's competitive power be accommodated by the policies of its principal trading partners?

Domestically, Japan's decade of the economic miracle was characterized by various aspects of unbalanced growth. One aspect was the disproportionate degree of investment in directly productive facilities while investment in social and economic infrastructure was neglected. Another aspect was the role of economic dualism in Japan—a modern, high-productivity sector coexisted with a traditional, low-productivity sector, the former partly sustaining and partly exploiting the latter. At the international level, "exports first" was the counterpart of "production first" on the domestic plane. Indeed, while Japan attempted to reduce the degree of its import dependence on the world economy, the growth rate of Japan's exports exceeded the rate of growth of its gross national product (GNP).[1] Thus, export dependence increased greatly. Moreover, by means of interaction between the international and domestic sectors, unbalanced growth was accelerated. For example, key export industries were subsidized while consumers were kept hungry for cheap foreign food and decent housing.

The growth potential of Japan's export industries, however, was greater when Japan's share of the world market was smaller. "The importance of being unimportant" conferred benefits on Japan that were lost when she acquired the role of a "major industrial nation." Japan's share of the world export market increased from 3.2 percent in 1960 to 6.2 percent in 1970. The ratio of exports to GNP has also increased during the decade.[2] Moreover, as GNP increased, the absolute increment to exports expanded. Now, as a major occupant of the world market, Japan's export expansion meets with increasing resistance. The Japanese have finally appreciated the fact that a free-trade system in the world at large is preeminently in their national interest. Ironically, protectionism has made striking gains elsewhere while Japan belatedly embraced the free-trade principle. However, what does Japan mean by *free trade?* At present, one of the points of contention between Japan and her trade partners concerns the definition of terms such as free trade and protectionism; another concerns the criteria that should be adopted multilaterally or bilaterally for the implementation of antidumping measures, orderly marketing, and the like. In these controversies, although the importance of the free-trade strategy to Japan is clear, the decision-making authorities in Japan are being conservative in adapting Japan's peculiar version of capitalism to the market system of the West.

Role of Japan's Foreign Trade in World Economy

During the decade of the 1960s, world trade (including that of Eastern Europe and China) expanded 2.4 times, from $128.1 billion to

$311.3 billion. In the same period, Japan's exports rose from $4.1 billion to $19.3 billion, almost a fivefold increase or approximately double the world average. According to projections of the Japan Economic Research Center (JERC) prepared under the direction of Hisao Kanamori, world trade (in undeflated values) will increase to $850.0 billion in 1980, to which Japan's exports will contribute $92.2 billion. Thus, as compared with a world market share of 3.2 percent in 1960 and 6.2 percent in 1970, Japan's market share in 1980 is projected at 10.8 percent.[3] (The share of the United States in world exports was 13.7 percent in 1970.) According to the JERC study, the average annual rate of increase in world exports during the 1970s is projected at 10.6 percent per annum. For Japan, the projected annual rate of expansion is 16.9 percent. In terms of Japan's demand elasticities, on the other hand, a progressive decline that is expected to persist has been observed in recent years. During the period 1955–1960, the average annual price elasticity of demand for Japan's exports was 2.34; during 1960–1965, it declined to 2.03; and during 1965–1970, it declined further to 1.67. In the decade of the 1970s, it is projected at 1.59. These figures imply that the expansion of Japanese exports by means of price-cutting offensives will be more difficult during the 1970s than ever before.

Where, then, will the projected increase in Japan's exports during the 1970s be sold? Table 20 shows a comparison of the change in Japan's share of various markets at ten-year intervals, including a projection for 1980. Despite the conspicuous projected growth in Japan's share of the markets of the United States, the ANS (Australia, New Zealand, and South Africa) region, Asia, and People's Republic of China, this distribution confirms an already existing pattern and does not imply a significant degree of geographical diversification of Japan's exports during 1980 as compared with previous years. In terms of another breakdown, the same impression is conveyed by Table 21. In 1980, as during former years, it is projected that the United States will receive approximately one-third of Japan's total exports, by far the largest volume of any individual country. However, whereas in 1970 Japan's share of United States imports amounted to 15.5 percent, the projected share increases to 23.3 percent by 1980. In contrast, Japan's exports to Western Europe in 1970 constituted less than 3 percent of the imports of that region, and Japan's share is expected to remain below 5 percent even by 1980.[4] In the planned-economy region, although China will receive a smaller absolute

TABLE 20. Japan's Share in Imports, Specified Regions,
1960, 1970, and Projection for 1980 (percent)

Region	1960	1970	1980 (projected)
World	3.2	6.2	10.9
North America	6.1	12.8	18.7
United States	7.5	15.5	23.3
Western Europe	0.9	2.6	4.7
ANS region[a]	5.0	12.1	28.0
Latin America	3.5	6.6	12.4
Asia	11.4	20.7	33.1
Africa	4.5	9.0	15.5
Planned-economy areas	0.5	3.4	9.3
USSR	1.1	3.1	10.0
People's Republic of China	0.1	28.3	40.4

[a]Australia, New Zealand, South Africa.
Source: JERC study.

volume of imports from Japan than the USSR in 1980, Japan will play a far larger role in the trade of China than in that of the USSR.

Japan's foreign-trade performance in 1971 is of special interest inasmuch as the yen was revalued by 16.88 percent in December of that year. In 1971, world imports increased by 12.1 percent (as compared with an increase of 14.5 percent in 1970). Japan's exports increased by 24.3 percent during 1971 (as compared with an increase of 20.8 percent in 1970). On the other hand, Japan's imports increased by only 4.4 percent during 1971 (as compared with an increase of 25.7 percent during 1970). These figures reveal that along with the remarkable performance of exports, the comparatively low level of imports was an important contributing factor to Japan's recent export surplus. The lag in imports, in turn, was due partly to the fact that raw materials and fuels figure prominently in Japan's import structure; demand for these commodities was depressed by the business recession that began in the autumn of 1970 and from which recovery did not occur until the spring of 1972.[5] These matters are discussed below in the context of Japan's dependence on the world economy and in the analysis of its competitive power.

Impact of Japan's export surplus. In 1971, the surplus in Japan's overall balance of payments amounted to $7,677 million (as compared with a surplus of $1,374 million in 1970), the largest in her history. In terms of customs statistics, the merchandise trade surplus was $4,307 million, including a surplus of $2,834 million in trade with the United States.[6] As an exporter, Japan ranked third in the world during 1971, after the United States and West Germany. As an importer, its rank was fifth. The role of Japan's trade in the world economy was affected by the relative decline in the competitiveness of the United States, by the increasing regionalization of trade, as in Western Europe, and by the stagnation of the trade of developing nations. The net interaction of these trends together with Japan's export drive stimulated protectionist elements in the international economy.

In terms of Japanese customs statistics, the balance of merchandise trade with the United States turned from deficit to surplus in 1965, followed by one more year of deficit in 1967. If the balance for the period 1960–1967 is calculated as a whole, the net total deficit of −$2,729 million is almost exactly offset by the income received from U.S. Special Procurement expenditures in Japan during those years, a sum amounting to $2,646 million. These receipts are classified within the invisibles category of the balance of payments rather than within the merchandise account. In 1971, U.S. military procurement of goods and services in Japan was valued at $623 million.

Unfortunately, from the point of view of their balance-of-payments relations, the United States and Japan were economically out of phase during 1971–72. Japan's exports to the United States tend to expand during the recovery period of the U.S. business cycle. They also tend to expand during the recessionary period of the Japanese cycle. On the other hand, U.S. exports to Japan (especially industrial machinery, industrial raw materials, and fuels) tend to decline during an industrial recession in Japan. All these factors coincided to aggravate the U.S. deficit with Japan during 1971–72.

TABLE 21. Distribution of Japan's Foreign Trade with Specified Regions, Selected Years, 1955 to 1970 and Projection for 1980 (percent)

Year	United States	Canada	EEC	EFTA	Latin America	Southeast Asia	West Asia	Africa	China	USSR	Other	Total
Exports												
1955	22.6	2.3	4.0	4.5	9.0	35.8	4.1	8.5	1.4	0.1	7.7	100.0
1960	27.4	3.0	4.3	5.7	6.8	32.3	3.3	7.2	0.1	1.5	8.4	100.0
1965	29.7	2.5	5.7	5.4	4.9	26.0	3.3	7.9	2.9	2.0	9.7	100.0
1968	31.8	2.7	5.3	5.9	4.6	27.8	3.5	5.8	—	1.8	12.6	100.0
1970	31.2	2.9	6.7	5.5	5.1	25.2	2.8	5.5	3.0	1.8	10.3	100.0
1980°	29.0	3.4	9.9	6.2	3.5	20.7	5.1	4.4	2.5	4.5	10.8	100.0
Imports												
1955	31.3	4.2	4.2	2.7	10.6	26.3	5.8	1.6	3.7	0.1	9.5	100.0
1960	37.1	4.8	5.4	3.5	6.2	19.6	7.7	1.9	0.5	2.2	11.1	100.0
1965	30.2	4.3	5.0	3.7	7.0	17.3	13.0	2.4	3.3	3.5	10.3	100.0
1968	26.8	5.2	5.9	3.9	6.0	15.4	15.1	3.3	—	—	18.4	100.0
1970	29.4	5.0	6.3	4.7	6.5	15.1	13.3	4.0	1.6	3.1	11.0	100.0
1980°	27.8	3.6	9.0	6.2	4.0	13.6	12.1	4.0	2.4	6.1	11.2	100.0

Source: JERC study.

°Projected.

Japan's relations with its principal trading partners. Although Japan's imports from the United States are complementary to an extremely high degree, her exports to the United States are almost exclusively competitive. Japan's imports are concentrated in products at both ends of the commodity spectrum—primary goods on the one hand and sophisticated technology-intensive products on the other. Japan's exports to the United States, however, consist primarily of manufactured goods in the intermediate section of the commodity chain. During 1971, products of the heavy and chemical industries constituted 75 percent of Japan's total exports, while industrial raw materials constituted 67 percent of her imports. Japan's complementary imports are one result of her persistent effort in the 1950s and 1960s to reduce the degree of her dependence on the world economy. As indicated below, some of the policies contributing to this result have been discriminatory and have been reinforced by institutional factors within the Japanese economy.

In 1971, Western Europe received 14 percent of Japan's exports, half of which went to the European Economic Community (EEC). The rate of increase in exports to EEC was 25.5 percent over the preceding year, almost as high as the increase in exports to the United States. Thus, the invasion of European markets by Japan occasioned some alarm. For example, exports of steel to EEC increased 73 percent in 1971 while Japan was negotiating an agreement for the voluntary control of its steel exports to the United States. However, Japan's share of the total imports of Western Europe in 1970 amounted to only 2.6 percent; thus the percentages prospered on a small base.

In general, as compared with those of the United States, the policies of Western Europe toward Japan are much more restrictive. Moreover, in addition to the policy factors, there are several structural reasons for the likelihood that Japan's trade with Western Europe will never approach the volume of her trade with the United States. In the first place, the horizontal division of labor between Japan and Western Europe is less conducive to trade than the vertical complementarity of Japan's relations with the United States. At the same time, rivalry between Japan and Western Europe has been enhanced by their competition for sales of similar products in third markets and by their search for similar raw-material sources.[7] The geographical barrier is also greater. By air, the distance between Tokyo and Rotterdam is about 1.5 times as great as the distance between Tokyo and San Francisco. By sea, the comparison is even less favorable. Furthermore, internal trade barriers and a lesser degree of legal and linguistic unification exist in Western Europe as compared with the United States. The European market is thus more difficult for the Japanese exporter.

Among its "natural" trading partners, moreover, Japan's attempt to diversify further its imports and exports is subject to problems of other kinds. In the case of People's Republic of China, for example, three "political principles" were expressed in 1958 as a precondition for trade. Japan was enjoined (1) not to regard China with hostility; (2) not to support the conspiracy to create two Chinas; and (3) not to obstruct progress of the normalization of Sino-Japanese relations. In August 1960, a similar set of three principles was stated anew by Chou En-lai. Again in April 1970, four principles were announced by Chou En-lai (and confirmed in a communiqué of March 1971) concerning the basis of trade with Japan. These principles declared that China would refuse to do business with any of the following types of enterprises: (1) trading or manufacturing companies assisting Taiwan's drive against the Mainland or South Korea's northward advance; (2) enterprises investing in Taiwan or the Republic of Korea; (3) enterprises supplying weapons or ammunition for American aggression in Vietnam, Laos, or Cambodia; or (4) Japanese-American joint-venture enterprises or U.S. subsidiaries in Japan. In the attempt to "shake hands" with China, these principles have been accepted by Japan's major trading companies and manufacturing firms. Thus, the approach to China implies an increase in the political role of Japan's foreign trade in the world economy.

Role of Foreign Trade in Japan's Economy

The role of foreign trade in the Japanese economy is a function of the structure of industry in relation to the geographical and commodity structure of trade. Aspects of this relation include the ratio of exports to output (in the aggregate and for individual commodities), the ratio of imports to consumption of principal industrial inputs, and the role of supply-oriented exports in Japan's business cycle.

At the macroeconomic level, the ratio of Japan's merchandise exports to GNP was 9.4 percent in 1960, 9.9 percent in 1970, and 10.6 percent in 1971. During the recessionary year 1971, the ratio was raised by supply-oriented exports, a special type of export drive stimulated by high fixed cost. Characteristically, there are two elements of high fixed cost in Japanese industry. The first is a high level of fixed interest, resulting from the fact that investment is financed chiefly by loans rather than by equity capital. Second is high fixed labor cost, associated with life-tenure employment. These costs create enormous pressure on the supply side during a recession, tending to push commodities out of the sluggish domestic stream and into foreign commerce. In 1971, a high level of excess industrial capacity and excess inventories were the statistical indicators of pressure promoting supply-oriented exports. Of the $4.8 billion increase in Japan's exports during 1971, about $1.6 billion resulted from the export drive. As a device for speeding up business recovery, supply-oriented exports clearly constitute an important element of Japan's dependence on the world economy, but one that is usually ignored in the evaluation of her foreign-trade dependence.[8]

By supporting an attitude of export optimism, supply-oriented exports have had an influence far beyond the recessionary phase of the Japanese business cycle. Speculative investment in plant facilities was actively promoted during the period of the economic miracle by confidence on the part of entrepreneurs that output that could not be sold at home could always be sold abroad. Therefore, investment was undertaken not in response to, but rather in anticipation of, realized home market demand. In this sense, Japan's economic miracle was export oriented. Dampening of the export option due to the increasing difficulty of expanding Japan's world market share means that future investment will have to be based on more careful calculations concerning the size of both the home and the foreign markets—calculations that entrepreneurs have had a tendency to neglect.

In the absence of institutional arrangements for the conversion of supply pressure into exports, however, the phenomenon of supply-oriented exports would not exist. In Japan, these institutional arrangements are centered on the trading company, a basic key to Japan's competitive power in the world economy. Trading companies have permanent offices in all major trading centers of the world, and they are continuously in touch with market conditions and with buyers and sellers in those centers. They are particularly adept at achieving rapid turnover of large quantities of goods at narrow margins of profit. Japan's ability to perform sudden feats of expert expansion as well as to develop system-

TABLE 22. Ratio of Exports to Total Production in Key Industries, Selected Years, 1969 to 1971

Industry	Export Ratio (percent)		
	1969	1970	1971
Iron and steel	25.4[a]	26.5[a]	—
Motor vehicles	18.3[a]	—	32.7[a]
Color television sets	20.7	—	23.0
Machine tools	9.1	7.6[a]	—
Ships	60.4	60.7	—
Petrochemical products			
Polyethylene	23.6	28.6	—
Polypropylene	18.7	23.8	—
Synthetic rubber	24.8	29.6	—
Fertilizer	21.7	22.3	—
Textiles	32.8	—	34.0
Synthetic fiber	38.5	—	47.0
Industrial machinery	15.2	—	18.4

[a]Fiscal year.
Source: Industrial Bank of Japan, Industrial Research Department.

atically both markets and import sources owes much to trading-company activities.

The role of foreign trade in the Japanese economy is usually underestimated not only for the reasons mentioned above but also because the aggregate ratio of trade to national income conceals the dependence of key industries on exports. In particular, although manufacturing produces about 31 percent of Japan's GNP, it accounts for more than 90 percent of Japan's exports. In the case of iron and steel, exports amount to more than one-quarter of total production. If steel embodied in products such as ships and automobiles were included, the proportion would be much higher.[9] Table 22 lists the ratios of exports to output for key individual commodities.

Import dependence is another aspect of the role of foreign trade in the Japanese economy. Industrial supplies (raw materials and fuels) and capital equipment comprise four-fifths of Japan's total imports. This ratio is about twice as high as in the case of Italy and about four times as high as in the United States. Consumer goods constitute only about one-fifth of total imports in Japan. The counterpart of these statistics is the apparently high degree of "self-sufficiency" attained by Japan in the main articles of personal consumption. In 1970, for example, Japan's self-sufficiency was 88 percent in meat, 89 percent in dairy products, and 84 percent in fruit. However, these ratios are partly the result of various kinds of import restrictions. In the absence of such restrictions, Japan's total imports would be higher, and the aggregate ratio of imports to GNP (8.7 percent in 1971) would also be higher.

The role of foreign trade in the Japanese economy may also be observed in terms of the impact of the external sector on the banking system. In 1965, the balance of payments began to show a pattern of surplus in the current account and deficit in the long-term capital account, with substantial surpluses accruing in the overall balance beginning in 1968. Accordingly, the increase in net foreign assets of the banking system has made an important contribution to the money supply. In 1971, the balance-of-payments surplus accounted for 22 percent of the increase in the money supply. This new trend has introduced a complicating factor that disturbs the effectiveness of the Bank of Japan's management of monetary policy.

Market Power and Competitive Strategy

In terms of Ministry of Finance (MOF) customs statistics, Japan's surplus in merchandise trade is a relatively recent accomplishment. Since World War II, deficits were incurred annually prior to 1970 with only two exceptions. This fact is one reason for the conservative policy generally practiced by the Japanese government in foreign-trade matters. In assessing this policy the author would like to identify the factors that brought the merchandise account into surplus and to estimate the prospects for Japan's future competitive position.

Sources of market power. It is sometimes difficult to distinguish elements of weakness from elements of strength in Japan's export performance. A problem of interpretation arises especially when export expansion takes place as a result of recession in the domestic economy, as in the case of supply-oriented exports. A new variation on this theme occurred in September 1969, when a credit squeeze was implemented for the purpose of combating inflation. This was the first time in the post-war period that overheating of the domestic economy rather than a balance-of-payments deficit was the occasion for a tight-money policy.[10] However, the tight-money policy cooled off investment and contributed to the recession that began in the autumn of 1970. As domestic demand declined, excessive competition set in, and supply-oriented exports were generated. (Typically, the latter include a significant quantity of exports sold at prices that cover little more than their variable costs of production, a fact that implies weakness rather than strength in terms of competitive position.) In the 1970 episode, however, excess plant capacity remained high even though Japan's exports were increased to an unprecedented level. This may mark another important element of Japan's economic transition—namely, a decline in the power of supply-oriented exports to revive capital investment in a recession. Heretofore, Japan has boasted of a "virtuous circle" in which capital investment based on anticipated market demand led to a self-fulfilling prophecy of growth in the GNP. Will the chronic presence of excess plant capacity disrupt this sequence?

On the positive side, the foundations of Japan's productive capacity and market power are well known. Her inherited structure of attributes include ethnic, cultural and linguistic homogeneity, the work ethic, inter-class mobility, absence of religious conflict, group-oriented incentives, literacy, adaptability, and discipline. At the policy level, productive efficiency has been advanced by administrative guidance with regard to technological innovation, rationalization, and mass production. Collaboration between government and business through administrative guidance has achieved prodigies of economizing which contribute to Japan's ability to compete.

Special factors have promoted efficiency in the production of exports in key industries. In the shipbuilding industry, for example, all major suppliers are also producers of heavy machinery, and the construction of ships is managed as one of a series of diversified and integrated operations. In the steel industry, coastal siting and the use of extremely large ore carriers have reduced transportation cost. Imports of technology have been systematically exploited, and a high degree of industry-wide collaboration in technical and economic activities has occurred in ways consistent with the provisions of the antitrust laws. Relatively low labor cost has been a further general advantage enjoyed by Japanese producers.[11] Moreover, the average annual increase in labor productivity during the 1960s exceeded 10 percent in Japan, as compared with approximately 3 percent in the United States.

Beyond the stage of production, policies of export promotion have made a positive and more visible contribution to Japan's market power. As of February 1972, Japanese government export-promotion programs included two categories: (1) export-related tax incentives and (2) export financing and export insurance facilities.

Among the tax incentives, accelerated depreciation, taken in the form of a reserve for special depreciation on machinery used for export production, was abolished as of March 31, 1972. A tax-free reserve for overseas market development and a tax deduction on foreign currency earned by the export of technical services, likewise scheduled to be revised or abolished, were extended for an additional three years after April 1972. A resources-development investment-loss reserve (which does not directly promote exports) also remained in effect. In the second major category of government export-promotion programs, special facilities are provided by the Bank of Japan for short-term preexport and postexport financing, as well as a foreign-exchange loan-fund system. Medium- and long-term financing facilities for plant exports are provided by the Japan Export-Import Bank. Supplemental to the latter are facilities provided by the Overseas Economic Cooperation Fund (OECF) for transactions with developing countries.

In June 1972, plans were completed for the inauguration of an exchange-risk insurance program to supplement the export insurance system already in effect. The new program originated in the aftermath of the international monetary crisis that erupted in August 1971. As a countermeasure to external monetary instability, Japanese foreign-exchange controls were defensively tightened. (This represented negative progress in terms of the government's formal policy of economic liberalization.) The controls prevented Japanese exporters from protecting themselves by hedging on long-term dollar contracts. Accordingly, the foreign-exchange insurance program contemplated giving Japanese exporters coverage against the risk of foreign-exchange fluctuations free of charge for an initial two-year period. (In this respect it was more liberal than its European counterparts.) In addition to the above, a tariff rebate system, which does not constitute an export-promotion system in the usual sense, is also in operation. The latter relieves exporters of the burden of paying customs duties on the import component of exports.

According to an evaluation by the United States Embassy in Tokyo, export-related tax incentives have never played a significant role in Japan's export performance. They have been relatively insignificant even in their heyday.[12] This conforms with an estimate by MOF which states that export-related tax benefits to all corporations in fiscal year 1971 amounted to $195 million, an amount that is less than 0.01 percent of Japan's total export sales of $25.1 billion during that year.[13]

In the private sector, as the vehicle for an overwhelmingly large proportion of Japanese domestic and foreign trade, trading companies are in a position to pursue an export-promotion policy of their own.[14] In some instances, they have been accused of disruptively penetrating established markets in preference to creating new markets of their own. In 1972, for example, the secretary of state for trade and industry of Great Britain criticized the Japanese practice of "identifying a narrow range of products in a major area and subjecting it to intense attack, cutting prices as much as necessary to secure a strong position within that narrow range." Here the lack of generally accepted definitions and criteria is a critical matter, for it becomes difficult to evaluate such accusations even on a case-by-case basis.

Japan's Export Restraints

What are the principles that should be applied in adjusting the current account imbalance between Japan and its trading partners? Should the responsibility and the burden of adjustment be shared equally by the surplus and the deficit country? Should the adjustment be accomplished by unilateral, bilateral, or multilateral measures? Should the adjustment be arranged by means of currency measures or by trade controls? And if agreement can be reached in terms of principles, how should criteria and definitions be formulated?

Orderly marketing. Legal instruments for export *control* in Japan were established promptly after World War II. For the most part, they were designed to promote export expansion; now, however, they are also being used to impose export restraint.[15] A conspicuous example is the case of the Export and Import Transactions Law (1952), which provided for the formation of voluntary export cartels.[16] The purpose of the law was to reduce "excessive competition" among Japanese exporters and to encourage their cooperation in the long-run development of export markets. For this purpose, export cartels were exempted from the provisions of the antitrust laws. In the 1970s, however, export cartels are being used as a means of enforcing "orderly marketing."[17] They may also receive administrative guidance from MITI concerning export levels and the distribution of export quotas among the cartel's members. This form of orderly marketing, which is the most typical kind of export restraint, is also a typical product of government-business collaboration.

A second type of orderly marketing is performed under the Export Trade Control Ordinance, an enactment of the cabinet in accordance with the provisions of the Foreign Exchange and Foreign Trade Control Law (1949). In this case, orderly marketing is not voluntary on the part of the private sector and is entirely and explicitly enforced by the government.[18] A third type of export restraint exists in the form of an agreement between an industry association in Japan and its counterpart in some other country. Only a single example exists at present, namely, the agreement between the Electronic Industries Association of Japan and the corresponding association in France. Formally, the agreement restricts the two-way flow of electronic products between the two countries, but because France does not export a substantial amount of such products to Japan the agreement in effect constitutes a restriction on Japan only.

With regard to the problem of definitions and criteria, the various examples of orderly marketing presented above make it clear that no simple definition of this concept can be formulated. Even within Japan, there are differences of opinion about its appropriate forms and degrees. MITI in April 1972 prepared a statement concerning orderly marketing as follows:

> What Japan means by "orderly marketing" . . . is not merely a policy of export restraint, but a planned systematic development of international trade on the basis of free and fair competition and the spirit of international division of labor. It certainly does not mean an arbitrary

curtailment of the growth rate of individual Japanese export items. The definition of what is a truly healthy expansion of trade must be determined by taking into account a great many factors, such as the present state of trade between Japan and any other country, and the specific situation of industries and markets in all nations concerned.

At the policy level, a highly influential body concerned with this matter is the Orderly Marketing Committee of *Keidanren* (Japan Federation of Economic Organizations).[19] However, the committee is composed of Japan's principal export champions. They do not find orderly marketing a particularly congenial concept, and it is difficult for them to agree about it. Moreover, the Japanese government is reluctant to commit itself to a firm bargaining posture on orderly marketing because it anticipates that for various reasons, including the yen revaluation of December 1971, exports may have a progressive tendency to level off or even to decline by 1974 or thereafter. Furthermore, the Japanese government fears that escalating the enforcement of orderly marketing from the voluntary private level to the government level for any particular commodity, industry, or export destination may lead to demands from abroad for further restrictions on other commodities, industries, or destinations.[20] Likewise, it fears that bilateral agreements for export restriction may be generalized into multilateral demands for similar restrictions.[21] In that event, Japanese products would be excluded from world markets at large in the name of orderly marketing.

There are also other reasons for misgivings or criticism concerning orderly marketing. In the first place, it offends the principle of free trade; and it does so in a manner particularly calculated to discourage the Japanese government in its rather desultory progress toward liberalization with regard to other matters. Second, it raises some very sensitive questions concerning the antitrust laws of both Japan and her trade partners. Third, it encourages MITI to interpose itself in matters of private commerce.[22] Orderly marketing also leads to the formation of international cartels—there is a very thin line between a legal export cartel formed by an association of Japanese firms and an illegal international cartel formed by an agreement between Japanese firms and foreign firms.[23] Furthermore, because of the base-period method of distributing quotas among the members of an export cartel, orderly marketing discriminates against newcomers to foreign trade. By discouraging the entry of new firms, especially small firms, orderly exports promotes the further concentration of the Japanese economy. Even among the established members of a cartel, preferred members get preferred quotas. There are known cases in which export cartels were formed specifically for the purpose of allocating export quotas rather than for the ostensible purpose of orderly marketing.

Although the concept of orderly marketing covers a wide range, it is evident that the United States and Japan have interpreted its meaning in inconsistent ways. From the American point of view, orderly marketing simply means that Japan will exercise control over exports and adhere to export quotas. From the point of view of the Japanese government, the concept refers to structural change, with special reference to the economic transition that is now in progress in Japan. The Japanese government wishes orderly marketing to contribute to the shift in emphasis from quantitative growth to qualitative reform, from mass-production goods to knowledge-intensive, sophisticated goods, and perhaps even from secondary industries to welfare, leisure, and education.

Because of the difference in their respective notions of what orderly marketing means, its results are likewise subject to different interpretations by the United States and Japan. As mentioned above, for the most part the quotas are not public information; consequently, the restraint cannot be quantitatively evaluated. In any event, restraint is usually not applied until exports have already arrived at a high level. Thus, restriction of exports to a "moderate" rate of increase does not signify a withdrawal by Japan from export competition. Differences of opinion also exist about what constitutes a moderate rate of increase. The exporting nation may believe that a growth rate of 20 percent is moderate, whereas the importing nation may believe that the growth rate of imports should be limited to the rate of growth of its domestic market, say 5 percent annually.[24]

Enforcement of export restraints. In some cases, the activities of outsiders to a cartel agreement constitute a loophole to the export quota. For example, a fringe of small firms anxious to increase their market shares may be uncooperative with the cartel arrangement. In this situation, adherence to the cartel's regulations may be enforced on outsiders by MITI. The discretionary authority of MITI to enforce such adherence, however, is considered inadequate by MOF. In April 1972, the latter ministry proposed that an export bill providing for mandatory export cartels should be submitted to the Diet. As seen by MOF, voluntary export controls, organized and operated at the industry level, have rarely been effective. Essentially, in urging the adoption of mandatory export controls, MOF was attempting to forestall pressure on Japan for a further revaluation of the yen. MITI, however, has thus far been unwilling to endorse this further attack on exports. Interministerial struggles on export control, among other issues, have become more visible in the process of Japan's economic transition.

The Japanese government has various options in responding to foreign pressure for adjustment of the current account surplus. The conservative approach resists yen revaluation—which in totally different circumstances precipitated a disastrous depression in 1930—as the least desirable of these options. In further remembrance of things past, an alternative option in the form of an export tax has received consideration. Prior to World War II, Japan had some experience with an export tax, which at that time was called an *export levy*. An export tax would in some respects have the characteristics of a temporary revaluation of the yen. It appeals to the Japanese authorities by virtue of being autonomous and not subject to review by foreign governments. Also, to the extent that an export tax would forestall the imposition of higher import duties abroad, the proceeds of export restriction would be collected by Japan rather than by her trade partners.

There are various arguments against the export tax. First, the tax would be difficult to administer inasmuch as the heaviest penalties would presumably be levied against Japan's most efficient export industries. Also, if it were applied on a global basis, it would penalize Japan's exports to all destinations for the sake of an export surplus generated primarily in trade with the United States. (In this respect, it would resemble yen revaluation without some of the accompanying benefits of the latter.) In a broader context, however, it could be argued that comprehensive pressure to export has been created by Japan's fundamental economic policies and it might be desirable to adjust those policies rather than to suppress the evidence of their results. In the context of the balance of payments as such, economists often argue that the export tax and export restraints in general approach the problem of adjustment on the wrong foot: The desired adjustment should be sought by increasing imports rather than by restricting exports. Imports, in turn, can be stimulated by measures promoting economic expansion; export restriction is inherently recessionary and would have the convulsive effect of generating further supply-oriented exports, which were simultaneously being suppressed.

Of late there has been increased unwillingness on the part of Japan's trade partners to rely exclusively on her enforcement of export restraint. Even when Japan is seen to exercise restraint in one market, the specter of an attack rises in another. Thus EEC has been wary of Japan's restriction of exports to the United States. As a complement to orderly marketing, EEC has demanded that a safeguard clause be included in the proposed trade agreement that EEC and Japan have been negotiating since 1970.[25] At present, a safeguard clause is included in each of Japan's trade agreements with the United Kingdom, France and Benelux, respectively, and formerly safeguard clauses were included in Japan's trade agreements with West Germany and Italy.

The content of the safeguard clause may be illustrated by reference to Japan's trade agreement with France. The essential element of the safeguard clause in that agreement states that if, as a result of unforeseen developments, products are imported into the territory of one party in such quantities as to cause or to threaten to cause serious injury to domestic producers of like or competitive products, the importing country may, after consultations with the partner country, introduce quantitative import restrictions. If the two sides do not reach a common position, the exporting country may apply appropriate and proportionate countermeasures. Among her trade partners collectively, the safeguard clause has been invoked against Japan in only several instances during the past decade.

Although ostensibly the safeguard clause is reciprocal, Japan regards it as discriminatory. A controversy on this point has arisen between MITI and the Ministry of Foreign Affairs. The former maintains that on a multilateral level Article 19 of the General Agreement on Tariffs and Trade (GATT), which contains explicit rules for emergency import restriction, already provides a sufficient safeguard. MITI contends that an additional "bilateral safeguard" is thus gratuitous and unfair. Also, Japan's granting special safeguards to EEC might set the stage for further demands by the United States.[26] The Ministry of Foreign Affairs, however, accepts the counterargument that Article 19

TABLE 23. Restrictions Discriminating against Japanese Exports Applied in Western Europe, April 1972

Country	Number of Restrictions[a]
Benelux Economic Union	27
France	44
Italy	46
United Kingdom	44
West Germany	21

[a]These are at the four-digit level of the Brussels Tariff Nomenclature (BTN). They exclude the following "voluntary" restrictions on Japanese exports of cotton products to Western Europe: Benelux Economic Union, 40; France, 45; Italy, 47; West Germany, 25.

Source: Japan. Ministry of International Trade and Industry, *Nichibei Keizai Shihyō* [Japan–United States economic indicators] (Tokyo, 1972).

is too restrictive to be readily invoked.[27] MOF and *Keidanren*, as well as the Foreign Ministry, are more flexible than MITI in this matter. Their strategy is to cooperate with EEC in order to expedite an agreement and to achieve harmony in a growing export market.[28]

Japan's competitive position. In addition to the measures initiated or acquiesced in by Japan for the restraint of her own exports, she has been subject to discriminatory import restrictions on the part of other countries. Table 23 presents a summary for Western Europe. In the case of exports to the United States, Japan accepted "voluntary" export restraints on 115 commodities as of May 1972.

When Japan joined GATT in 1955, fourteen countries including France and England invoked Article 35, which permits members of GATT to decline to accept GATT obligations with regard to any new member at the time of the latter's accession. Later, when colonies of France and England became independent in the 1960s, they followed their former mother countries in likewise invoking Article 35 upon their accession to GATT. In most cases, these restrictions were relinquished in the 1960s, but as of April 1972 nineteen countries (mostly African) still invoked Article 35 against Japan.[29]

As a major trading nation, Japan's impact on the United States and other countries has certainly been a leading factor in the preparation of defensive measures such as the U.S. import surcharge of August 1971 (terminated in December 1971) and the more restrictive administration of the U.S. antidumping and countervailing duty laws. Do such defensive measures, applied equally against all other countries, constitute discrimination against Japan? Conversely, are restrictive trade, capital, and nontariff barrier (NTB) policies applied by Japan discriminatory against the United States—upon which their greatest impact falls— even though legally they apply equally to all other countries? These are some of the problems of criteria and definitions that mark the present controversy about discrimination.

In any event, the announcement by the U.S. Treasury Department in April 1972 that the administration of the Anti-Dumping Act of 1921 would be strengthened was a very sensitive matter for Japan. Japan protested that this domestic U.S. law was inconsistent with GATT Article 6, the so-called International Dumping Code.[30] In defense of its own exporters, on the other hand, the Japanese government maintains that because of "excessive competition" small and medium-sized enterprises *cannot* raise their prices even though they may desire to do so; thus they are particularly vulnerable to U.S. antidumping penalties. The Japanese case includes several further points in reply to dumping accusations. First, Japan argued that simplistic price comparisons between export goods and home goods are inappropriate because they are not identical in specifications or performance. Second, whereas the domestic shipping price includes excise tax, selling expenses, and the like, these fees are not part of the export price, such costs being normally borne by the importer. Third, export goods are moved in larger lots than those shipped domestically, and the risk in sales returns is borne by the importer. Thus, export prices are naturally lower than domestic shipping prices.

In addition to the export restraints mentioned above, Japan's competitive position is subject to various difficulties and constraints that may have a strong cumulative impact in the long run. Among these difficulties are an increasing degree of economic instability and rising costs of production.[31]

Japan's Protectionism

In the conflict of interest between the United States and Japan over protectionism, several sources of controversy may be distinguished. In the first place, protectionism resulting from official policy is qualitatively different from protectionism inherent in the nature of economic institutions. Tariffs and quotas may be included in the former category, whereas some of Japan's NTBs may be included in the latter. Sometimes the Japanese government is blamed for import restrictions over which it has no control.

Second, in matters over which it does have control, the government follows a policy of reducing import dependence by heavily protecting Japan's weakest producers, those in the declining or infant industries such as agriculture or computer software. But the greatest comparative advantage of the United States lies precisely in these industries; thus Japan's official protectionism affects the United States more adversely than it does any other supplier.[32]

A third source of controversy concerns reciprocal privileges and obligations in relations between the United States and Japan. Legally, according to the United States-Japan Treaty of Friendship, Commerce and Navigation, each country is bound to provide unqualified "national treatment" to the other. Japan's failure to do so is a principal source of complaint on the part of the United States. Once again, this attitude is partly the result of policy decisions and partly the result of institutional facts of life.[33]

Protectionism has both direct and indirect repercussions on Japan's international sector. A conspicuous example is the contrast between the strong external yen due to the surplus in the balance of payments and the weak internal yen due in part to protectionism. Imported consumer goods remained expensive in Japan following the yen revaluation of December 1971, and the retail price of some goods actually increased. Protectionism thus contributed to the delay in the effectiveness of yen revaluation in adjusting the balance-of-payments surplus.

In contributing to this delay, protectionism played several roles. First, at the policy level, import quotas were a countermeasure to the yen revaluation. The limited availability of foreign commodities kept their prices high. Second were institutional practices, such as the *general-agent* system. More accurately, the latter should be described as a *sole-agent* system, for in accordance with Article 21 of the Tariff Law it confers monopoly import privileges on firms that act as the agent of a foreign supplier.[34] Such firms impose their private quota decisions on imports, and many of them absorbed the currency gains of the yen revaluation. Third, a similar effect occurred on the institutional plane as a result of inefficiencies in the domestic system of processing and distribution of imported goods, which further drained off the profits of yen revaluation instead of passing them on in the form of lower retail prices.[35]

At the close of 1969, Japan retained 118 residual import restrictions (at the four-digit level of the BTN). These were reduced to 33 items as of April 1972 (fewer than the residual import quotas of West Germany or France), of which 24 were agricultural products.[36]

Although protectionism by means of outright quotas is gradually being reduced, the removal of a quota may be neutralized by the imposition of some alternative measure, such as a restriction on imports in accordance with standards for public health or safety. Such measures may or may not be justified, but it is difficult to quarrel with them. In other cases, the removal of a quota is accompanied by the imposition of a tariff.[37]

In view of its balance-of-payments surplus, Japan's residual import quotas are embarrassing. However, they are defended with the argument that quotas exist not for the protection of the balance of payments but rather for the protection of industries.[38] On the other hand, estimates of the potential contribution of complete quota removal to adjustment of the current account surplus have not produced impressive figures.[39] Nontariff barriers other than quotas are probably collectively of greater significance than quotas, because in the extent to which its import list includes complementary rather than competitive products, Japan is conspicuously in a separate category from other major industrial nations.

A detailed discussion of the varieties and impact of NTBs is not possible within the scope of the present paper. Their principal types, however, may be identified as follows:

> Administrative guidance
> Import quota system
> Import quota administration
> State trading system (tobacco, rice, wheat, and dairy products)

TABLE 24. Average Tariffs since Kennedy Round (percent)

Country	Raw Materials	Semi-manufactures	Finished Manufactures	Average
EEC	0.6	6.2	8.7	6.0
United States	3.8	8.3	8.1	7.1
United Kingdom	1.2	8.3	10.4	7.6
Japan	5.5	9.3	12.0	9.7

Source: GATT, *Tariff Study* (1971), Commission of the European Communities, "The Monetary and Commercial Relations between the Community and the United States," Information Memorandum p. 36 (Brussels, October 1971).

Customs practices (such as arbitrarily raising the invoice value—known as "uplift"—prior to the assessment of customs duties)

Standard method of settlement (applies asymmetrical standards to exports and imports with regard to settlement of financial accounts)

Discriminatory ocean-freight rates (freight costs from Japan to the United States are lower than costs in the opposite direction)

Japanese government procurement ("Buy Japanese" policy)

Industrial standards

Sanitary restrictions

Controls on sales and service of foreign firms in Japan

Labeling requirements

Since the reduction of tariff levels following the Kennedy Round, NTBs have become a prominent target for foreign criticism as a protectionist device on the part of Japan. According to a GATT survey made in 1968, Japan's tariffs were considerably higher than those of other advanced nations, but at present they are more or less in the same range. The structure of rates in Japan's tariff system provides for low, medium, and high rates on imports of raw material, semiprocessed goods, and finished goods, respectively. Infant industries, luxury goods, and "sensitive consumer items" are also protected by high tariffs. Japan utilizes a system of temporary duties that may be imposed, altered, or withdrawn by administrative ordinance, whereas regular duties require action by the Diet.[40] According to GATT, the average post–Kennedy Round tariffs for selected regions were as shown in Table 24.

Patterns of Adjustment: Internationalization of the Japanese Economy

Having practiced the art of balance-of-payments defense assiduously since World War II, the Japanese authorities still find uncongenial the necessity for adjusting a surplus. They are very reluctant to take steps that might jeopardize the security of the balance of payments, and they are especially reluctant to do so by the irreversible relinquishment of balance-of-payments controls.

MOF and MITI have emphasized different approaches to the problem. MITI has concentrated its attention on reducing the size of the foreign-exchange reserves, which is essentially a cosmetic matter having little to do with the continuing surplus in the current account. MOF is more concerned with the current account surplus. As we have seen, that surplus is the result partly of cyclical and partly of secular factors. Japan has been urged by the United States to adopt a mixture of policies, some of which would have short-term and others long-term effects. In Japan in 1971–72, the most popular approach to balance-of-payments adjustment was the proposal to promote economic expansion, which in turn would increase imports and reduce supply-oriented exports. But basically it was the Japanese position that responsibility for balance-of-payments adjustment lies primarily with the deficit rather than with the surplus nation.

In order to offset foreign pressure, however, measures for defense of the balance of payments eventually gave way to measures for defense of the yen. On June 4, 1971, the Japanese government announced an Eight-Point Program for the purpose of forestalling yen revaluation. An outline of its provisions was as follows:

1. Acceleration of import liberalization
2. Implementation of preferential tariffs in favor of developing countries
3. Promotion of tariff reduction
4. Promotion of capital liberalization
5. Removal of nontariff barriers
6. Promotion of economic cooperation (foreign aid)
7. Orderly marketing and acceleration of imports
8. Elastic operation of fiscal and monetary policy

On September 3, 1971, the government announced that implementation of the program would take place. In the meantime, the Nixon shock of

August 15, 1971, had occurred, and the trade surplus was increasing heavily. In December 1971, the yen was revalued by 16.88 percent, still with no immediate effects on the merchandise account. Therefore, to forestall a second yen revaluation, on May 20, 1972, the cabinet announced a new Seven-Point Program, which included the following provisions:

1. Use of monetary and fiscal policy to stimulate the domestic economy by the construction of public works, reduction of interest rates on bank deposits, postal savings deposits, and loans.
2. Import promotion by enlargement of import quotas and by steps to rationalize the distribution system.
3. Promotion of orderly export marketing by the use of legislation to reinforce the voluntary efforts of businessmen.
4. Transfer of foreign currency from the foreign-exchange reserves to the foreign-exchange banks so as to enable them to repay their external liabilities, increased use of foreign-currency assets for the development of resources abroad, expansion of the import-financing activities of the Export-Import Bank of Japan, and authorization for the Export-Import Bank to extend untied loans to foreign banks.
5. Measures to liberalize the acquisition of unlisted foreign securities by residents and facilitation of the flotation in Japan of yen-denominated bonds by international institutions and foreign governments.
6. An attempt to increase the use of untied credit in the Japanese government's foreign-aid program.
7. Quick introduction of legislation to implement the above measures.

Collectively, these measures for liberalization of trade and capital movements, foreign aid, and tariff preferences to developing countries form the core of Japan's program to "internationalize" her economy. Other elements of the program include the inauguration in April 1972 of a dollar call market in Tokyo, authorization of direct sales of Euro-dollar bonds by foreign-securities companies in Japan, permission for the retention of foreign currency by private individuals, and issuance in Japan of Asian Development Bank bonds and World Bank bonds. However, by its preservation of foreign-exchange controls, the Japanese government still carefully restricts the evolution of the yen toward becoming an international currency.

Because of the underlying system of government controls and restrictive institutional practices, liberalization did not prevent the present current account surplus from coming into existence, nor by the same token has internationalization as yet resulted in any adjustment of that surplus. Moreover, from a conservative point of view, the Japanese case presents the argument that a continuing surplus is necessary in order to pay the costs of domestic priorities with regard to renewal of infrastructure, removal of environmental hazards, and improvement in social services and facilities.[41] Not yet evaluated is the extent to which this surplus is offset by the fact that in maintaining an undervalued yen Japan is giving away real resources to other countries. Such an evaluation would be difficult to make because of the extent to which the yen is insulated from free market forces by foreign-exchange controls.

Patterns of Adjustment: Effects of Yen Revaluation

After Washington's "New Economic Policy" of August 15, 1971, Japan defended the ¥360 = $1 rate until August 27, at which time a floating rate was adopted. The floating rate was also a defended rate, and it foreshadowed the revaluation that Japan was obliged to accept at the Washington conference of December 17, when the rate was changed to ¥308 = $1. Coming in the midst of a recession, the revaluation was regarded in Japan as "too soon and too much."[42] As it turned out, however, the effect of the revaluation on the trade balance was slow in coming.[43] Some were of the opinion that the full effect of the revaluation would not appear until 1974.

A combination of short-term and long-term factors contributed to the delayed response. In the first place, a large proportion of total exports in the six-month period following revaluation had been arranged by prerevaluation contracts. In addition, substantial amounts of advance payments were received in Japan immediately prior to the revaluation for additional exports that were supposed to be shipped within one year. Second, some key commodities, such as steel and automobiles, were sufficiently competitive to maintain export strength despite price increases resulting from yen revaluation. Third, because of movements in the rate of exchange of other currencies along with the yen, Japan was able to increase her exports in countries where the relative rate of revaluation of the yen was not pronounced. Fourth, after an initial pause, exports to the United States increased as a result of the latter's economic recovery, lifting of the import surcharge in December 1971, and settlement of the U.S. dockworkers' strike. Fifth, in the short run, foreign buyers found it necessary to reorder from Japan items such as components and replacement parts required for the maintenance of Japanese equipment.

In the export market, moreover, the price effect of revaluation was much smaller than the degree of revaluation might suggest. In the case of high-quality consumer products (such as cameras and binoculars), for which the profits of distribution were high, a large proportion of the price effect of the revaluation was absorbed by Japanese exporters. In other cases (such as passenger cars, motorcycles, and household electrical appliances), in which foreign marketing was performed by producers without the services of trading companies, export quotations in terms of foreign currencies remained fairly stable. The failure of Japan's export prices to reflect the full extent of revaluation prompted strong complaints on the part of the U.S. government.[44] Also, as mentioned above, the United States complained about the fact that the reduced cost to Japan of imports of consumer goods became a source of higher profits to distributors rather than of lower retail prices. Collectively, these factors tended to create the impression that the price elasticities of Japan's import and export demand were smaller than was formerly believed.[45] However, the effects of the revaluation were difficult to interpret because of the masking effect of the recession from which Japan had not yet recovered. Furthermore, there were various overlapping and partially offsetting factors including excess capacity (leading to supply-oriented exports), reduced cost of imported raw-material inputs, voluntary export restraints, varying types of marketing procedures with varying markups, varying degrees of occupancy by Japan in the market structures of her trade partners, varying degrees of profit margin (and thus varying ability to absorb price cuts as a countermeasure to the revaluation), and varying degrees of difficulty in concluding sales on a long-term, deferred-payment basis. Consequently, the role of revaluation in the adjustment of Japan's balance-of-payments surplus was ambiguous and subject to misinterpretation both in Japan and elsewhere. Among Japanese, the possible contribution of revaluation to the reallocation of resources in favor of domestic welfare objectives was all but disregarded.

Revaluation not only failed to result in a rapid adjustment of the current account surplus but also failed to induce an outflow of the foreign capital that (despite the exchange controls) had entered Japan in anticipation of the revaluation. Evidently, speculators were not convinced that the new rate was firmly established. This opinion was soon widely adopted. In the summer of 1972, the pessimistic view of a second revaluation anticipated that it would induce a vicious circle, leading from deflation to recession to excess capacity to supply-oriented exports and thus to further yen revaluation. By the autumn of 1972, however, economic recovery was firmly established. With window-dressing measures, the Bank of Japan endeavored to keep the level of foreign-exchange reserves below $20 billion, which was considered to be the flash point beyond which pressure for revaluation would become irresistible. For example, funds from the foreign-exchange reserves that were invested in medium- or long-term U.S. government securities were technically excluded from the foreign-exchange reserves inasmuch as they were not "short-term assets." Despite management of the reserves, however, their level continued to rise. By October 1972, many private foreign-exchange contracts were being concluded at the rate of ¥278 = $1. Thus there seemed a strong probability that a second revaluation would occur after the general election that was in the offing around the end of the year.

Patterns of Adjustment:
Projection of the Balance of Payments

If Japan's current account surplus is neither adjusted nor accumulated in the foreign-exchange reserves, it will have to be utilized in the capital account. The scope, the speed, and the form of Japan's capital exports, and the extent to which the foreign-exchange control system is removed, will in turn reveal the degree of optimism or pessimism with which Japan's authorities regard the future course of the merchandise trade balance.

Foreign investment. In the postwar period, Japan has been a net exporter of long-term capital only since 1965, when for the first time both the current account and the merchandise account showed a surplus. At that time, Japan's total overseas investments amounted only to about $500 million. By the end of 1970, the total outstanding balance of

Japan's overseas investments amounted to $2,680 million (compared with about $5 billion each for France and West Germany and over $70 billion for the United States). The horizon for foreign investment by Japan is now widening sharply in accordance with her increasing ability and need to perform it.[46] It is noteworthy that the rationale for foreign investment by Japan is supported by an identity of macro- and micro-economic interests, as is not wholly the case with regard to liberalization of foreign-exchange controls.

The purposes of Japan's foreign investment, within its brief career, have already undergone considerable change. Establishment of over-seas branch offices of Japanese trading companies, which required relatively little outlay, was one of the earliest priorities. This step was followed by investment for the expansion and diversification of stable sources of raw-material supply. To the extent that such supplies were available in developing countries, Japan's foreign investment became a component of her foreign-assistance programs, as in the case of Indonesia. However, as of March 1970, almost half of Japan's total foreign investment was in the form of extractive and processing activities located in advanced regions such as Alaska, Canada, and Australia.[47]

Subsequently, foreign investment was prompted by the labor shortage and the rising cost of labor in Japan. Taiwan and Hong Kong, having been sources of labor-intensive components for Japanese finished manufactured goods, became destinations to which Japanese light industries could be transferred.[48] This transfer will be progressively associated with the concept of Japan's domestic industrial transition, with its emphasis on new sophisticated activities in information, atomic energy, and space. Japan is impelled to transfer to developing countries not only her traditional labor-intensive industries but also some of her modern heavy and chemical industries in order to overcome the diseconomies of production in Japan.[49]

Lately, Japan's foreign investment has been stimulated further by the growth of protectionism and inward-looking regionalism in the world economy (associated in part with the decline of the dollar as an international currency). Japan will increasingly attempt to avoid import barriers abroad by undertaking production behind those barriers. Thus, exports of capital and technology, and the advance of Japanese multinational corporations, will contribute to the further "internationalization" of the Japanese economy.[50] In the long run, the present transition

TABLE 25. Alternative Projections of Japan's Balance of Payments, 1975 and 1980 (millions of current dollars)

	1975[a] (JERC)	1975[b] (Kuwayama)	1980[c] (JERC)	1980[b] (Kuwayama)	1980[d] Sato (millions of 1970 dollars)	
Trade balance	8,314	6,700	16,674	9,100		
Exports (FOB)	42,376	37,200	92,184	69,100	51,400[e]	36,300[f]
Imports (FOB)	34,062	30,500	75,510	60,000		
Invisible trade balance	−4,395	−1,800	−5,965	−1,800		
Transfer balance	−743		−2,738			
Current account balance	3,176	4,900	7,971	7,200[g]		
Long-term capital-account balance	−2,310		−7,971			
Basic balance	866		0			
Overall balance	866		0			

[a]Japan Economic Research Center, *The Outlook for a Trillion Dollar Economy* (Tokyo, 1971). Assumes ¥360 = $1. Reference is to fiscal year.

[b]Patricia Kuwayama, "Japan's Balance of Payments and Its Changing Role in the World Economy" (March 1, 1972). Assumes ¥308 = $1.

[c]JERC, *Sekai no Nakano Nihon Keizai—1980* [Japan in the world economy—1980] (Tokyo, 1972). Assumes ¥280 = $1.

[d]Kazuo Sato, "Japan's Foreign Trade: Retrospect and Prospect" (May 20, 1972). Assumes ¥360 = $1.

[e]"A" projection: export of manufactures only, projected at annual growth of 11.0 percent.

[f]"B" projection: export of manufactures only, projected on the assumption of constant marginal shares of 1962–1969 through the 1970s.

[g]Discrepancy in the sum of the current account items appears in original source.

in Japan's industrial structure will likewise promote internationalization by enhancing Japan's competitive power in world markets.

Projections. For purposes of comparison, balance-of-payments projections for Japan in 1980, prepared by the Japan Economic Research Center (JERC), Patricia Kuwayama, and Kazuo Sato, are presented in Table 25. The JERC projection is fairly detailed, whereas Kuway-

TABLE 26. Alternative Projections of Japan's Balance of Payments, 1975 and 1980
(billions of yen, converted at specified rates of exchange)

	1975ᵃ (JERC)	1975ᵇ (Kuwayama)	1980ᶜ (JERC)	1980ᵇ (Kuwayama)	1980ᵈ (Sato)	
Trade balance	2,993	2,064	4,669	2,803		
Exports (FOB)	15,255	11,458	25,812	21,283	18,504ᵉ	13,068ᶠ
Imports (FOB)	12,263	9,394	21,143	18,480		
Invisible trade balance	−1,582	−554	−1,670	−554		
Transfer balance	−267		−767			
Current account balance	1,143	1,509	2,232	2,218ᵍ		
Long-term capital-account balance	−832		−2,232			
Basic balance	312		0			
Overall balance	312		0			

Notes: See Table 25.

ama's projection refers only to the current account and Sato's only to Japan's merchandise exports. The present discussion will therefore be confined to the merchandise trade projections.

The projections lack comparability in several respects. First, they are not comparable in terms of their exchange rate data and price or their degree of commodity coverage. In dollar terms, they incorporate different assumptions about the exchange rates that will prevail in 1980. In terms of yen (see Table 26), this discrepancy has been eliminated. Even on a yen basis, however, the projections are not comparable inasmuch as the data of Kuwayama and JERC reflect anticipated price increases, whereas Sato's data are calculated in terms of 1970 prices. Furthermore, Sato's projection refers only to exports of manufactured goods, whereas JERC and Kuwayama refer to Japan's total exports.[51]

Second, the projections are not comparable in terms of their various assumptions about growth rates during the 1970s. JERC assumes that Japan's average rate of growth during the decade will be 17.2 percent annually, whereas Kuwayama and Sato each assume it will be 8.0 percent. Sato forecasts that, except for Japan, the growth rate of GNP for the world at large in the 1970s will be the same as the trend rate for 1955 to 1969; JERC, however, assumes that the annual rate of growth of world GNP will increase from 8.2 percent in the 1960s to 9.6 percent in the 1970s. Concerning world imports, JERC estimates an annual average rate of growth of 10.6 percent during the 1970s, whereas Kuwayama estimates a rate of 7.0 percent and Sato a rate of less than 7.0 percent. All three projections forecast that, as in the 1960s, the rate of growth of Japan's exports will exceed the rate of growth of world imports, although perhaps by a diminishing margin. JERC assumes an average annual rate of growth in Japan's exports of 16.9 percent; Kuwayama assumes a rate of 10.0 to 11.0 percent and Sato a rate of 11.0 percent.

Corresponding to these discrepancies in assumptions and in data, the actual projections are quite divergent. Sato's projection is in two parts. Assuming that Japan's marginal shares of increasing imports of manufactures purchased by its established markets would remain constant during the 1970s at their 1962–1969 level, Japan's exports in 1980 would amount to ¥13,068 billion ("B" projection). Implicit in the constancy of historical marginal shares is Sato's assumption that "Japan's export prices will keep going down relative to others' prices," which will be more difficult to achieve during the 1970s than heretofore. This feat would still be insufficient, however, to enable Japan to attain an annual average growth rate of 11 percent in exports during the 1970s, leading to exports valued at ¥18,504 billion in 1980 ("A" projection). The rate of 11 percent annual growth in exports would be required in order to enable Japan's imports to grow *pari passu* with Sato's estimate of Japan's growth in GNP during the 1970s. However, because world trade will expand at a rate less than 11 percent during the 1970s, the "A" projection requires Japan to increase her incremental market shares beyond their 1962–1969 proportions. In view of many problems not discussed by Sato, it would be difficult for Japan even to maintain her present high marginal shares, to say nothing of expanding them. Sato's projection, nevertheless, is the least optimistic of the three.

According to Patricia Kuwayama, Japan's exports in 1980 will amount to ¥21,283 billion, an amount that is 15 percent greater than Sato's "A" estimate. Kuwayama provides no breakdown of the foreign markets in which she anticipates these exports may be sold. Whereas Sato's projection has been derived by finding the exports required to support an assumed rate of GNP growth in Japan, Kuwayama derived her projection from an assumed rate of growth in world trade combined with assumptions about relative price changes.[52] The JERC estimate is the highest of the three, projecting Japan's exports in 1980 at ¥25,812 billion. As compared with Kuwayama and Sato, the JERC projection incorporates assumptions concerning the growth rate of world GNP, of Japan's GNP, of world trade, and of Japan's trade, all of which are highly optimistic.

The descending order of optimism in these projections perhaps reflects the chronological sequence in which they were prepared. Of late, the problems of Japan's transitional decade have begun to loom large in relation to its promises. Even so, few of the relevant problems have been discussed or even identified in the three papers compared above. For this reason, it may be best to rely on a moderate version of Japan's prospective balance-of-payments position in 1980.

Notes

1/ In constant prices (1965 = 100), exports increased relatively faster than GNP during the period 1955 to 1970. This was partly due to the fact that prices of non-exported goods (nontraded services and primary products) rose faster than those of manufactured goods, which are Japan's principal exports. In current prices, the rate of increase of exports and imports was about the same as that of GNP during this period.

2/ In current prices, the ratio of exports (in terms of exports of goods and services and factor income received from abroad) to gross national expenditure (GNE) increased from 9.6 percent in 1963 to 11.7 percent in 1970. In constant prices (1965 = 100), the ratio increased from 9.0 percent in 1963 to 13.2 percent in 1970. During the same period, in current prices, the ratio of imports (in terms of imports of goods and services and factor income paid abroad) to GNE varied by less than one percentage point from 10 percent. In 1965 prices, the ratio of imports to GNE increased from 9.7 percent in 1963 to 12.1 percent in 1970. Japan. Economic Planning Agency, *Kokumin Shotoku Tōkei Nenpō* [Annual statistics of national income] (Tokyo, 1972).

3/ Japan Economic Research Center, *Sekai no Nakano Nihon Keizai—1980* [Japan in the world economy—1980] (Tokyo, 1972). Hereinafter cited as the JERC study.

4/ If the intraregional trade of Western Europe were considered to be domestic rather than foreign trade, however, the disparity would not be so large.

5/ Japan attempted to negotiate a reduction in contractual imports of ferrous and nonferrous ores from sources such as Australia, Bougainville, and Canada during 1971. These efforts met with sharp resistance and created considerable dismay among her suppliers. The episode is an example of possible similar difficulties in the future.

6/ According to Department of Commerce statistics (in which both exports and imports are reported on an FOB basis), the deficit in U.S. merchandise trade with Japan during 1971 amounted to − $3,206 million.

7/ In the case of automobiles, a key export product, Japan's servicing network in Western Europe is comparatively weak. Thus, Japan will not be able to become a serious competitor to European manufacturers in the near future.

8/ According to a calculation of the Economic Planning Agency, exports contributed 19 percent to the real GNP growth of 10.5 percent during the prerecession year 1970, whereas in the recession year 1971 they accounted for 41 percent of the real GNP growth rate of 6.1 percent. In performing their antirecessionary role, supply-oriented exports also are partly accountable for the failure of the yen revaluation of 1971 to yield results as soon as anticipated. Furthermore, supply-oriented exports play a role in dumping to the extent that exports are sold at less than domestic prices in Japan and occasionally at prices that cover only slightly more than the variable cost of production.

9/ In the case of individual companies, the ratio of exports to output may be very high. Sony, for example, exports over half of its production. Exports also account for about half of the sales of Sharp, Pioneer, and Honda.

10/ The tight-money policy was adopted in September 1969 and was not relaxed until October 1970. It reinforced various autonomous factors such as a slowdown in business investment and consumer demand for durable goods, which were leading causes of the recession beginning in the autumn of 1970.

11/ Because of the weak internal purchasing power of the yen, conversion of Japanese wages at the official rate of exchange makes their purchasing power seem higher than it is. On the other hand, Japanese wages are usually reported with a downward bias inasmuch as fringe benefits are usually excluded.

12/ In 1969, a tax expert in the U.S. Department of the Treasury calculated that for a particular Japanese firm whose accounts he reviewed, all available export-related tax benefits would have yielded savings of only 0.79 percent on its total export earnings of $94.7 million during the accounting year ending October 31, 1967.

13/ U.S. Embassy Airgram A-134 (Tokyo, February 18, 1972). Despite this testimony, the intangible benefits of government cooperation, favors, and encouragement to exports are not readily quantifiable in the form of such calculations. In particular, it is difficult to separate the effects of tax-incentive measures for export promotion from other incentive measures.

14/ The Securities and Exchange Council in the Ministry of Finance reported that in 1970 the ten largest trading companies acounted for 47 percent of Japan's total exports, 63 percent of total imports, and 10 percent of all domestic transactions. For most of the major trading firms, export business represents about 20 percent of their total transactions.

15/ Other cases could also be mentioned of rules created for a given purpose in Japan which later were used to enforce other or even opposite purposes.

16/ Under Section 5 of the law, Japanese firms wishing to form an export cartel are authorized to do so merely by notifying the Ministry of International Trade and Industry (MITI). However, if the export cartel has any repercussions on domestic production, then Section 53 of the law requires that the producer as well as the exporter must agree to formation of the cartel. In the latter case, moreover, formation of the cartel is subject to the approval of both MITI and the Fair Trade Commission. Formation of an export cartel (between Japanese firms) should also be distinguished from an international cartel (between a Japanese firm and a foreign firm). The latter is not authorized under Japanese law.

17/ For a list of export cartel agreements, see *Koseitorihiki Iinkai Nenji Hōkoku* [Fair Trade Commission annual report] (1971), p. 294 ff.

18/ As of June 1972, exports of twenty-one major commodities (which may be broken down into sixty-four items at the four-digit level of the Brussels Tariff Nomenclature classification) were subject to the Export Trade Control Ordinance. These included the items of the three-year Japan–United States government-to-government textile agreement (signed in January 1972, retroactive to October 1, 1971). The latter limits Japanese exports of wool and manmade fiber goods. Prior to this agreement, a purely voluntary private program of export restraint had been in effect with regard to noncotton textiles since July 1971. (Cotton textile exports from Japan are subject to a separate governmental agreement, the "long-range arrangements regarding international trade in cotton textiles," or LTA, which has evolved through various stages since it was first initiated in 1957. It is presently scheduled to expire in September 1973.)

19/ As of July 1972, an Orderly Marketing Committee was also established within MITI.

20/ For this reason, the Japanese government is very reluctant to allow details of existing orderly marketing agreements to become public information.

21/ From the point of view of the United States, on the other hand, a serious flaw in the present procedure of organized marketing is its bilateral orientation. U.S. government advisors have argued that orderly marketing cannot be effective unless it is simultaneously enforced by many countries. By instigating Japan to take action to forestall such multilateral restrictions, this argument has the effect of putting pressure on Japan for greater bilateral concessions to the United States.

22/ According to the Fair Trade Commission, MITI has been encouraging the formation of voluntary export cartels beyond what FTC considers proper. This tends to undermine the Anti-Monopoly Law.

23/ For example, in June 1972 Japanese makers of synthetic fiber were charged with having concluded an illegal agreement with West German producers concerning a division of the market for nylon and staple fibers. The West German parties to the agreement were fined by their government. This raises the interesting point that, although European demands for orderly marketing on the part of Japan may be in the interest of private European firms, it is not invariably European governments that take a restrictive attitude toward Japanese exports.

24/ A cartel organized by the Japan Machinery Export Association, scheduled to go into effect on July 15, 1972, restricted itself to an increase of 40 percent annually in shipments of desk-top electronic calculators to the United States and Canada, and an increase of 20 to 30 percent in shipments to Western Europe. *Nihon Keizai Shimbun* [Japan economic journal] (June 6, 1972).

25/ The first round of negotiations took place in September 1970, followed by a second round in July 1971. Preparations for a third round were made in hopes of concluding an agreement during 1973.

26/ In this case, to hold down export restrictions as much as possible, MITI prefers a multilateral accommodation in GATT, whereas for the same purpose in the case of orderly marketing, it insists on the bilateral approach. The reason for the discrepancy is that with regard to GATT Article 19 the multilateral limits of restrictive action have already been established, whereas in the matter of orderly marketing they have not.

27/ On the other hand, some argue that GATT Article 19 is not restrictive enough. They say it should be revised to require the importing country to provide industrial-adjustment assistance to its disadvantaged producers before the restrictions of the article can be invoked. This is a very important argument on the Japanese side. Japan would also require that Article 19 should specify the sequence in which various types of import restrictions may be applied, beginning, for example, with tariff increases, quantitative restrictions, and so forth.

28/ Since December 16, 1969, members of EEC no longer have the authority to arrange individual trade agreements. Japan can make only a single agreement with EEC as a group. Such an agreement would tend to be influenced more heavily by the more restrictive rather than by the less restrictive policies of various EEC members. Consequently, Japan was anxious to induce England to drop its discriminatory restrictions against Japan before its accession to EEC.

29/ Article 35 has often been invoked as a bargaining device by developing countries to obtain foreign aid or tariff preferences from Japan. Portugal, for example, received import tariff preferences from Japan in April 1972 after withdrawing its implementation of Article 35. In other cases, Japan has purchased such withdrawal by accepting the inclusion of a safeguard clause in trade agreements.

30/ Japan claimed that the international code calls both for presentation of evidence concerning price differentials and evidence of injury to U.S. producers, whereas the U.S. code merely requires evidence of differentials. Under the international code, suspension of tariff assessment is contingent upon presentation of sufficient evidence of injury, whereas the U.S. code does not require such evidence. The international code requires that the standards and reasons underlying the anti-dumping action of the importing country be reported to the exporting country, whereas the U.S. code does not. Japan claimed further that the international code, unlike that of the United States, forbids retroactive application of suspension of tariff assessment. Under the international code, any decision concerning losses must be based on the results of study of all factors affecting the industries concerned. In the U.S. code, however, consideration is given to the effects of dumping alone. Japan also maintained that under the international code the decision to apply countervailing tariffs is left to the discretion of the government concerned, whereas the U.S. code makes the imposition of penalties mandatory.

31/ For further discussion, see Leon Hollerman, "Economic Factors in Japanese Planning for the Twenty-first Century," *Proceedings of the Fourth International Symposium on Regional Development* (Tokyo, January 1972).

32/ Protection for the purpose of reducing import dependence was of particular importance in the early postwar period. Protection of weak or declining industries has also been prompted by domestic political considerations, such as the dependence of the Liberal-Democratic party on its rural constituents. In recent years, however, when politically feasible, an opposite and overlapping policy of phasing out weak and declining industries has been adopted. The labor shortage and the high rate of economic growth, facilitating the reallocation of factors of production, have assisted the implementation of the new policy.

33/ Lack of reciprocity is conspicuous, for example, in Japan's rules for capital liberalization. Foreign capital participation in joint ventures is defined as liberalized when the limit of foreign participation is 50 percent. No limitation exists on U.S. import of capital from Japan. Examples of lack of reciprocity in the form of Japanese NTBs are numerous.

34/ In fiscal year 1971, 484 sole-agency contracts, covering a wide variety of imported commodities, particularly branded goods, were reported to FTC. Mitsui Bussan alone was the general import agent for about 150 of these commodities. Some modification of the general-agent system was planned by MOF, to become effective September 1, 1972.

35/ As a nontariff barrier, this institutional factor certainly restricts imports, although it is not a deliberately constructed protectionist device. In most cases, imported consumer goods automatically become luxury goods because of the high margins and multiple markups that are imposed by Japan's distribution system. This treatment is not discriminatory inasmuch as domestically produced as well as foreign goods are subject to the same treatment. In only very few instances have foreign suppliers been able to bypass the bottleneck by performing their own distribution independently.

36/ Residual import quotas are those in conflict with GATT. As of April 1972, these included coal, rawhide and leather products, machinery and instruments (digital computers, their components, and peripheral equipment), and integrated circuits. Primary products included beef, milk and cream, processed cheese, preserved meat, fresh and salted fish, oranges and tangerines, grapefruit, fruit purée, fruit paste, canned fruit, fruit juices, tomato juice, tomato catsup, tomato sauce, mixed seasonings, starch, grape sugar, wheat flour, rice flour, wheat and rice groats, malt, beans, peanuts, edible and nonedible seaweed, tubers of *konnyaku*, denatured dates, and food preparations containing sugar, milk, and so forth. At the same date, import restrictions other than residual were applied to light airplanes, components for light airplanes, radar apparatus for aircraft, and radio and remote-control apparatus for aircraft.

37/ For example, when the quota for importation of beef cattle was liberalized in October 1971, a tariff of ¥75,000 per head was then imposed on cattle weighing 300 kilograms or more and a tariff of ¥45,000 per head on cattle weighing less than 300 kilograms. Between April 1969 and April 1972, among eighty liberalized commodities, tariff increases were imposed upon six commodities, according to MITI.

38/ This is a private and political explanation, rather than an official one, inasmuch as it would be inadmissible under GATT.

39/ In his testimony before the House Subcommittee on Foreign Economic Policy, Hugh Patrick referred to a U.S. government estimate that the cost in U.S. exports forgone of Japanese quotas on manufactured goods was about $200 million. U.S. Congress. House. Committee on Foreign Affairs, *United States Foreign Economic Policy toward Japan* (Washington, D.C.: U.S. Government Printing Office, 1972), p. 91.

40/ Temporary duties are authorized by the Provisional Measures Law for Import Liberalization. Effective October 1, 1971, temporary duties were imposed on live bovines, live swine, pig meat, fish and fish products, menthol, peppermint oil, dextrins, and "finishing paste."

41/ In itself, the current account surplus is perhaps less important than its role as an indicator of the viability and growth of the Japanese economy. The authorities fear that loss of the surplus (as a result of yen revaluation or other causes) would be accompanied by a slowdown in the rate of growth of the economy and thus impair Japan's ability to install new social-overhead capital.

42/ Indeed, it was regarded as a defeat inflicted by the United States—a "reverse Pearl Harbor."

43/ During the first six months of 1972, the trade surplus in terms of customs statistics was $3.7 billion; the overall balance-of-payments surplus was $1.4 billion.

44/ In the case of steel, however, which was subject to quantitative export restraints, the export price was raised by about 20 percent during the first six months following revaluation.

45/ On the import side, however, the income elasticity of demand is greater than the price elasticity because of the commodity structure of Japan's imports, which is heavily concentrated on industrial raw materials and intermediate industrial products.

46/ Various authorities have prepared projections of Japan's capital exports during the decade of the 1970s. According to the Industrial Bank of Japan, about $6 billion will be invested abroad during 1971–75, bringing the total of Japan's overseas investments to about $10 billion at the end of that period.

47/ As of March 1970, 44.0 percent of Japan's foreign investment was located in advanced countries and 56.0 percent in developing countries. At the same time, only 12.6 percent of her foreign investment was in the form of direct investment. Loans accounted for 47.8 percent of the total, securities for 38.6 percent, and investment in overseas branch offices of Japanese trading companies for 1.0 percent. Japan External Trade Organization, *Economic Cooperation of Japan* (special edition of *Trade and Industry of Japan*), August 1971.

48/ At the same time, Japanese interests could participate in the benefits received by developing countries in the form of tariff preferences conferred upon their exports to Japan.

49/ These include air, water, and noise pollution; congestion and bottlenecks in production, transportation, and storage; and the diminished availability of new industrial sites.

50/ Indeed, in terms of the significant increase in world production of agricultural goods which will be generated by Japanese foreign investment during the 1970s, Japan's activities imply a direct threat to the international economic position of the United States in 1980. See Clarence E. Pike, *Japanese Overseas Aid and Investments —Their Potential Effects on World and U.S. Farm Exports* (Washington, D.C.: U.S. Department of Agriculture, Economic Research Service, 1972).

51/ The ratio of manufactured-goods exports to total exports from Japan has risen from 86 percent in 1955 to 94 percent in 1971. Conceivably, this trend may continue in the future.

52/ In another particular, Kuwayama's projection of the invisible trade-balance deficit for calendar year 1975, −$1.8 billion, is about half as much as the projection for fiscal year 1975 based on The New Economic and Social Development Plan (April 1970), −$3.8 billion.

7.

JAPAN'S FISCAL INCENTIVES FOR EXPORTS

Yoichi Okita

THE PURPOSE OF THIS CHAPTER is to clarify and to evaluate the role of fiscal incentives in the efforts of the Japanese government to stimulate exports in the postwar period. Although there has been no legislation nor a system called *export subsidies* as such, various so-called favorable discriminatory systems of taxes favoring export industries have been adopted. This "subsidy" is, of course, only a small part of the measures taken by the Japanese government as well as by the private sector to enhance, in other countries, the popularity of the goods made in Japan and to facilitate their import by foreign buyers.

Postwar History of Preferential Tax Systems

The Shoup Recommendations, announced in 1949, form the basis of the tax system of present-day Japan. The recommendations embodied the ideal notion of an equitable and consistent tax system, but since their implementation, this ideal has gradually been eroded by various provisions designed to promote general economic development and, more frequently, to promote particular economic activities. This chapter analyzes those tax provisions relating specifically to exports and does not consider other schemes, such as special depreciation allowances and tax deferments on reserves, that did aid exporters but that were designed to stimulate economic growth in general.

Table 27 summarizes the types and dates of tax-incentive schemes for exports that have been employed in the period beginning August 1953. These provisions are described in detail below, but it may be useful at the outset to have a broad idea of the history of changes in the subsidization of Japanese exports. Some incentives have been abolished or replaced; others remain in force today. It is apparent from the table that most of the systems were initiated or renewed in 1964. These changes were due to a restructuring of many Japanese trade provisions designed to bring these provisions into conformity with the articles of the General Agreement on Tariffs and Trade (GATT). In 1963, the Anglo-Japanese Treaty of Commerce and Navigation was ratified. Under this treaty, Japan agreed to abide by Article XVI (4) of GATT as of March 31, 1964.[1] In accordance with this article, which prohibits export subsidies, the Export Income Deduction System was abolished.[2] Revision of export-promotion policies took the form of the replacement of the Export Income Deduction System and the Special Depreciation (the old name of the Additional Depreciation System for Export Promotion) by several other systems that did not subsidize firms according to their export income or their sales revenue. Thus, export-promotion policies became more dependent on tax deferments rather than outright tax deduction.

Another change occurred in June 1971, two years after the Organization for Economic Cooperation and Development (OECD) had pointed out in its annual country review that Japan had begun to be faced with "the problems of surplus countries trying to avoid undue strains on international liquidity."[3] The government publicized an Eight-Point Program for Avoiding Yen Revaluation, whose recommendations included the abolition of preferential financing of exports and special tax benefits for exporters, and also the establishment of "orderly marketing to prevent export growth annoying to a specific market."[4] The program reflected a basic change in the government's view of the situation and an awareness of the problems pointed out in the OECD study. Although all the incentives to exports were not abolished in 1971, several major changes were made: The Additional Depreciation System was drastically reduced, the Technical Export Income Deduction was

TABLE 27. Dates of Tax Subsidies to Export Industries

Tax Systems	1953	1959	1962	1964	1969	1971, 1972
Export Income Deduction	* August			* March		
Technical Export Income Deduction		* April			* March	* March ?
Export Loss Reserves	* August		* March			
Overseas Market Development Reserve				* April	* March	* March ?
Overseas Market Development Reserve for Small and Medium-Sized Firms				* April	* March	
Additional Depreciation				* September * March	* March	* March
Special Deduction on the Travel and Hotel Expense of Foreign Buyers				* April	* March	

Note: Solid lines indicate the period of the system's existence; asterisks on these lines indicate dates for implementation, renewal, or expiration.

TABLE 28. Revenue Criterion
for Export Income Deduction System

Exports	Percent of Gross Revenue	
	Manufacturers	Trading Companies
Consumption goods	3.0	1.0
Investment goods	5.0	1.0

halved, and in 1972 the whole Additional Depreciation System was terminated.

The position paper by the U.S. delegates to the 1972 U.S.–Japanese Conference of Commerce asserted that Japan should utilize more tax policies to correct the disequilibrium of her balance of payments with the United States. As a result, the government studied the possibility of abolishing the remaining export incentives. These incentives, together with both the export products' exemption from the indirect tax and the Tariff Drawback System for exported goods, will probably be discontinued. In searching for a policy with an immediate impact, the government was first inclined to levy export surcharges but then decided to use export quotas. These became effective in September 1972.

Deductions. The Export Income Deduction System was the most important tax measure for export promotion over the period from 1953 to 1964. This law permitted part of corporate income to be exempt from tax, that is, a deduction from total income in calculating taxable income. Two alternative measures were allowed in the calculation of this deduction, the income criterion and the revenue criterion, with the final deduction being the smaller of the two calculated figures. The *income criterion* permitted the deduction to be a certain percent of all income (profit) generated from exports, and the *revenue criterion* allowed the deduction to be based on total export sales. When the law was enacted in 1953, the income criterion was set at 50 percent of net income from exports but in 1957 was increased to 80 percent. The revenue criterion is shown in Table 28. Investment goods that qualified for the 5 percent deduction consisted largely of plant exports.[5]

TABLE 29. Revenue Criterion
for the Additional Deduction System

Exports	Percent of Gross Revenue	
	Manufacturers	Trading Companies
Consumption goods	4.5	1.5
Investment goods	7.5	1.5

The reason for two alternative tax bases is quite simple. On the one hand, if the government had allowed as the deduction a percent of profit from exports sufficient to provide a meaningful subsidy to companies with low profit-to-revenue ratios, then exporters with high profit-to-revenue ratios would have received extremely large subsidies. On the other hand, if a certain percent of gross export revenue had been deductible, then the percentage needed to provided adequate subsidies to manufacturing exporters would provide a very large deduction for firms, such as the Japanese trading companies that have high revenue but low profit-to-revenue ratios. Thus, by introducing both the income and the revenue criteria and using the smaller of these two deductions, the government was able to stimulate exports by high-revenue and high-profit companies without sacrificing too much tax income. However, the government was concerned only with maintaining "horizontal equity" between manufacturers and trading companies. No consideration of GATT rules on export subsidies was necessary until 1964.

In 1957, the Additional Deduction System was introduced. This permitted a further deduction from total income to be made in calculating taxable corporate income. This extra deduction was again taken as the smaller of the income- or the revenue-based figure and was related to the increase in sales or profit over normal export activity, defined as the gross revenue or income from exports in the preceding year. The income criterion allowed 100 percent of the increase in export income to be deducted from this year's taxable income. The revenue criterion applied to the increase in export sales according to the rates given in Table 29. For example, suppose that a company's profit ratio was such that it was subject to the income criterion for both the ordinary and the additional part of its export activity. Then, 80 percent of its export income within its normal export activity was not subject to tax, and in addition, the entire increase of net income from exports over that of the previous year was exempt from taxation.

In 1961, the Additional Deduction was abolished in order to simplify the system, although the ordinary deduction system established in 1953 was extended to 1964. As noted earlier, this turned out to be the last extension. However, the Technical Export Income Deduction, a minor part of the system, has survived until the present day with some revision and a change of name to Special Deduction in Connection with Overseas Transactions in Technology and Services.[6] Because this system covers invisibles only, the requirement of GATT Article 16, which refers to products, does not apply.

The Technical Export Income Deduction was added to the system in 1959. When a corporation obtained revenue by overseas sales of technology, it was allowed to deduct 50 percent of that revenue or 50 percent of the total income of that corporation, whichever was smaller. Here, the total income was defined to include not only the net income from overseas transactions but also the profit from domestic transactions.[7] For reasons similar to those presented in the explanation of the Export Income Deduction, two alternative criteria, the income and revenue criteria, were again necessary in order to take account of the possibly wide range of profit-to-revenue ratios. The reason why the total income was used instead of export income is as follows: Unlike the case of the export of commodities, it is difficult to identify the cost of the invention or production of technologies; in fact, new technologies may simply be generated out of the ordinary operation of machines. Thus, although the gross revenue from export of technology may be clearly defined, it is difficult to separate from total ordinary operating cost those costs that are necessary for the creation of new technologies. The deductions under both criteria are much higher than those used in the Export Income Deduction System. In the case of the revenue criterion, the percentage was made higher. In the case of the income criterion, the base was made larger.

Here it may be worth discussing how export income should be calculated given the existence of joint costs. In the case of the DISC proposal of the United States, because of the existence of joint costs, it was necessary to approximate the export income as the base of tax deferment by applying a fraction to the whole income of a company. If a fixed fraction of this nature is considered satisfactory, the notion of export income can be dispensed with, and the deduction can be computed directly from the total income (including that from domestic transactions) of the company. For a closer approximation, it sometimes makes sense to use the ratio of export sales to the total of domestic and export sales as the fraction that should be applied to total income.

The direct derivation of the deduction from a firm's total income was adopted for technology exports as explained above. Later, when the items listed under the category of transportation and like services came to be covered by the system, the export income was approximated by applying the ratio of export sales to total sales.

The Technical Export Income Deduction System was revised in 1964 when the deduction for specified categories of technology export was increased from 50 to 70 percent of revenue. The system was extended to cover exports of consulting and shipping services. Under the revenue criterion, the allowable deductions were 20 percent and 30 percent, respectively, for revenue from the export of consulting and shipping services. The income criterion permitted the deduction of 40 percent of the approximated export income, rather than total income, in the export of services and the deduction of 50 percent of total net income for firms exporting technology. In subsequent years, the deduction was extended to cover sales of copyrights, construction services, and repairing and processing (1965); export and reexport of primary products, services of travel agents, surveying services (1967); and qualifying conditions for the consulting services were relaxed (1966). Since April 1972, the system has been operating as indicated in Table 30. In the table, *export income* is an approximation as explained in the previous paragraph. Specifically, export income is defined as:

$$\text{Total income} \times \frac{\text{sales revenue from transportation and other services}}{\text{total of domestic and export sales}}$$

Another minor deduction, a special treatment of travel and hotel expenses for foreign buyers paid by exporting corporations, was introduced in 1964. In Japan, only a fraction of expenses for entertainment is deductible in computing taxable income. The special treatment permitted corporations to deduct the full amount of entertainment expenses for foreign buyers as ordinary operating costs. In 1967, expenses for buyer

TABLE 30. Technological and Service Export Income Deduction System

Kinds of Transactions	Revenue Criterion (percent)	Income Criterion (percent)
Transactions on technology		
Export of patent rights	70	50[a]
Sales of patent rights to trading companies	70	50[a]
Export of copyrights	30	50[a]
Consulting services	20	50[a]
Transportation and other services		
Export of motion picture rights	15	40[b]
Outbound shipping	1.5	40[b]
Other transportation services	1.5	40[b]
Repair, processing, and construction	1.5	40[b]
Travel-agent services	1.5	40[b]
Export of primary products, direct and indirect	1.5	40[b]
Reexport of primary goods	1.5	40[b]

[a]Percent of total income.
[b]Percent of export income.

receptions paid at overseas branches were also permitted as ordinary operating costs. These measures lasted until 1971.

Fast depreciation. Before discussion of depreciation systems relating to export incentives, two observations are necessary. First, all the systems discussed in this section are only accelerated depreciation. Also, in all these systems, the sum of depreciation cannot exceed the cost of the asset. Second, in Japan, capital gains of incorporated firms are treated as ordinary income. This contrasts with the United States, where firms can adopt the following tactics to increase capital gains: Firm A buys an asset, depreciates it rapidly, and then sells it to firm B, which does the same. Although the same kind of tactic is possible in Japan, it is not worthwhile to reduce cost adjusted for depreciation and thereby increase the capital gain, simply because capital gain is treated as ordinary income.

In 1961, a Special Depreciation System was introduced. It permitted corporations engaged in export business to accelerate depreciation over and above regular depreciation by using the following formula:

Additional depreciation allowance =

$$
\begin{array}{c} \text{regular} \\ \text{depreciation} \\ \text{allowance} \end{array} \times \left(\dfrac{\begin{array}{c}\text{amount of export sales} \\ \text{in current period}\end{array}}{\begin{array}{c}\text{total sales in} \\ \text{current period}\end{array}} - \dfrac{\begin{array}{c}\text{amount of export sales} \\ \text{in prior period}\end{array}}{\begin{array}{c}\text{total sales in} \\ \text{prior period}\end{array}} \right)
$$

(By law, the term in parentheses could not exceed 50/100.) This system was replaced by an Additional Depreciation System in 1964. Leon Hollerman explains the change as follows[8]:

> Under the former system, if domestic and export sales increased at the same rate, the permitted additional depreciation would be zero. Thus, regardless of the amount by which it had increased the absolute volume of its exports, a firm might receive no benefit whatever. This was especially adverse to traditional industries such as textiles and sundry goods which find it difficult to increase their export ratio. On the other hand, it was favorable to firms newly entering the export field. In any event, effective April 1, 1964, the amount of additional depreciation (again over and above regular depreciation) was to be computed by multiplying the ordinary depreciation allowance for a specified period by the following:
>
> $$80\% \times \dfrac{\text{export sales for preceding accounting period}}{\text{total revenue in preceding accounting period}}$$
>
> The new formula was favorable for firms employing a high proportion of fixed assets.

The ratio of export sales to total revenue that appears as the last term of the formula quoted above will be called the *export ratio*. The percent figure in front of the export ratio in the formula was raised to 100 percent in 1966. In 1968 came another revision. Under it, a corporation that was designated by the Minister of International Trade and Industry (MITI) as an "Exporter with Distinguished Merits," defined as a firm that had achieved an export sales increase of more than 1 percent in the previous year, was allowed to avail itself of still higher additional depreciation. When the firm's export ratio exceeded that of the previous period, or when the rate of increase of its exports relative to the previous period was higher than two-thirds of the rate of increase of Japan's total exports, it was called *Exporter with Merits of Class A*. As such, the firm qualified for an additional depreciaton of 160/100 × export ratio × regular depreciation. Otherwise, it was called an *Exporter with Merits of Class B* and qualified for an additional depreciation of 130/100 × export ratio × regular depreciation.

As partial implementation of the Eight-Point Program, the special treatment of the Exporter with Distinguished Merits was repealed in 1971, and the additional rate of depreciation was reduced to its intial 80/100 (from 100/100) × export ratio. Finally in 1972, the system itself was abolished.

There is no legal conflict between the tax schemes outlined here and Article 16 of GATT. The article prohibits subsidies on exports, but because the depreciation schemes amount only to deferment (rather than reduction) of taxation, there is no contravention of Article 16 (although it might be considered a bribe). In other words, the accelerated depreciation scheme takes advantage of a legitimate GATT loophole.

Tax deferment. Various reserve-allowance schemes have been tried since 1953. The main purpose of these schemes was to encourage internal retention of funds by private enterprises, but a secondary effect was an incentive to export. In 1953, a tax deferment on export loss reserves was initiated, ostensibly for the purpose of providing against contract cancellation and claims. A small percent of the amount of an export contract could be credited to this reserve and exempt from taxation for up to five years. Little use was made of this scheme, and it was terminated in 1962.

In 1964, the Export Income Deduction System was replaced by a range of other measures designed to encourage development of overseas markets. Included in the new package were incentive schemes, one principally for large corporations, the other for small and medium ones. Because the accelerated-depreciation system stimulated investment in industries manufacturing for export but did not greatly help the trading companies, the incentive system for large corporations was designed primarily to encourage the activity of these trading companies. It was officially explained by MITI that the Overseas Market Development Reserve helped corporations to average over several years those expenses subject to wide fluctuations, such as those incurred during the establishment of overseas branches and for advertising abroad. But because corporate taxation is not progressive unless a corporation's profits fluctuate from negative to positive, the merit of averaging is not significant. Rather, the true object of this reserve was simply to give firms tax deferments. The maximum allowable credit to this reserve was set as a fraction of the revenue earned from exports during the previous year, specifically 0.5 percent in the case of trading companies and 1.5 percent in the case of industries manufacturing for export. This Overseas Market Development Reserve contained a provision restoring at least one-fifth of the credited fund to income for tax purposes in each of the next five years.[9] "Additional amounts may also be required to be restored to income based upon the actual deductible expense for overseas operation incurred in the years after the reserve was created."[10] In other words, when a firm made an actual expense that exactly fitted the purpose of the reserve, it was not deductible because the operation had to be financed by the reserve rather than by the ordinary income. The deduction of the actual deductible expense for overseas operation had been already carried backward. Thus, the reserve could be shrunk by the amount of that actual expense. The firm was therefore free from the burden of restoring taxable income in later years by that amount because the planned expense had already materialized. If the reserve had remained intact even when the expenses were made, the reserve would not have been called a reserve for a certain purpose but a generally applicable tax deferment.

The Overseas Market Development Reserve for Small and Medium-Sized Firms differed from the system just described in that the reserve had to be deposited with an authorized commercial and industrial association. The deduction, which was limited to 2.5 percent of revenue from the previous year, was therefore given only to a member corporation of such an association.[11] Because the number of firms utilizing it was so small, the system was abolished in 1969. But the system that was started initially for the larger firms only was expanded in 1966 to include other firms. A corporation with authorized capital of less than ¥100 million could place in a reserve (and defer tax on) 1.0

TABLE 31. Percent of Revenue That Can Be Placed in Overseas Market Development Reserve

Size of Capital (yen)	Trading Companies	Manufacturers
Less than 100 million	1.7 (1.1)	2.3 (1.5)
0.1–1.0 billion	1.0 (0.5)	1.5 (1.5)
Less than 1 billion	0.5 (0.5)	1.5 (1.5)

Note: Figures in parentheses are percents before the revision.

percent (rather than 0.5 percent) of its revenue from exports. In 1968, the special treatment of the Exporter with Distinguished Merits was introduced in exactly the same way as in the Additional Depreciation System. An Exporter with Merits of Class A qualified to place in the reserve 1.6 times as much as a nonprivileged firm; and an Exporter with Merits of Class B, 1.3 times as much. In 1969, the percent of export revenue placeable in the reserve was raised to 1.1 for smaller trading companies (those with capital of less than ¥100 million). Then, in 1971 the percentages were again revised. The data presented in Table 31 describe the system as it operated in 1972. Also, in the 1971 revision special treatment of the Exporter with Distinguished Merits was abolished.[12]

Estimation of Revenue Lost through Export Incentives

Each year, the Ministry of Finance (MOF) makes public estimates of corporate tax revenues lost through tax incentives provided in the Special Measures Act of the Revenue Code. Table 32 shows the figures relevant to export promotion. Figures for the Export Loss Reserve are missing in this table because they are not available on a basis comparable

TABLE 32. Tax Revenue Lost through Export Promotion Measures (millions of dollars)

Fiscal Year	(1) Additional Depreciation	(2) Export Income Deduction[a]	(3) Overseas Market Development Reserve	(4) Total (1) + (2) + (3)	(5) Total, All Special Measures[b]	(6) Corporate Tax Revenues[c]
1957	—	20.8	—	20.8	169.7	1,011.4
1958	—	34.7	—	34.7	197.5	856.4
1959	—	27.8	—	27.8	229.7	1,085.0
1960	—	31.9	—	31.9	280.8	1,592.7
1961	—	30.5	—	30.5	284.7	1,984.1
1962	5.6	54.2	—	59.7	349.4	2,167.7
1963	2.8	62.5	—	65.3	471.1	2,396.9
1964	32.5	1.9	31.7	66.1	596.6	2,709.4
1965	31.9	3.1	33.3	68.3	613.3	2,575.2
1966	43.3	7.2	21.9	72.5	650.3	2,865.8
1967	45.8	7.8	18.1	71.7	660.3	3,633.0
1968	70.0	11.9	22.2	104.2	735.5	4,421.8
1969	100.6	11.1	28.1	139.7	896.1	5,580.1
1970	152.2	16.9	41.7	210.8	1,066.9	7,130.9
1971	143.1	15.8	38.3	197.2	1,220.5	7,976.2
1972[d]	—	11.1	22.2	33.3	N.A.	N.A.

[a] Including the Technical Export Income Deduction.
[b] Including measures other than those for export promotion.
[c] Actually collected.
[d] Preliminary estimate by MITI.
Source: Japan. Ministry of Finance. Tax Bureau, Research Section.

to other figures. However, the amount of funds accumulated in the reserve are available from 1953 to 1960 in unpublished data of MOF.[13] According to these data, reserves were negligible before 1955. Applying the statutory rate of corporate income tax that existed from fiscal year 1958 to 1960 (about 38 percent) to amounts added to the reserve in each year, we find that revenue loss is at most ¥1.6 billion in 1960. In other years, a tax reduction of more than ¥0.8 billion never occurred.

Note that the nature of the data in Table 32 differs in columns 1, 2, and 3. Although no negative figures appear in the table because revenue from exports has been increasing throughout the period, the figures in column 3 are net of tax on previously exempted reserves transferred to taxable income. The estimate of the effect of the Additional Depreciation allowance is probably based on the estimate of the sum of the book value of assets belonging to the firms eligible for the system. Thus, the increase of tax revenue after the completion of the write-off of an asset is automatically taken into account.

Most of the entries in Table 32 are not revenue completely lost to tax but rather tax liabilities that are postponed in time; that is, they are not tax deductions but tax deferments. Although these deferments are not specifically subsidies, they do have a similar effect in that the tax deferment reduces the present value of the tax. The exact amount of the benefit is, however, difficult to estimate, but it is certainly less than the amount of tax deferred.

Furthermore, three other facts explain why the tax deferments benefit private enterprises: (1) When prices are rising, tax deferment decreases the burden in real terms. (2) When the statutory rate of corporate tax is declining, tax deferment reduces the tax liability even in current dollars. (3) When the investor applies both a risk premium and a normal discount rate to more distant returns because of uncertainty, an accelerated depreciation means a still bigger reduction of present value to tax flow.[14] All three reasons are relevant in Japan. The movement of prices has never been toward deflation; the statutory rate of corporate tax has been declining from 42 percent to a level between 35 and 26 percent[15]; and corporate income has been fluctuating so much that, in spite of complete loss-offset refund from the tax system, the uncertainty of future return has never been negligible. Although these benefits may deserve the name "subsidy," it is almost impossible to weigh the importance of these factors quantitatively.

TABLE 33. Calculation of Subsidy Rates
and Hypothetical Change in Exports, 1957 to 1963
(millions of dollars)

Year	(1) Export Income Deduction[a]	(2) Commodity Exports (FOB) at Current Prices	(3) (1)/(2) (percent)	(4) (3) × (η−1.0)	(5) Change in Exports (yen)
1957	20.8	2,399.1	0.7	0.7	20.31
1958	34.7	2,888.5	1.2	1.2	34.67
1959	27.8	3,565.5	0.8	0.8	28.53
1960	31.9	4,030.4	0.8	0.8	32.25
1961	30.5	4,242.7	0.7	0.7	29.69
1962	54.2	4,954.3	1.1	1.1	54.50
1963	62.5	5,594.0	1.1	1.1	61.53
					261.48

[a]Figures are from Table 32, column 2.
Note: η denotes the price elasticity of exports.

Effects on Exports

Because incentives were given directly in the form of tax deduction (rather than deferment) until 1963, it is possible to calculate a rate of subsidy to exports. However, because the system was not an explicit ad valorem subsidy but rather a mixture of ad valorem subsidy and a subsidy proportional to export income, only a proxy to the ad valorem rate of subsidy can be calculated. Dividing the figures in column 2 of Table 32 by the total value of commodity exports (FOB), we obtain the results shown in Table 33. The figures in column 3 of the table are considerably lower than the revenue criterion deduction rates of 3 and 5 percent for manufacturing firms. Probable explanations of this are: (1) trading companies, for which the criterion is 1 percent, accounted for a large proportion of exports; (2) deduction is limited to the lower of that given by the revenue criterion and that resulting from the income criterion; (3) underestimation of the effect of tax revenue reduction due to insufficient coverage; and (4) underutilization of the system by minor exporters.

In any case, the rate of the export price reduction due to the subsidization seems not to exceed 1.5 percent. Column 4 applies the price elasticity of −2 estimated by several researchers.[16] Finally, in column 5 the hypothetical percent change in the value of exports is translated into yen. The figure that appears at the last line of column 5 is the sum of the figures of six years.

A rough, back-of-the-envelope approach can also be used to check these calculations and to place an upper limit on the estimated effects of the incentives on exports over the 1957–1963 period. If the same price elasticity of exports is applied to a postulated subsidy rate of 1.5 percent, instead of the rates of column 3, and the resulting figure taken as an upper bound on the effect of the subsidies, one discovers that the export subsidies might have increased the value of exports by 2 percent in every year before 1964. The summation of this contribution of the incentive programs to the reserve of foreign exchange over the six-year period comes to ¥203 billion instead of the ¥86.8 billion calculated in Table 34. Thus, if the system of export subsidies and incentives had not existed, Japan's foreign-exchange reserves would have been about $240 to $560 million smaller at the end of fiscal year 1963 than was their actual figure.

Turning to the effects of measures taken after 1964, we could use the same method as that used for the 1957–1963 period only if all the tax incentives were actual tax deductions. But in the period beginning in 1964, the major export incentives (shown in columns 1 and 3 of Table 32) are not tax reductions but merely tax deferments. Thus, it is difficult to place a precise value on the incentive to export given by these measures.[17] However, if one puts an upper bound on the induced increase in exports by treating these deferments as outright tax reductions, the result is a very conservative estimate in the sense that it avoids any danger of underestimating the increase in exports induced by the export-incentive programs. This analysis, summarized in Table 34, suggests that the result of the export-incentive programs after 1963 was similar to those systems used prior to 1963. If the figures in column 4 of Table 32 are divided by the total value of exports including the invisibles (to

TABLE 34. Calculation of Subsidy Rates and Hypothetical Changes in Exports, 1964 to 1970 (millions of dollars)

Year	(1) Tax Revenue through Export Incentives[a]	(2) Export of Goods and Services at Current Prices	(3) (1)/(2) (percent)	(4) (3) × (η−1.0)	(5) Change in Exports (yen)
1964	66.1	8,325.9	0.9	0.9	74.94
1965	68.3	9,905.8	0.9	0.9	89.17
1966	72.5	11,411.6	0.7	0.7	79.89
1967	71.7	12,391.0	0.7	0.7	86.75
1968	104.2	15,621.2	0.8	0.8	124.97
1969	139.7	19,175.3	0.8	0.8	153.42
1970	210.8	23,073.0	0.9	0.9	207.67
					816.81

[a]Figures are from Table 32, column 4.

take account of the Technical Export Income Deduction), the result again rarely exceeds 1 percent, as Table 34 demonstrates. Thus, we can assert that the size of the incentives relative to the volume of exports was smaller in the period after 1964 than in the period before 1963, especially if we take account of the fact that most of the incentives taken after 1964 were tax deferments.

We can conclude that the influence of these policies was substantial and that even in the last several years, it has never become negligible. This conclusion seems quite reasonable especially when these tax measures are compared in Table 35 with the 1970 DISC proposal in the United States. Because the current law based on the DISC idea consists of a kind of tax deferment rather than tax deductions, the comparison does make sense.

TABLE 35. Comparison of Tax Revenue Lost because
of Tax Deferment Measures in Japan and United States,
1970 (billions of dollars)

	(1) Revenue Lost	(2) Total Export	(3) (1)/(2) (percent)
Japan	0.2	19.3	1
United States	0.5–1.0	43.2	1–2

Other Measures

In addition to the so-called Export Promotion Tax Measures discussed above, two other policies relate to exports via indirect taxation. They are usually grouped under the class of international tax-coordination policies or of border tax-adjustment policies rather than tax-incentive programs because they simply save commodities moving across borders from double taxation. This double taxation arises when exports are taxed both by the exporting country (taxation according to the origin principle) and by the importing country (taxation by the destination principle). A shift to origin taxation, when competing export countries do not make the same shift, will reduce the competitiveness of a country's exports. Because the Japanese government did consider this change, its probable impact upon Japanese exports had to be considered. The change would have involved subjecting export goods to the Commodity Tax, a tax already applying to goods sold for domestic consumption. The rates of this tax, as it would apply to several important export commodities, are listed in Table 36. But it was calculated that the effects of this policy would not be significant because the most important export goods, iron and steel, were not subject to the commodity tax in the first place.

The second indirect tax measure, introduced in 1965, is the drawback of tariffs on material and fuel used in making export goods. The refund is given not to the exporter but to the manufacturer of the goods. This system applied to seventy-one items, and the refunds amounted to ¥3 billion in 1971. This represents an example of the use of the destina-

TABLE 36. Rates of the Commodity Tax (percent)

Export Commodity	Tax Rate
Automobile (compact)	30
Air conditioner	20
Small television set	15
Subcompact automobile	15
Radio	10
Tape recorder	10

tion principle to avoid double taxation. Recently, MOF decided to exclude steel, automobiles, motorcycles, ships, and some fifty other items from the tariff drawback. It is estimated that this will reduce refunds to business by ¥2.4 billion.[18]

The increase in government revenue resulting from the two changes considered in this section, that is, the possible levying of the Commodity Tax on export goods and the restriction of the tariff drawback, is estimated on the basis of 1972 trade figures to be some ¥20 billion.[19] (This is a hypothetical figure as the Commodity Tax extension has not been implemented but instead is only under consideration.) Thus, if both were implemented, the two measures discussed in this section would offset the effects of the existing export-incentive measures —the Technical Export Income Deduction System and the Overseas Market Development Reserve—which, as indicated in Table 32, brought about a ¥12 billion reduction in tax revenue in 1972.

Subsidies to JETRO and Japan Plant Export Association

The Japan External Trade Organization (JETRO) was established in 1958 to promote exports by means of overseas market research, operation of trade centers, and advertisement. It has 19 trade centers in

TABLE 37. Export Promotion Budgetary Items
and Their Budgets, 1970 (millions of dollars)

JETRO	16.0
Asian Economic Research Center	2.5
Japan Plant Export Association	
Machine Tool Export Promotion Project	1.6
Japan Sundry Goods Export Center	0.6
Silk Export Promotion Project	
Overseas Construction Promotion Project	
Design Improvement of China, Textiles, and Machinery	1.0
Small Firms Export Promotion Project	
General Overseas Economic Research	1.1
Administration of Quality Test of Export Goods	6.9
Promotion of Tourist Industry	2.8
Total	32.5

major cities, 41 overseas branches all over the world, about 190 Japanese employees dispatched abroad, and about 200 foreign employees. Its activities include participation in international fairs, constant exhibition· of goods at the branches, mediation of commercial inquiries, research on the general economic situation and systems of foreign countries and tone of markets, marketing research on specific commodities, various advertisements, improvement of design of export goods, and so on.

The Japan Plant Export Association was established in 1955 to promote the export of heavy machinery and factories by performing technological consulting services and participating in industrial development projects in advance of the construction of equipment. These two organizations are financed almost entirely by the national budget.

Several other similar projects and organizations, with their budgets of 1970, are listed in Table 37. The time series of the total of them, the so-called Export Promotion Budgetary Items, is presented in Table 38.

TABLE 38. Total of Export Promotion Budget
and JETRO Budget, excluding the budget of EXPO '70
(millions of dollars)

Fiscal Year	(1) Total	(2) JETRO	(3) Total Export of Goods and Services (percent)	(4) Total Tax Incentives[a] (percent)	(5) (1) + Total Tax Incentives[a]
1958	4.2	2.8	0.13	12.0	38.9
1959	5.6	3.1	0.13	20.0	33.3
1960	6.7	3.9	0.14	20.8	38.6
1961	11.1	4.2	0.22	36.3	41.7
1962	13.3	5.0	0.23	22.3	73.1
1963	15.3	6.1	0.23	23.4	80.6
1964	17.2	7.2	0.21	26.0	83.3
1965	20.0	15.8	0.20	29.2	88.3
1966	29.2	12.5	0.26	40.2	101.7
1967	34.7	14.4	0.28	48.4	106.4
1968	27.2	14.2	0.17	26.1	131.4
1969	29.7	16.1	0.15	21.2	169.4
1970	32.8 (24.7)[b]	16.1	0.14	15.5	243.6
1971	27.2[b]	17.8	—	—	—
1972	29.4	19.2	—	—	—

[a]From column 4 of Table 32.
[b]Budgets administrated by MITI only.

Because these budget totals, unlike tax deferments, are definite figures on budgetary contributions to export stimulus, the size of the budget may deserve some attention. One could argue that export prices are lower because of the government's assumption of public relations functions. But evaluation of these prices is less clear than evaluation of tax incentives, especially with regard to items like the Asian Economic Research Center and the general research of foreign economies by

227

MITI, JETRO, and the Ministry of Foreign Affairs. Furthermore, because of the externalities and scale economies inherent in this kind of promotion activity, one cannot tell how much higher export prices would be if private firms took over the functions of these organizations. Therefore, there is no attempt to translate the figures in column 3 of Table 38. However, these budgetary measures have never been small in the course of the growth of exports.

Conclusion

None of the individual export incentive measures discussed in this paper seems to have had an extraordinary significance. Generally, the Japanese government tends to provide specific policies to cover specific needs, thereby making the scale of each measure small. This fact makes the evaluation of the total effect of all the measures difficult, particularly when the effects cannot be aggregated in a simple way. Partly because of this and partly because of the inadequacy of available data, it is difficult to reach a definite conclusion on the effect or the system of direct incentives given to export industries.

Still, an estimate of the effect of total export subsidies, including tax incentives, is attempted in column 5 of Table 32. Although such an estimate cannot accurately represent the true effect of the system, the system as a whole has had some significance, especially in the middle 1960s. However, the vigor of the private sector in the Japanese economy should not be neglected. The high rate of increase in exports is more probably the consequence of industrial development itself rather than the result of export subsidies. In this context, two industrial development strategies, namely the protection of domestic enterprises by restriction on both imports and capital inflow and the monetary policy favorable to export industries, deserve further analysis. These issues form the logical sequel to this study.

Notes

1/ This provision states that "contracting parties shall cease to grant either directly or indirectly any form of subsidy on the export of any product other than a primary product which subsidy results in the sales of such product for export at a price lower than the comparable price charged for the like product to buyers in the domestic market."

2/ Prior to the abolition, GATT adopted a "Declaration of Abolishment of Subsidy on the Export of Products Other than a Primary Product" and a declaration of maintenance of status quo on such subsidies. Japan signed the latter only in 1963, but the government decided to let the system expire as of March 31, 1964.

3/ Organization for Economic Cooperation and Development, *OECD Economic Surveys: Japan* (1969), p. 5.

4/ The other seven points are: (1) further removal of import quotas, (2) preferential tariffs for imports from developing countries, (3) additional general tariff reductions, (4) liberalization of capital movements, (5) reduction of nontariff barriers, (6) increased aid to developing countries, and (7) monetary and fiscal policies to stimulate the domestic economy. Points 2, 7, and parts of 1 and 4 were already carried out in 1971 and 1972.

5/ When plant or investment equipment is exported through a trading company, it is the manufacturer of the plant who is eligible for the 5 percent deduction of sales, even though the sale to the trading company is a domestic transaction.

6/ This system aimed at improvement of the invisible account that was a particularly weak point of Japan's balance of payments. Though it does not make much sense to attempt such a thing, a belief in its necessity was seriously held by the Japanese government.

7/ Two items are excluded from the definition of income: the rental income from real estate and revenue from the sales of real estate, bonds, and stocks. On the other hand, several kinds of deductible income must be included in the calculation of the total income.

8/ Leon Hollerman, *Japan's Dependence on the World Economy* (Princeton: Princeton University Press, 1967), pp. 191–192.

9/ One-fifth of this reserve must be returned to taxable income in the second year, another one-fifth in the third year, and so on until the sixth year. Because of this compulsory partial dissolution of the reserve, there was also a limit to the ratio of accumulated reserve relative to the revenue of the corporation, as long as the firm's revenue was either stable or increasing. For example, imagine that the revenue of a trading company is constant at ¥1 billion for several years. The amount of money that then remains in the reserve at the end of the first year is ¥5 million (applying 0.5 percent). It then declines by ¥1 million every succeeding year. Therefore, in the second year, ¥4 million plus ¥5 million are reserved since the company can again add ¥5 million to the reserve: in the third year, $3 + 4 + 5$. Thus, in the fifth and each succeeding year the company has ¥15 $(1 + 2 + 3 + 4 + 5)$ million. If revenue increases, this total will increase in absolute value but will decrease in value relative to the firm's total revenue after the sixth year.

10/ Price Waterhouse & Co., Clients' Circular No. 64/4 (Toyko, May 22, 1964).

11/ Hollerman sees in it an effect of encouragement of forming the authorized associations, which may make the control by MITI of small firms more effective. However, the history of such associations dates back to the prewar period.

12/ This revision was also in accord with the Eight-Point Program.

13/ The accumulated funds in the reserve were as follows (in million dollars):

1953	1954	1955	1956	1957	1958	1959	1960
0.3	1.1	1.7	5.8	11.7	13.6	15.0	24.4

14/ See R. A. Musgrave, *The Theory of Public Finance* (New York: McGraw-Hill, 1957), p. 337.

15/ Until 1960, corporate tax had a single statutory rate. Thereafter, the tax rate on dividends was set lower than that for the rest of corporate income. The weight of the former in the total corporate income was about 25 percent. Yet, because of the loss offset and numbers of special treatments, it does not make sense to calculate the weighted average of statutory rates. But the effective rate of national corporate tax calculated from national income statistics has been decreasing steadily from 39 percent in 1954 to 28 percent in 1968.

16/ For example, see Hendrik S. Houthakker and Stephen P. Magee, "Income and Price Elasticities in World Trade," *Review of Economics and Statistics.* Also, Japan. Economic Planning Agency, *Keizai Hakusho* [White paper on Japanese economy] (Tokyo, 1971), p. 244.

17/ According to unofficial comment by an officer in the government, only one-fifth to one-tenth of the figures in columns 1 and 3 can be considered as genuine subsidies.

18/ *Nihon Keizai Shimbun* [Japan economic journal] (Dec. 7, 1972).

19/ Ibid. (July 23, 1972).

8.

RAW-MATERIALS POLICY:
Japan and the United States

J. J. Kaplan

RAW-MATERIALS SUPPLIES have recently become the subject of topical concern in both the United States and Japan. In the United States, the Resource Recovery Act of 1970 established a National Commission on Materials Policy which reported its findings in the summer of 1973. It was the first such exercise since the 1952 report of the President's Materials Policy Commission, headed by William S. Paley. In Japan, a white paper on natural resources was issued by the Ministry of International Trade and Industry (MITI) while the U.S. commission was still at work. In the fall of 1973, an oil embargo was followed by steep price increases. In 1974, for the first time in many years, minerals and metals are in short supply, and prices have climbed in response.

Common Concerns

The concerns of Japan and the United States about raw materials have some common roots. Both countries have sustained their economic growth by importing increasing quantities of raw materials. Both foresee progressive growth in their need for such imports and wonder whether supplies will be available as needed or whether excessive prices may have to be paid in order to assure their delivery.

The most immediate concern is the flow of imported petroleum, which has been repeatedly disrupted over the past twenty years. The major producing countries have banded together in an Organization of the Petroleum Exporting Countries (OPEC) and since 1971 have successfully negotiated higher prices and other increased benefits. The 1973 embargo dramatized the possibilities for using control of exportable supplies of petroleum for political as well as economic ends. Production in some OPEC countries has been limited below the level desired by the producing companies and below market demand.

Doubts about raw-materials availability in general have been nurtured by the most recent wave of Neo-Malthusian prophesy of a prospective exhaustion of resources. Pessimists foresee a cataclysm as the rising demands of expanding populations impinge on the earth's finite supply of resources. The rate of increase in the demand for materials has indeed been unusually high during the 1950s and 1960s, with Japan in the forefront. Rapid rates of growth could persist in the case of the developing countries, as they proceed with the modernization of their societies. Moreover, the United States is beginning, for the first time, to enter the world market as a buyer of large quantities of the major minerals. Normal plans for expanding production of energy and other materials in the United States have been thwarted by widespread public concern about the environment. Eventually, environmental regulations should become stabilized, and procedures should be firmly established permitting orderly resumption of investment in expanding domestic output. However, in the meantime, the United States may have to look to production in other countries for more of its requirements than has previously been the case. Unforeseen increases in U.S. import demand would compete for supplies with other importing countries, among which Japan is most prominent.

Increasing demands for exportable supplies appear to coincide with a possible retardation in the growth of production. The traditional system of developing exportable quantities of minerals through foreign private investment confronts national demands for ownership and control of the use of domestic natural resources, for increased domestic processing and for larger payments to host governments. While such problems are negotiated and new arrangements are developed, production in the developing countries may not expand as rapidly as world demand.

Resource Histories

Although these problems are common to both Japan and the United States, the two countries have very different resource histories, accounting for some divergence in the way they approach the issues.

Reliance on imported materials. Economic development in the United States took off from a rich materials base and a high ratio of readily available resources to population. Basic materials such as coal and iron ore, petroleum, and copper were abundant and could be exported at competitive prices, despite relatively high U.S. labor costs. Only as the richer deposits were depleted did the United States begin to import significant quantities of basic minerals and then only because imports were cheaper than was the cost of exploiting lower-grade domestic deposits. To be sure, the United States has long imported virtually all its consumption of certain materials used in smaller quantities —chrome and magnesium, tin and rubber. Only in times of national emergency has dependence on such imports proved difficult, and even then, it has not been crucial. The cost of these imports has not been a significant factor in determining the general price level of U.S. industrial output or foreign-exchange requirements.

Japan, on the other hand, began its industrialization with a densely populated land area and minimal supplies of basic minerals and fossil fuels. It has been completely dependent on imports, not only for the same materials that the United States obtained primarily from foreign sources but also for those that the United States produced at home. In 1970, 36.6 percent of all Japanese imports consisted of mineral fuels and metallic raw materials; the comparable figure for the United States was 10.5 percent.

The extent to which the two countries used imports to meet their needs for some basic materials in 1950 and in 1970 is shown in Table 39. The Japanese economy was, of course, operating at a very low level in 1950, and foreign-exchange limitations forced resort to domestic supplies of materials, wherever possible. As the economy expanded, needs for materials had to be met almost completely from foreign sources. By 1970, Japan was importing 50 to 100 percent of its consumption of every basic mineral and fossil fuel. The lowest percentage applied to coal, but it understates dependence on foreign sources be-

TABLE 39. Dependence on Imported Resources,
Japan, and the United States, 1950 and 1970,
by volume of imports (percent of apparent consumption)

	1950		1970	
	Japan	United States	Japan	United States
Iron ore	62	9	99	36
Aluminum (bauxite)	100	63	100	88
Copper, ore and concentrates	20	2	73	1
Zinc, ore and concentrates	8	28	64	47
Coal	2	—	56	—
Petroleum, crude	82	8	100	16
Natural gas	—	—	35	4

Sources: U.S. National Commission on Materials Policy, *Toward a National Materials Policy, World Perspective: Second Interim Report* (Washington, D.C.: U.S. Government Printing Office, January 1973).

Percent of natural gas imported by Japan in 1970: Ministry of International Trade and Industry, *Shigen Hakusho* [White paper on natural resources] (Tokyo, 1972).

cause about 80 percent of Japanese needs for coking coal were met by imports.

For the same list of basic materials, U.S. dependence on imports was very much less in every instance. Moreover, a 50 percent price rise would probably have elicited a large increase in U.S. domestic production within a relatively brief period of years. Japanese industry had no such alternatives. Much higher prices would have meant a correspondingly larger bill for imported materials.

Role of materials in economic growth. The Japanese economy of 1950 was operating at a low level of per capita production and at a fraction of its potential; the United States was already relatively affluent and fully employed. In the interim, Japan has maintained an exceptionally high rate of economic growth, based on a particularly rapid expansion of its manufacturing industry. Economic expansion in

TABLE 40. Intensity of Use of Major Materials,
United States and Japan (metric tons per billion dollars GDP)

	Japan		United States	
	1951–1955	1966–1969	1951–1955	1966–1969
Crude steel (1,000 tons)	129	266	157	136
Iron ore (1,000 tons)	54	217	102	76
Refined copper	2,020	3,500	2,240	1,920
Primary aluminum	830	3,120	2,090	3,480
Zinc	1,790	2,650	1,480	1,230
Fluorspar	480	2,220	890	1,140
Total energy (1,000 tons)	1,600	1,290	2,160	2,070

Source: Wilfred Malenbaum, "Materials Requirements in the U.S. and Abroad in the Year 2000" (March 1973).

the United States has proceeded at a slower pace and has placed more emphasis on meeting rising consumer demands for services.

Thus, U.S. gross domestic product (GDP) at constant prices in the late 1960s is estimated at 77 percent above its average level in 1951–1955; the comparable estimate for Japan is 500 percent.[1] Between 1960 and 1970, Japanese gross national product (GNP) in real terms grew at an average annual rate of 11 percent, compared to 4 percent in the United States.[2] Between 1960 and 1970, Japanese industrial production increased 270 percent; U.S. industrial production increased 54 percent.[3] Nevertheless, in 1971 U.S. per capita GNP was twice that of Japan.

Such different rates of increase in production, starting from very divergent bases, have led to significant variation in the importance of materials supplies. The white paper by MITI estimated that in 1969 Japan used $76 worth of major minerals to produce $1,000 worth of GNP while the United States used only $41 worth of the same minerals. An analysis of materials demand in the United States and abroad, prepared for the National Commission on Materials Policy by Wilfred Malenbaum of the University of Pennsylvania, shows the role of major materials in the economic output of the two countries, both in the early 1950s and the late 1960s (see Table 40).

In the United States, energy demand per unit of output fell slightly over the two decades, as technological advances offset a huge increase in the use of energy by final consumers for personal transportation and household purposes. Japan experienced a much sharper decline in its use of energy per unit of output. It benefited more from increased efficiency in industrial consumption because growth in consumer uses of energy was much more restricted.

With the exception of aluminum and fluorspar, U.S. consumption per dollar of output declined for every mineral. For all the metals, the Japanese increase in intensity of use is very striking; more metals were used per unit of output at a time when output itself was expanding at an unusually high annual rate. Japanese economic growth in the 1950s and 1960s was heavily concentrated in metal-using industries. Despite technological advances that raised the efficiency with which Japanese industry converted metals into final products, the nature of Japanese economic growth required much larger quantities of metals per unit of output.

The U.S. economy was expanding at a much slower rate. Moreover, the composition of its output placed decreasing emphasis on metal-using products. Fixed investments require large quantities of materials; whereas services make very modest demands on resources per dollar of expenditure. In 1970, gross private fixed capital formation in Japan was equal to more than 30 percent of GDP. For the United States, such expenditures equaled 13.5 percent of output. Accordingly, the availability of a rapidly expanding supply of imported materials at reasonable prices was much more critical to the Japanese than to the U.S. economy.

Control of foreign supplies. In the 1950s and 1960s, Japanese supplies had to be purchased currently and paid for on the open market. Neither the government nor industry could turn to Japanese investments in foreign materials-producing enterprises nor to special relations with the governments of materials-producing countries to assure an orderly flow of imports. Only in the latter part of the 1960s did the Japanese balance-of-payments position strengthen sufficiently to permit large-scale capital exports. Before that, foreign credits were needed even to finance current imports.

The United States, on the other hand, was the principal source of capital for financing the large expansion in materials production that took place in third countries. Between 1957 and 1970, net new U.S. direct foreign investment in petroleum, mining, and smelting totaled $19.1 billion, of which some $14 billion was invested in countries that exported the larger part of their output. During this period, the average annual rate of increase in production of aluminum and petroleum outside the United States was almost 11 percent. Iron production increased by almost 9 percent a year; zinc and copper production, by almost 6 percent. For the most part, such increased production of minerals was marketed in Western Europe and Japan.

Prospective Requirements

Neither Japan nor the United States to date has had its economic growth hampered either by a shortage of materials supplies or by the prices that had to be paid for such supplies. In both countries, there is considerable speculation that this condition may not persist into the indefinite future.

To some extent, the speculation is based on projections that assume a continuation of recent trends into the medium- or long-term future (five to thirty years ahead). Some studies assume that requirements will continue to grow exponentially, some linearly, at recent rates. The Malenbaum study is particularly valuable in demonstrating that such trends have never persisted for long periods of time and in explaining why they are unlikely to do so. The available historical data indicate that the world as a whole has never experienced average economic growth at the rate of 3 percent per year for a thirty-year period. Indeed, in only a few thirty-year periods has any major subdivision of the world expanded its total product by as much as 3.8 percent per year. The study assumes that gross domestic output in the world as a whole will increase at this latter rate between 1970 and 2000, with the United States expanding slightly below the world average. Japanese economic growth is projected at 5 percent—high relative to general historical experience and to that projected for the rest of the world, but half that experienced over the past decade.

Whereas developing countries are projected to increase their use of materials per unit of output, both Japan and the United States would decrease theirs, at least for the traditional basic metals. The projections are based on the probable evolution of the two economies from their present position and on the historical experience of expanding economies. In the year 2000, use of metals per unit of output would be higher in Japan than in the United States during the late 1960s and much higher that that projected for the United States (see Table 41). Japanese energy consumption would increase as household uses expand, but Japanese requirements per unit of output would remain below the U.S. level. The two countries would account for a smaller, but nonetheless large, proportion of total world requirements for materials—a third or more in the case of each of the materials listed in Table 41.

Carefully researched projections such as the Malenbaum study incorporate a sophisticated reading of the human and technological forces that have shaped economic growth in the past and are likely to be operative in the future. Nevertheless, long-term economic projections should be treated, not as precise forecasts, but rather as indicators of what may evolve under stated conditions. They are necessarily based on assumptions about changing tastes and technology that have an element of the heroic. Nevertheless, signs are already appearing that point to a slackening rate of growth in GDP and in consumption of materials per unit of GDP.

Japan has already begun to experience the stresses implicit in sustaining exceedingly high rates of economic expansion. Prime Minister Tanaka's program *A Proposal for Remodeling the Japanese Archipelago* calls for diverting Japanese industrial potential away from goods for export and toward the domestic supply of public goods. He proposes relocation of industry in rural areas, the building of new towns, an improved transportation network, more emphasis on housing and leisure activities, better facilities for waste disposal, and pollution abatement. His emphases are comparable to current U.S. discussions about improving the quality of life. As a result, Japanese economists predict that economic growth in the 1970s will occur at the rate of 9 percent, slowing to 6 percent in the 1980s. As this occurs, requirements for materials will also grow more slowly than during the 1950s and 1960s. The kind of economic growth foreseen by Tanaka will require less materials and more services per unit output than did the heavy-industry, export-oriented production growth of the past.

TABLE 41. Materials Requirements in the Year 2000

	Intensity of Use[a]		Total Requirements (thousand tons)		
	United States	Japan	United States	Japan	World
Crude steel	85	190	266,000	203,000	1,552,000
Iron ore	45	150	141,000	161,000	1,086,000
Refined copper	1,400	2,800	4,389	2,996	19,693
Primary aluminum	5,000	6,000	15,657	6,420	46,761
Zinc	900	1,725	2,822	1,846	13,448
Fluorspar	1,300	2,500	4,076	2,675	15,870
Total energy	1,875	1,500	5,878,000[b]	1,605,000[b]	21,040,000[b]
Solid fuel			1,058,000	161,000	6,518,000
Liquid fuel			2,116,000[b]	1,172,000[b]	8,498,000[b]

[a]For definition of concept and unit of measurement as well as historical data, see Table 39.
[b]In coal equivalents.
Source: Wilfred Malenbaum, "Materials Requirements in the U.S. and Abroad in the Year 2000" (March 1973).

Prospective Supply

Despite slower rates of growth in demand for materials, both Japan and the United States will require larger absolute quantities than they have been using. The long-range projections would require a considerable expansion in production outside the United States if the needs of the rest of the world, including Japanese and U.S. import demand, are to be satisfied at the end of the century. They imply a quadrupling of aluminum production, a tripling of iron and petroleum supplies, and a 250 percent increase in zinc output. Nevertheless, the average annual rate of increase would only be 3 to 5 percent, rather than the 6 to 11 percent experienced between 1950 and 1970.

There is no particular reason to believe that physical factors will impede the satisfaction of such demands. Despite a very high rate of growth in production, known world reserves of most minerals were larger in 1970 than in 1950. Moreover, the reserve figures relate to *current* prices and *current* technology and take little account of areas whose resources have yet to be explored and developed. These areas include the seabeds (which have known deposits of renewable manganese nodules), the outer continental shelves, and the upper slopes of the international seabed, as well as some major inland seas. To date, exploitation of the earth's crust has been confined essentially to the temperate zones and certain adjacent arid areas. Geologic mapping and preliminary surveys of the developing countries and of the less accessible regions of many developed countries are still in their early stages.

Attention has been focused particularly on the potential exhaustion of known resources of the fossil fuels. Twelve countries now produce about 90 percent of the world's petroleum, with the United States accounting for almost 20 percent. Four of the others—Libya, Nigeria, the Trucial states, and Indonesia—have become important sources of supply only in very recent years. Exploration is increasingly concentrated in new areas and on the continental shelves. The North Sea and the Arctic zones of Canada and of the United States will almost certainly become important in the 1980s as will the continental shelves. Better use of coal resources can also help to moderate any shortages of liquid and gaseous fuels that may be experienced over the next decade. For the longer run, nuclear, geothermal, and solar energy should help meet requirements.

The compelling question is not whether the resources exist but whether they will be exploited and become available. Four major sets of problems must be addressed.

Problems of environmental safeguards. Environmental in-interests must be satisfied, particularly in the United States, if the production of minerals and energy products within the country and on its continental shelves is to expand. Without such expansion, U.S. demands on exportable supplies of materials from third countries could impinge on Japanese requirements. Because its output is likely to remain relatively small, Japan's internal environmental interests lie more in the transportation and utilization of materials than in their production.

Technological problems. Substantial research-and-development efforts and expenditures are needed, to an extent that may well exceed the capabilities of the private sector. Some of the problems to be resolved relate to the disposal of mineral waste, the restoration of mining land, and the use of nuclear energy. Others concern recycling and the use of less concentrated mineral deposits. Coal gasification, safe overseas transportation of petroleum and natural gas, and more efficient processes for using minerals and energy products to satisfy industrial and consumer wants add to the list. Finally, increased research-and-development attention is required to the pollutant problems associated with the consumption of coal, petroleum, and other minerals in highly congested population centers.

Interaction between foreign-owned enterprises and local economies. The third set of problems relate to arranging for the necessary flow of capital and expertise to the less developed areas under conditions that satisfy their sense of sovereignty and their economic aspirations. The traditional wholly owned private foreign investment, operated essentially as an enclave enterprise, appears to be increasingly unsatisfactory to the governments of the areas containing large exportable resources.

Fluctuations in world supplies. Finally, the possibility exists that, for more or less limited periods, world supplies of one or another material may be inadequate to meet Japanese and U.S. demands for imports. The reasons may vary from an absence of sufficient production in supplying countries to unexpectedly large demands from other areas or the withholding of supplies for political or economic reasons.

Collaboration on Policy Issues

The preceding enumeration of current and prospective problems affecting the availability of adequate supplies of raw materials illustrates the interdependence of the two societies and their common interdependence with the rest of the world. U.S. environmental policies could sharply increase demand for imported raw materials, requiring competition for supplies that might otherwise be directed to Japan. The direction that Japan chooses for its future economic expansion could sharply reduce the rate of growth in its demand for imported materials. The possibility of concluding satisfactory arrangements for expanding materials production in third countries will affect the need for both countries to expedite the development of substitute materials and processes. The list of such interrelated policies is very long.

But if the fact of interdependence is strikingly evident, the correct path toward constructive collaboration remains uncertain. Among the possibilities are bilateral discussions and joint ventures, coordination of policies in multilateral bodies organized on a global scale or on a more selective basis, and operations through multinational institutions. All appear to have a role to play in dealing with one or another problem. Effective approaches to problem solving appear to vary from one situation to another. Each raw material appears to have its own set of problems, as does each exporting and importing country. Acceptability may be a more important criterion than logical or evidential merit in seeking solutions to problems. Accordingly, it is advisable to identify areas in which collaboration may be mutually beneficial and to suggest possible avenues that might be explored by both countries.

An intergovernmental raw-materials study group. The more worrisome raw-materials supply problems are prospective. A first logical step, therefore, would be to develop a common view of the outlook for the demand and supply of each major industrial material. Such an exercise would probably be more effective if conducted by a group in which both Japan and the United States are effectively represented. The Organization for Economic Cooperation and Development (OECD) has become a useful forum for collecting and analyzing data and exchanging views about policies and problems. It might be asked to perform this function for raw materials, building on the precedent of its Oil Committee. Although most OECD members are primarily importers of raw materials, a number are major exporting countries. Other exporting countries should be invited to participate.

The proposed raw-materials study group could organize subgroups for each major raw material. Each would be charged with collecting data on past and prospective supply and demand. Careful statistical analysis would provide a solid foundation for a forum in which information and views on current and prospective problems could be freely exchanged.

Coordinated industrial-materials policies. The proposed study group might further be charged with the coordination of industrial-materials policies, much as the Development Assistance Committee (DAC) has become a forum for coordinating policies with respect to assisting developing nations. Other OECD countries have come to share Japanese and U.S. concerns about the availability of supplies of raw materials. They are introducing new programs to encourage both domestic production and the efforts of their industries to develop and acquire foreign supplies.

The United States has long financed the export of raw materials on favorable terms through its Export-Import Bank. The bank has also financed the export of equipment to other countries, including equipment for use in materials-producing enterprises. The United States has further supported materials production abroad through its foreign-aid programs and its investment-insurance schemes. Various tax incentives have encouraged U.S. companies to accept the risks associated with the exploration and development of mineral production at home and abroad.

As its balance-of-payments position strengthened and the need for imported materials grew, Japan took comparable steps. Its Export-Import Bank has financed both materials imports and overseas investment in developing raw-materials resources. Its Overseas Economic Corporation Fund makes loans to Japanese firms for resource development. The Japan Petroleum Development Corporation supplies risk capital to firms engaged in oil and natural-gas projects abroad and on the Japanese continental shelf. The Metallic Minerals Exploration Agency subsidizes geologic surveys and extends or guarantees loans for developing nonferrous minerals at home and abroad. Tax benefits are used to share with private firms the investment risk associated with overseas investment in raw-materials industries.

Other OECD countries have had similar policies, and new programs appear to be under consideration or in the early stages of implementation. Policies to protect the environment while encouraging minerals production are an issue in almost every country. As in the case of DAC, a continuing and systematic exchange of experience and views about the effectiveness of all these policies should be mutually beneficial.

International agreements to facilitate expanded production. Expanding production in third countries to meet prospective Japanese and U.S. demand for imported materials is largely a matter of an adequate flow of capital and expertise to explore and develop resources and market the resulting production. Nationalism and political instability have heightened the risks associated with such investment and are discouraging the efforts of private investors.

Effective international agreements are needed to define the rights and the responsibilities of foreign investors and to provide for compulsory arbitration of disputes. Such agreements could be helpful with respect to long-term purchase and service contracts, as well as in the case of direct equity investments or loans. International insurance or guarantees of such investments, including appropriate sharing of the risks among the governments of both the investors and the host country, could further reduce risks and facilitate production.

Many years of effort in OECD and the World Bank have produced conventions on these matters, but they have yet to receive widespread adoption or implementation. The preparations for the Law of the Sea Conference suggest that a similar fate may await proposals for international agreement on the exploitation of the international seabed and the outer continental margins.

It might prove fruitful for Japan and the United States to coordinate their views on these matters, both to expedite international agreement where possible and to seek broader adherence to those agreements that have already been reached. Until such efforts reach fruition, unilateral and bilateral approaches to the specific problems are bound to continue and will probably proliferate. They might be more effective if Japan and the United States could coordinate their own interim arrangements for expanding foreign materials production—whether bilaterally or together with other major importing countries. Such arrangements should be compatible with the multilateral provisions that must eventually order a stable international system of investment, production, and trade.

Better use of the multilateral institutions. The various multilateral institutions—the United Nations, specialized agencies of the World Bank, and the regional banks—have all sought to facilitate the expansion of materials production in developing areas. However, their roles have been poorly defined and might be reexamined in the light of renewed concern about supply shortages. For example, the U.N. Development Programme has long financed pre-investment surveys, with particular attention to mineral resources; the World Bank and its affiliates have financed a considerable number of minerals projects. Both institutions might be asked to consider whether in the future greater priority should be given to such uses of their funds.

The multilateral financial institutions may be in a position to assist further by facilitating relations between international investors and marketers and their host countries.[4] Dr. Lincoln Gordon has suggested three possibilities: (1) By promoting explicit appraisal of the size and the allocation of the benefits, they can assure that each party receives some share of the total benefits; (2) they can provide technical assistance to less sophisticated governments to help equalize bargaining skills; and (3) they can provide a neutral third-party judgment on the fairness of the terms, especially where they are themselves directly involved in part of the financing. Perhaps major materials-importing countries, including Japan and the United States, should suggest that the multilateral institutions reexamine their role in encouraging expanded materials production.

Joint approach to the energy problem. The most immediate policy issue is the energy crisis. It was producing localized physical shortages in the United States even before the 1973 oil embargo. In Japan, the dramatic increase in energy costs has undermined efforts to control an inflationary surge in the price level and is threatening the international competitiveness of Japanese industry. Japan and Western Europe face significantly higher real costs of energy-producing materials that will be further exacerbated if government policies in the United States and other major consuming countries fail to encourage both conservation and increased domestic production of energy. Through a combination of such policy measures, U.S. requirements for imported energy need not long account for a large percentage of total demand.

More use of nuclear power with appropriate safeguards, together with conservation measures, can limit the growth of Japan's need for imported petroleum. However, neither Japan nor Western Europe has possibilities comparable to those of the United States for containing demand for imported petroleum without significant damage to domestic prosperity and welfare.

All the major importing countries would benefit from more cooperative arrangements with the OPEC countries, but a common approach has yet to be developed. Fears of confrontation and exaggerated response from the OPEC countries have been joined to hopes of concluding advantageous bilateral arrangements. The result has been a fragmented response to the coordinated policies of the major petroleum-exporting countries. Coordination among the consuming countries and between the consuming and producing groups nevertheless appears to be both essential and inevitable. In the long run, both producing and consuming countries should gain more from a joint approach to an orderly program for dealing with both demand and supply problems than from crisis-induced efforts to organize privileged supply circuits.

The producing countries should benefit from coordinated offers of assistance by the major consumers—directly or indirectly through multilateral institutions—with programming and implementing their economic and social development. Such assistance is well within the capacities of the industrialized countries, but its benefits may be less and the likelihood of future tensions may be greater if provided on a bilateral basis. The major consumers may also find it advantageous to offer special incentives to those petroleum-producing countries with small populations who may, for a more or less extended period of time, find themselves with more foreign exchange than they can spend effectively. Some of these countries have begun to wonder whether their petroleum reserves may be more valuable in the ground than exploited for foreign currencies. The prices that prevailed in the first half of 1974 may not be sustainable as higher prices lead to increased production and a slower rate of growth in demand. In any event, petroleum prices in exporting countries should not be expected to increase by more than 5 percent a year over the next decade or two. It should be possible to provide the producing countries with reasonably secure, exchange risk-proof investments for their oil revenues that would offer considerably higher rates of return than 5 percent per annum.

To protect themselves against any possible supply shortages, Japan and the United States might well concert efforts to develop alternatives—substitute fuels, more efficient processes for using energy in industry and transportation, and better means of minimizing pollution in large urban concentrations—while economizing on the consumption of energy materials. Should serious shortages threaten, perhaps they should develop standby arrangements for allocating available supplies among importing countries and for rationing internal uses.

Notes

1/ Wilfred Malenbaum, "Materials Requirements in the U.S. and Abroad in the Year 2000" (March 1973).

2/ International Monetary Fund, *Annual Report* (Washington, D.C., 1972).

3/ Organization for Economic Cooperation and Development, *Main Economic Indicators* (various issues).

4/ See Lincoln Gordon, "Multinational Corporations and the Less Developed Countries," paper delivered before Dusseldorf Conference on the International Control of Investment (January 1973).

9.

JAPANESE FOREIGN DIRECT INVESTMENT

M. Y. Yoshino

ONE OF THE MOST SIGNIFICANT RECENT DEVELOPMENTS in the Japanese business scene is the rapid rise of foreign direct investment. Japan has achieved her present eminence in the world market through exporting. In the last several years, however, in response to a variety of domestic and international pressures, Japanese corporations have begun to expand their foreign direct investment. Although this development is still in its infancy, given Japan's relative strength in the world economy and her still-growing economic potentials, Japan's emergence in this field is likely to add a new dimension to the world economy.

An Overview

This chapter will examine the overview of Japanese private foreign direct investment, its salient features and the prospect. In 1971, the cumulative total of Japanese foreign direct investment reached the $3.6 billion level with a total of 3,935 different projects in 104 nations. In international perspective, this involvement is still rather small. It is only a fraction of the total U.S. investment, which for the same year was at the level of $78 billion. Japan's total investment is less than 50

TABLE 42. Growth of Japanese Foreign Direct Investment, 1951 to 1970

Year	Number of Projects	Cumulative Amount (thousands of dollars)	Percent of Total Projects	Percent of Total Cumulative Amount
1951–1958	445	143,912	11.3	4.0
1959	123	53,062	3.1	1.5
1960	151	92,729	3.8	2.6
1961	133	164,811	3.4	4.6
1962	179	99,425	4.5	2.8
1963	223	125,977	5.7	3.5
1964	193	120,291	4.9	3.3
1965	209	156,739	5.3	4.4
1966	253	227,008	6.4	6.3
1967	306	274,867	7.8	7.6
1968	384	557,174	9.8	15.5
1969	568	667,579	14.4	18.6
1970	768	913,449	19.5	25.4
Total	3,935	3,597,023	100.0	100.0

Source: Japan. Ministry of International Trade and Industry.

percent of the U.S. investment in West Germany. In the postwar period, Japanese foreign investment began in 1951, but not until 1966 did the cumulative total exceed the $200 million mark. Since then, as shown in Table 42, it has been growing at an exponential rate. Between 1967 and 1968 the investment doubled, and between 1968 and 1970 it almost doubled again. Roughly 60 percent of the total investment has taken place since 1967.

Looking at breakdowns by industries, nearly 31 percent of the total investment has gone to the extractive industries, 27 percent to the manufacturing sector, 10 percent to commercial activities, 9 percent to the financial sector, and 18 percent to miscellaneous activities. Geographically, the Japanese investment is widely distributed. It is interesting to note the fact that, at least in aggregate terms, Japanese investment is greatest in North America, accounting for 25 percent. Asia, Europe, and Latin America claim 22 percent, 18 percent, and 16 percent respectively; the remainder is scattered among the Middle East, Oceania, and Africa. The details are presented in Table 43. Much of the investment in North America has been in the commercial sector; the investment in Latin America largely consists of manufacturing activities supplemented by the extractive industries, whereas investments in Oceania and the Middle East are mainly in the extractive field.

A notable feature of the Japanese foreign direct investment is that nearly half is found in developing countries. This trend is particularly evident in the manufacturing sector, where over 70 percent is in developing countries, presenting a striking contrast to the American pattern.

The average size of an investment is rather small. There are only fifty projects with more than $1 million of investment, and furthermore these fifty projects, which constitute only 11 percent of the total number, account for nearly 90 percent of the total amount invested, indicating that the remaining 90 percent of the projects are indeed of limited size. Of the fifty projects, roughly half are found in resource development, and the majority of the remaining are in the commercial sector.

Postwar Japanese investment has gone through four rather distinctive stages of development. The initial stage, covering between 1951 and 1955, is characterized by small, sporadic investments in the development of mineral resources, particularly copper. This period also witnessed the reestablishing of branches of trading companies in a few key markets in the world. In the second stage, covering the period roughly from 1955 to 1959, a number of investments were made in the manufacturing sector in Latin America. Most notable was the establishment of several textile plants. In the third stage, covering 1960 through 1967, Southeast Asia—notably Thailand—attracted many small investments of the import-substitution type, but during this period, due to a serious deterioration in the political and economic climate there, investment in Latin America showed a definite sign of decline. Finally, there is the fourth stage, from the late 1960s to the present, when investment in offshore production facilities began to appear. Taiwan, Hong Kong, and South Korea have been the major localities for this type of invest-

TABLE 43. Cumulative Japanese Private Foreign Direct Investment, by Industry and Area, (thousands of dollars)

	Manufacturing	Mining	Agriculture	Fishery	Construction	Commerce	Finance and Insurance	Branches	Other
North America	249,345	17,750	4,146	2,105	6,595	293,434	116,173	7,937	70,643
Latin America	273,542	87,463	7,600	7,834	26,706	17,363	71,501	1,369	65,297
Asia	334,439	268,532	40,599	11,240	4,146	18,233	68,892	16,948	16,572
Europe	36,597	6,366	448	115	69	28,822	60,731	5,997	498,796
Middle East	4,257	328,088	—	143	—	579	934	111	—
Africa	24,831	58,614	—	1,380	—	671	296	358	6,149
Oceania	49,690	200,134	4,900	4,398	—	11,487	8,383	123	925
Total	972,701	966,947	57,693	27,215	37,516	370,589	326,910	32,843	658,382
Percent of total	26.80	31.3	2.4	0.8	1.1	10.3	9.0	0.9	18.3

Source: Japan. Ministry of International Trade and Industry.

ment. As for market-oriented investment, the focus has shifted to Malaysia, Singapore, Indonesia, and Brazil. During this phase, there have emerged a few sporadic manufacturing investments in advanced countries. This period is also characterized by a significant growth in investments on a large scale, at least by the past Japanese standard, in the resource industries.

Investment in Resource Industries: Japan's Need for Critical Raw Materials

Japan is sometimes referred to as a "museum of minerals"; the country is richly endowed with almost every variety of mineral, but usually in quantities only sufficient for museum displays. The postwar economic growth and the resulting changes in the industrial structure have led to a rapid growth in Japan's need for critical raw materials. As indicated in Table 44, the consumption of every critical raw material has increased at a rate surpassing the growth of the nation's gross national product. Between 1960 and 1970, Japan's dependence on foreign sources for iron ores increased from 68 to 88 percent, for copper from 51 to 76 percent, and for coking coal from 36 to 70 percent. For petroleum, aluminum, and uranium, Japan is completely dependent on foreign sources.

Moreover, the Japanese resource industries have followed a lopsided growth during the past two decades to cope with ever-increasing demands for processed materials; they have concentrated on expansion of processing capacities—refining and smelting—and have largely neglected the development of the resource bases. The petroleum industry, for example, now boasts the second largest refining capacity in the noncommunist world, with only very limited control over the upstream operations. Even in the hard minerals where the Japanese firms once had substantial mining interests, the postwar growth has been predominantly in the processing sector.

Need for a new strategy. Until recently, Japan had experienced little difficulty in procuring the needed natural resources from abroad, and much of her purchasing had been on the open market, occasionally supplemented by long-term purchase contracts. Such a pro-

TABLE 44. Growth of Japanese Consumption
of Key Raw Materials, 1960 to 1970

Raw Material	1960	1970	Average Annual Growth Rate
Copper (1,000 tons)	320.0	833.0	10.0
Lead (1,000 tons)	108.0	213.0	7.0
Zinc (1,000 tons)	199.0	634.0	12.3
Nickel	19.0	90.0	17.0
Aluminum	155.0	880.0	19.0
Iron ore (million tons)	21.1	111.0	18.0
Coking coal (million tons)	17.5	59.3	13.0
Petroleum (million kiloliters)	29.5	185.5	20.4

Source: Japan. Ministry of International Trade and Industry.

curement method has offered a number of advantages. It is flexible. As long as the quantity demanded is fairly limited, the level of procurement can be readily adjusted to the current need. Most importantly, the risk and high capital requirements that are invariably associated with extractive activities are assumed by another party. Freed from such a burden, the Japanese resource industries have been able to concentrate their limited capital on the expansion of their refining or smelting capacities to meet the ever-growing demand for processed materials. Such a strategy had worked well while the Japanese consumption of the key materials had been still on a modest scale. But the advantages of this policy began to erode gradually in the 1960s when Japanese demand for raw materials skyrocketed and the quantities required grew to account for a significant share of the world consumption. In the face of these developments, the Japanese resource industries have begun to perceive growing threats to their ability to procure raw materials in sufficient quantities at acceptable terms. This concern was reinforced by the fact that during the past decade in most of the raw-material fields there has been characteristically a seller's market and, with a rapid increase in demand, Japanese firms had to seek out needed raw materials aggressively, which placed them in a weak bargaining position.

The industry's potential vulnerability through exclusive dependence on foreign-controlled sources is heightened by the very structure of the world resource industries. The nature of natural resources is such that the supply is highly inelastic and will not respond readily to rapid increases in demand. Moreover, the production of almost all vital natural resources is controlled by a small number of major international firms, and this fact intensifies the danger of reliance on foreign-controlled sources.

These industries are also subject to volatility in the level of production. Long and serious labor disputes have repeatedly occurred, resulting in unexpected and forced reduction in output. Another threat to stability lies in the increasing tensions between the major international corporations and the host countries, growing out of their long and not always satisfactory relationship. Disturbances engendered by these tensions have often led to sharp curtailment of production and the resulting decline in their ability to supply the Japanese need. Even with long-term contracts, it is difficult, if not impossible, to fulfill contractual obligations in the face of these problems. For example, in 1966 the Japanese copper industry was forced to reduce the amount specified in a long-term contract by 10 percent. In some months, the supply was reduced to a half. Such unpredictable reduction in the supply of critical raw materials has happened with sufficient frequency to cause a real concern.

Moreover, as long as the Japanese resource industries confine their activities to processing operations, their performance is, in large measure, subject to forces outside their control. The price of ores undergoes volatile fluctuation, and since this price is the single most important determinant of their profitability, smelting firms are at the mercy of forces beyond their control. Moreover, in natural-resource industries, extractive activities are far more profitable than the processing operations. Thus, there is a real incentive for the firms engaged in downstream processing to achieve upstream integration.

Japanese processive industries have from time to time attempted to gain a degree of stability by financing development of certain mineral resources through extending long-term loans to foreign mining interests, thus binding them to supply certain quantities of minerals at a predetermined schedule as repayment of loans. This practice has been used in the purchase of copper, iron ores, and coking coal. It does reduce some instability, gives the Japanese companies the first claim over the output, and also affords some protection over the price, but the control is far from complete. Moreover, this method does not enable the processors to participate in the profit associated with upstream operations.

Implementation of the new strategy. Against this background, in the late 1960s the Japanese resource industries began their concerted efforts to expand investment in exploitation and development of natural resources overseas. The motives for Japanese investment in this area have been defensive: first, to attain a degree of stability and security in the procurement of raw materials for domestic consumption by reducing their dependence on foreign-controlled sources, and to improve the industry's bargaining position vis-à-vis the major international corporations; and second, recognizing the disadvantages of having become primarily processors in the course of rapid postwar economic growth, they wanted to gain partial access to the profit associated with upstream operations. Thus, during the past decade the risk preference of Japanese resource industries regarding the methods of procurement has undergone a perceptible change.

Procurement of natural resources in the open market, occasionally supplemented by long-term contracts, and once considered the only feasible method for Japan, began to threaten the security of the Japanese resource industries, as Japan emerged as a major consumer of these materials. In order to seek greater security, the Japanese resource industries have begun to diversify their procurement methods by undertaking their own investments. Such an alternative has become feasible and practical with the growing capabilities of the Japanese economy, which, among other things, has resulted in liberalization of the government's restrictions on capital investments by Japanese firms. To reduce the risk of instability resulting from the almost exclusive reliance on one method of resources procurement, the Japanese economy and the resource industries in particular have become willing and capable of assuming the risks that are associated with exploration and development of natural resources.

The investment in the extractive industries in 1971 reached ¥346 billion, approximately $1.1 billion, accounting for nearly one-third of the total investment. Significantly, the investment made in 1970 was almost a third of the cumulative investment up to that point; the increment in 1971 reached roughly ¥550 million, which was more than a half of the cumulative investment made through 1970, indicating the rapid rate of growth in very recent years.

We shall briefly examine the patterns that are now evolving in two critical industries—petroleum and copper—which together account for 85 percent of the total investment in the extractive industries.

The case of petroleum. Let us first examine the investment in petroleum. The importance of petroleum to the Japanese economy needs no elaboration except to note that 70 percent of the nation's primary energy now comes from petroleum. Most critical for our present consideration is the fact that for this vital resource Japan must rely entirely on foreign sources and, moreover, only about 8 percent of crude-oil imports come from sources under Japanese control. Further complicating the situation is the fact that it is the only major industry in Japan over which international corporations exercise a significant degree of control. Despite the Japanese government's persistent efforts to strengthen the 100 percent Japanese-owned refineries, over a half of the refining capacities within Japan are under the control of foreign interests which are obligated to purchase virtually all of their crude requirements from their affiliates. Moreover, a number of wholly Japanese-owned refineries have entered into long-term contractual obligations to buy crude supplies from the majors in return for receiving loans to help finance their expansions and to gain access to advanced refining technology. Thus, at present, a half-dozen international petroleum firms control 70 percent of the crude supplies to Japan.

The first Japanese effort to develop petroleum sources overseas began in the late 1950s when Taro Yamashita, an entrepreneur with considerable influence in the political circles as well as in the business community, successfully obtained a concession from the governments of Saudi Arabia and Kuwait for the right to explore the neutral zone off the coast of Khefji. The Arabian Oil Company was founded and soon discovered reserves of substantial size. It began its production in 1961 and has been supplying 120 million barrels of crude every year. Subsequently, another project, though much smaller than Arabian Oil, went into operation in Indonesia. This project has been producing 2.5 million barrels of crude oil annually.

So far, these two projects have been the only successful ones, and together they supply less than 8 percent of the total Japanese crude requirement. In the late 1960s, encouraged by the government's policies and assistance, as well as stimulated by the success of Arabian Oil, there emerged a rapid interest in petroleum exploration, and at present over thirty firms have been formed by several major groups, including refining firms, major users of petroleum products such as utility firms and steel mills, trading companies, equipment manufacturers, and financial institutions.

The case of copper. The copper industry, having had considerable mining experience since the early days of Japan's industrialization, was the first resource industry to undertake overseas investment. Beginning in the early 1950s, leading Japanese mining companies have made sporadic investments in the Philippines, Latin America, and Canada. The most successful of these earlier efforts was the Sumitomo's 30 percent ownership of a Canadian mine, from which the company has been exporting 20,000 tons of copper ores and receiving ¥200 million in dividends for the past decade.

The efforts until recently were small scale and sporadic. The overseas total investment for copper through 1970 was only slightly over ¥100 billion, or about $360 million, and in most cases ownership has been limited to a minority portion. The output of these mines accounts for only 6 percent of the total copper obtained overseas. As in the case of petroleum, in very recent years the copper industry, too, began intensifying its efforts to search for opportunities for investment. To date, this has resulted in two major projects.

One is the development of the Musoshi Mine in the Congo, which is reported to contain 100 million tons of high-grade ore. The project at this point is 85 percent owned by a consortium of several mining firms under the leadership of the Nippon Mining Company. The mine, once it begins its full-scale production, is expected to produce over 50,000 tons of ore every year. The other project is the Mumut Mine in Malaysia, whose development has just begun, also on a joint basis. This mine is expected to produce approximately 30,000 tons of ore annually.

Though on a much more modest scale, similar efforts are now being made in the development of iron ores, bauxite, zinc, and other critical raw materials. While the patterns vary among specific minerals, there are several common features. In every field, the Japanese efforts are still in their infancy. Certainly, in none of the fields has Japanese entry so far had a perceptible impact on the structure of the resource industry. The Japanese interests, as latecomers, are finding that the entry barriers, though gradually eroding in a number of industries, are still substantial.

So far, the Japanese efforts have been atomized. This is particularly notable in exploration of crude oil. There are over thirty projects, each of which is small. To overcome this fragmented method of the past, there is a growing trend toward cooperative approaches in resource development. In petroleum, several refining firms are joining hands; in copper and aluminum, joint projects are gaining popularity. Virtually all the large projects have been organized on this basis. Also, there have been several cases of Japanese firms participating in international consortiums.

The role of the government. As one might expect, the government's role in the development of natural resources has been rather extensive, but characteristically, it has been primarily supportive in its character. The actual operations have been undertaken on private initiative. The government has played an important role in creating awareness in the business community of the need for, and opportunities in, natural-resource development overseas. It has acted as a catalyst in close consultation with the business community in arriving at a general consensus as to the target to be sought and the directions to be pursued.

The government also provides funds to help finance exploration and development. In the case of petroleum, for example, the Petroleum Development Corporation, a public corporation founded in 1967, is authorized to invest in exploration projects up to 75 percent of the equity and to extend loans up to 50 percent of the total debt, the repayment of which is forgiven in case of failure. This participation by the Petroleum Development Corporation is to be gradually phased out if

TABLE 45. Cumulative Book Value of Japanese Foreign Direct Investment in the Manufacturing Sector, 1951 to 1970

Type of Industry	Number of Projects	Amount *(thousands of dollars)*
Foods	135	60,840
Textiles	259	189,797
Pulp	144	212,353
Chemicals	175	59,633
Metals	99	137,954
Machinery and equipment	138	67,206
Electrical machinery	206	70,890
Transportation	43	102,532
Others	292	61,494
Total	1,491	962,699

Source: Japan. Ministry of International Trade and Industry.

the exploration proves successful and as the project enters the production stage. Similar, but less extensive, assistance is extended to the development of other mineral resources.

Manufacturing: An Overall Pattern

In 1971, the Japanese foreign investment in the manufacturing sector reached an accumulative level of about $963 million, accounting for roughly 27 percent of the total foreign direct investment. As shown in Table 45, the investment is spread among a variety of industries. The pulp industry, which has had a small number of large investments, claims the largest share, closely followed by the textile and iron and steel industries. Fourth is transportation equipment, primarily automobiles.

The remainder is divided among electronics, electrical machinery equipment, electrical machinery, chemicals, and foods.

This investment is concentrated in three major regions of the world: 35 percent in Asia, 29 percent in Latin America, and 23 percent in North America. Significantly, in terms of the number of cases, Asia accounts for an overwhelming majority, 1,011 out of the total of 1,391. There are 172 projects, or about 12 percent of the total, in Latin America and 67 projects in North America.

Japanese direct investments in the manufacturing sector to date can be classified into two major categories—those initiated in response to import substitution policies of the host countries and those made to create offshore production facilities to take advantage of cheap labor resources in certain developing countries. Since the patterns of development are somewhat different, each category will be examined separately.

Import substitution—the key motive. The most common motive thus far for Japanese foreign investment in the manufacturing sector has been to avert the loss of the export market threatened by import substitution policies of a host country. Thus, these investments are typically made as an ad hoc, often reluctant, response to specific threats.

Of course, action by a leading firm in response to such a threat often elicits moves by its major competitors. In oligopolistic industries such as synthetic fibers, electrical machinery, and iron and steel, a major export market is almost invariably served by several manufacturers. In order to avoid total preemption of such a market by a single firm, investment by one company leads to similar actions by competitors. This trend is further intensified by the strong growth orientation of large Japanese corporations and their preoccupation with increasing their respective market share in every market in which they operate.

The fact that these manufacturing companies are linked to different trading companies intensifies such pressure, since there exists fierce competition among major trading companies. Thus, there have been numerous occasions where all the major firms in an industry swarm into a market of limited size, making it difficult for any single firm to achieve any degree of economy of scale in its local production facilities. Examples of defensive investment stimulated by import substitution policies of the host countries are found in such industries as textiles, home appliances, automobiles, and metal fabrication.

Major characteristics of import-substitution type of investment. These investments have several common characteristics. First, they are rather small, with a minimum of capital commitment. This is evident from a recent survey conducted by the Japan Export-Import Bank. Among 613 manufacturing subsidiaries surveyed, half were capitalized at less than $300,000 and, moreover, roughly a quarter of them were capitalized at $100,000 or less. Among the firms surveyed, only 12 were capitalized at $10 million or more. Another indication of the small size is the fact that among the 552 subsidiaries for which data were available, only 176, or 14 percent, had more than five hundred employees. In fact, 43 percent of the 552 firms had less than one hundred employees.

At least initially, these investments are designed to perform only the minimum amount of production consistent with the local government import restrictions and are not likely to result in a major shift in the company's export strategy. Thus, in textiles, the foreign plant performs only simple weaving operations, using yarns supplied from Japan. Among steel products, a typical case is the manufacturing of galvanized iron sheets for roofing, which are in great demand in developing countries in tropical or semitropical areas. The production performed locally is confined to the final galvanization process of sheet metals imported from Japan. For home appliances and automobiles, the local plant performs only the assembly operations. It is advantageous for large Japanese manufacturers to minimize the local production in order to allow as much processing or manufacturing as possible in Japan. Typically in this type of investment, the firms derive much of their profit from export of intermediate materials and component parts to the foreign production facilities. Such defensive investments have been made in a number of countries to the point where large Japanese corporations in certain industries now have manufacturing subsidiaries of very limited size literally scattered through the world on a highly fragmented basis.

Another notable feature of the market-oriented Japanese manufacturing investment is the widespread presence of joint ventures. According to the aforementioned survey by the Export-Import Bank of

Japan, 83 percent of the 514 subsidiaries were joint ventures; 14 percent of the subsidiaries had less than 25 percent Japanese ownership; 27 percent had between 25 and 50 percent; and Japanese interests held the majority of shares in only 16 percent of the subsidiaries surveyed.

Such a high proportion of joint ventures presents a striking contrast to the American pattern. Several reasons can be suggested. One obvious factor is the requirement of the host countries. As we have seen, in contrast to the American investment, the Japanese manufacturing investment is heavily concentrated in developing countries where local equity participation is required. Another reason is the fact that until recently, the Japanese government has maintained a restrictive policy toward the outflow of capital from Japan. Government approval has been required for each investment. Concerned with the foreign-exchange position and anxious to minimize the risks for Japanese corporations, the government tended to look more favorably upon proposals with local participation.

Still another factor to account for the prevalence of joint ventures is the very character of the Japanese foreign manufacturing investment up to this point. It is small, performing only limited production functions, thus involving the very minimum of financial and technological commitment on the part of the parent company. As far as the Japanese manufacturing firms are concerned, the venture's primary purpose is to provide the local presence to meet the government's requirements. Also, the investment is designed to serve only the local market. Under these circumstances, 100 percent ownership is by no means essential. In fact, local participation is usually preferred because there exists a widespread view among Japanese managers that joint ventures are less vulnerable to political risk.

A unique element of Japanese ventures is the extensive participation of Japanese trading campanies. Thus, most joint ventures have three partners—manufacturing company, trading firm, and local interests. In a number of industries, the trading company performs export functions for the manufacturing firm, and therefore it has as much vested interest in the protection of the market as the manufacturing company that it is representing. Indeed, it is almost always the trading company which first identifies a threat of the potential loss of the export market and brings it to the attention of the manufacturer. The trading company is interested in having an equity position in the venture so that it may continue to serve the market even after export is completely replaced by local production. The manufacturing firm, on the other hand, looks to the trading company for its knowledge and expertise in international business, financial resources, and local know-how.

Labor sourcing investment. The second category of Japanese foreign direct investments in the manufacturing sector consists of those motivated by a search for low-cost labor. The phenomenal economic growth during the last two decades has exerted tremendous pressures on labor supplies in Japan. Since the early 1960s, and for the first time in the nation's history, Japan has been experiencing a serious labor shortage, resulting in the steady rise of the wage level. During the past decade alone, the wage level in the manufacturing sector has nearly tripled.

The labor shortage and the resulting rapid rise of wages has been particularly serious among young female workers who have constituted the main source of labor to perform labor-intensive semiskilled manufacturing activities. Young workers have been particularly in demand because of their high productivity in relatively routine and simple manufacturing tasks requiring a high degree of dexterity. Moreover, the traditional seniority-based wage system makes this segment of the labor force least expensive and has intensified the demand for these workers during the past several years. Understandably, this segment has enjoyed the highest rate of increase in the wage level. The average wage for new graduates of junior high school has more than quadrupled during the past decade. In recent years, the absolute number of those entering the labor force with junior-high-school education has been steadily declining, inasmuch as the number seeking higher education is growing. For these reasons, recruitment of young female workers has become extremely difficult and competitive. The rapid rise in the wage level has had the first and most marked impact on Japanese ability to compete in the export market, particularly in the face of emergence of significant competition.

During the 1960s, a number of Asian countries, notably Taiwan and Hong Kong initially, and later South Korea and Singapore, have successfully developed labor-intensive light industries of their own and have begun to challenge Japan's preeminence in these fields. Their efforts certainly have been greatly facilitated by the rapid rise of wages in Japan. These developments have been further encouraged by the incessant search for the cheapest sources of supply by American buyers, particularly large American mass-merchandising firms, which have made foreign sourcing an important and integral part of their purchasing systems. Japan has been the major source of supply for many products but, faced with the rising cost of production reflecting the wage increases, the American buyers have begun to shift their supply sources elsewhere. Also, the suppliers of large American retail outlets, or even the outlets themselves, have acquired considerable experience and know-how in helping to promote supply sources in developing countries.

Meantime, another significant development has led to further erosion of Japanese competitive ability in the export market. In certain industries, notably electronics, a number of American manufacturers have established offshore production facilities in such places as Mexico, Taiwan, and Hong Kong to manufacture parts as well as to engage in assembly activities. Anxious to maintain their competitive position in export markets, the Japanese manufacturers have been compelled to match the very actions the American corporations had made in the first place to cope with the Japanese import threats in the U.S. market. This type of investment also is defensive in character and export induced. It is an effort by Japanese manufacturers to prolong competitive viability in the export market. Such responsive action has become even more compelling since the currency revaluation in 1971.

Until recently, Taiwan has been the major recipient of Japanese investment in offshore production facilities. The island is geographically close, and since it was a former Japanese territory, language and cultural barriers are less acute. Moreover, the Taiwan government has provided incentives for foreign investment designed for reexporting. The latest political developments, of course, are likely to make a drastic change in this situation, forcing Japanese investors to look elsewhere for such investments. South Korea, Hong Kong, and Singapore are receiving increasing attention. Japanese investment to seek cheap labor supplies overseas has been largely concentrated in two types of industry. One is the consumer electronic industry, and the other is the manufacture of inexpensive sundry goods varying from shoes, apparel, or baseball gloves to household items. The Japanese electronic companies have been particularly aggressive. As of 1971, the industry had made a $36.8 million investment overseas, and almost half of the amount had been invested within the preceding two years. Over 70 percent of these ventures are concentrated in Taiwan, South Korea, and Hong Kong.

The offshore investment in the electronics industry can be further broken down into two major types—assembly operations and parts manufacturing. Almost all major Japanese manufacturers of consumer electronics products now have offshore assembly facilities. Most of the component parts are shipped from Japan, while some are locally procured. Products assembled are monocolor television sets and inexpensive lines of transistor radios, and they are exported primarily to the United States and Europe. For understandable reasons, most of these assembly operations are usually wholly owned by the Japanese parent companies.

The Japanese manufacturers of component parts that had been supplying large American companies have been forced to shift their bases of operations to stay competitive in the export market as the latter began to look to cheaper sources of supply. This move is further prompted by the growing trends on the part of major American as well as Japanese customers to shift their assembly bases to offshore facilities.

In the sundry goods fields, the patterns vary somewhat among specific products, but two dominant features are apparent. One feature is that investment in this field is dominated by small to medium-size firms, reflecting the nature of the structure of these industries in Japan. In fact, active participation of small to medium-size firms in direct-investment activities is one of the distinguishing characteristics of the Japanese investment. It is estimated that roughly 30 percent of the total investment projects are undertaken by such firms, and altogether, they are responsible for 8 percent of Japan's total foreign investment.[1] Roughly 90 percent of the offshore investment projects by these firms are found in Southeast Asia, two-thirds of which are concentrated in Taiwan, Hong Kong, and South Korea. The great majority of these investments by small to medium-size firms have been made in light, labor-intensive industries in order to maintain competitive ability in the export market.

Another noteworthy feature of investment in offshore production facilities in the sundry goods fields is the extensive participation of trading companies. With few exceptions, trading companies handle export of these products. The trading company, first perceiving the eroding position of the Japanese manufacturers in these fields, is forced to find cheaper supply sources and, rather than cultivating new foreign sources, the trading company encourages its Japanese suppliers to move abroad in partnership with it.

The discussion of Japanese investment in offshore production facilities is incomplete without considering the presence of a rather unique governmental restriction. The Japanese government has had a policy of discouraging large Japanese firms from establishing offshore facilities to produce for the Japanese market. The chief reason is to protect small to medium-size enterprises which may be adversely affected by such a practice. Thus, offshore production for the domestic market has been quite limited. There are, however, increasing signs that this policy will be gradually relaxed to enable the large Japanese manufacturers to capitalize on cheap labor sources in the neighboring countries. As a matter of fact, a leading firm in the electronics industry now produces 60 percent of its integrated circuits at one of its foreign plants, and all the output is imported back to Japan.

Recent developments. In the foregoing section, salient features of the Japanese foreign direct investment in the manufacturing sector have been discussed, but during the past year or two a number of new trends are emerging, which we shall briefly examine. First, confronted with slowing down of growth in the domestic market and deteriorating climate for Japanese export in key world markets, a number of firms have begun considering expanding direct investment as an alternative way of reaching these markets. These firms no longer make foreign investment merely as a defensive response to avert the possible loss of the export market. They aggressively seek out promising investment opportunities.

Some manufacturing firms have established a system of scanning the world market with the expectation of identifying new areas not related to their established export markets. In this process, a few have developed a set of explicit criteria for seeking out and evaluating new investment opportunities.

It has been observed that a number of developing countries, having achieved the initial objective of import substitution, begin to tighten their restrictions to further promote their industrialization. The Japanese firms already committed to the market had little choice but to comply with such a requirement by increasing their local value added. As a result, a small-scale operation to perform limited manufacturing or only assembly operations is forced to undertake backward integration. Anticipating such a requirement, and in the face of the rapidly growing demand, some firms have expanded into upstream operations to discourage subsequent entry into the market by competitors.

An outstanding example of such a development is found in the synthetic-fiber industry which has been one of the first to undertake foreign investment. Particularly active have been the two leading firms in the industry, Toray and Teijin. The fiber manufacturers have built up, through trading companies, a substantial control over downstream operations including spinning, weaving, dyeing, and even manufacturing of ready-made apparel. When exports in the form of finished products began to be threatened in a number of developing countries, the fiber manufacturers, together with trading companies and local interests, established weaving operations in these markets to which the yarns are supplied. In Thailand, for example, synthetic fibers have enjoyed very ready acceptance resulting in the rapid growth of demand for these products. Confronted by a growing market and at the same time incessant governmental pressure for a higher degree of import substitution, the firms have escalated their investment from weaving to spinning and dyeing and eventually to production of the fiber itself.

The two major manufacturers jointly established a nylon plant with sufficient capacity to supply the entire local needs for some time to come. In this process, imports from the parent company had been completely terminated. Within a few years, an investment which began with a small and classical case of import substitution has been totally transformed to become a fully integrated operation, with considerable financial and technical commitment by the parent company. Interestingly, this experience in Thailand has had a substantial impact on the manner in which the two competitors have subsequently entered other major markets. Implicit division of the key world markets began to emerge between the two leading firms, and in entering the key markets, both adopted the policy of making their initial investment in an upstream operation, namely, a fiber plant. Toray entered Indonesia in this manner and was matched by Teijin in Brazil.

The third recent trend is away from an atomized approach whereby each subsidiary serves only the market in which it is located. Among a few firms, there is a move toward achieving some semblance of product specialization and crosshauling of products among subsidiaries located in different countries. Though they are still small in number and quite crude in their approaches, it is significant to note that some firms have begun to instigate a formal logistics network involving several foreign subsidiaries.

We should note in passing that the last two recent developments discussed—the changing character of the subsidiaries and the need and opportunities for integration among subsidiaries—are now leading to growing tensions between joint-venture partners. Particularly, signs of strain have begun to appear between the manufacturing firms and the trading firms. Manufacturing firms have gained considerable experience in international business and are finding it increasingly necessary to make greater financial, technical, and managerial commitment to joint ventures as they expand. In this process, the initiative is shifting from the trading company to a manufacturing firm. As the reader can readily see, this problem is likely to have a profound implication.

The fourth recent development is an increasing involvement of Japanese corporations in large capital-intensive and technologically oriented projects. A good example is the case of Japanese investment in a petrochemical complex in Iran and Thailand. In the Iranian project, a half-dozen Japanese chemical and petrochemical firms have agreed to make substantial joint financial and technical commitments with the Iranian National Petroleum Corporation in the development of a petrochemical complex, capitalizing on abundant locally available petroleum resources. The Iranian project is now under way at the instigation of the Mitsui Trading Company. Negotiation of the petrochemical project in Thailand was initiated by the Mitsuhishi Trading Company. Interestingly, in both cases, trading companies are playing the central role as project organizer and coordinator.

Finally, some of the leading Japanese corporations have begun to explore the feasibility of becoming multinational enterprises, like their major international competitors. There is a growing recognition of the fact that development of multinational corporations is likely to represent a major thrust for corporate growth in the coming decade. For Japanese corporations, this is an uncharted and untested field, and for that very reason, the possibility holds considerable excitement. Management of a number of Japan's leading corporations have begun to grope for directions and strategies to achieve this goal.

Thus, the Japanese foreign direct investment is now at a turning point, departing from the initial stage of small, fragmented, and marginal export-induced operations to the next stage of development.

Looking Ahead: Future Prospects

As we have seen, the Japanese direct foreign investment is still rather small. But it has grown at a very rapid pace in the past two or three years, and the trend is likely to continue throughout the 1970s. According to a recent prediction by the Ministry of International Trade and Industry (MITI), Japanese direct investment is likely to reach the level of $12 billion by 1975 and $27 billion by the end of the decade, which is roughly eight times the 1971 figure. By 1980, the annual level of investment is predicted to reach $35 billion, equivalent to the cumulative investment up to now. According to MITI prediction, most significant growth will be achieved in the resource industries. By 1975, the investment in this sector is expected to be $6 billion, and by 1980 it will reach the $16 billion level, accounting for nearly 60 percent of the total investment in contrast to 33 percent in 1971.

What is the likelihood of Japanese foreign direct investment achieving such a rapid growth? No doubt, there will be opportunities and pressure for increasing foreign direct investment. Moreover, with enormous foreign-exchange reserves coupled with an increasing value of the yen, Japan indeed has sufficient financial resources to undertake expansion. To provide a proper perspective, however, we should recognize that there are a number of obstacles, which, unless overcome, are likely to impede future growth of Japanese foreign investment.

Major problem areas. First, the future growth depends to a large degree on the ability of Japanese management to adapt their highly culturally bound management practices. The Japanese managerial system, which has proved so effective within its national context, is essentially a product of a cohesive, monolithic, and homogeneous culture. Faced with a new and different environment, Japanese management must evolve a different managerial system. The very fact that the Japanese system has been evolved in a highly insulated environment and derives its strength mainly from culturally induced values poses a difficult challenge for Japanese management in the operation of a large multinational enterprise. There is no clear evidence that Japanese management can achieve the substantial adaptation which would be required.

Another problem lies in the reactions from the host countries toward Japanese direct investment. Conflicts and tensions resulting from the presence of multinational corporations have received considerable attention in recent years. Japanese investment, though small in relative terms, has already come under rather severe attack in a number of countries, particularly in Southeast Asia. Many familiar accusations are echoed, providing more discomforting evidence that the tensions resulting from the presence of foreign direct investment transcend the national origins of the investing companies. There are, however, several noteworthy features of the Japanese investment which create special sources of tension.

First, the investments are highly concentrated in a few countries in Southeast Asia—Taiwan, Thailand, and Indonesia. The case of Thailand, where the Japanese investments dominate the scene, is a particularly striking one. Such a relative dominance makes Japanese investment an easy target of attack. Closely related to the foregoing is the very character of the Japanese manufacturing investment, which, as we have noted, is chiefly the import-substitution type. As a result, many of the investments are found among those products which require only limited capital and technology. These are precisely the areas which local entrepreneurs could well enter, but their entry is prevented by the dominant position of the Japanese. In a number of fields, the Japanese investment has preempted opportunities which local businessmen feel are rightfully theirs. The second source of tension has been the Japanese tendency to keep local production to a minimum in order to maximize export from the parent company to the foreign subsidiary. Local government officials find the Japanese investment objectionable on the ground that too often it is no more than a disguised form of export. The almost chronic presence of large trade deficits with Japan found in most Southeast Asian countries, despite continued efforts of local governments toward import substitution, tends to accentuate further the host country's concern over the nature of Japanese investment. A third source of tension is the fact that wartime experiences are still too vivid to be forgotten.

The local political and intellectual elite feel uncomfortable over the presence of a large enclave of Japanese businessmen in their major cities. These enclaves are characteristically closed, exclusive, and almost impregnable. The elite also find the Japanese preference to deal only with other Japanese distasteful. The Japanese businessmen overseas are often accused of using the Japan Airlines, staying at Japanese hotels, eating at Japanese restaurants, and doing business exclusively with their fellow Japanese. The Japanese cultural insularity and almost total lack of skill in effective communication often aggravate unnecessarily and quite unintentionally the local feelings.

Investment in the United States. In examining the future trend of Japanese foreign direct investment, a topic of considerable interest and speculation is whether or not during the next several years there will be a significant increase in Japanese manufacturing investment in the United States and Europe. Available evidence indicates that the probability of this occurring is not very high. No doubt, a gradual increase will occur, but it is likely to remain sporadic and to be confined to limited areas. Some manufacturing investments are beginning to appear in those areas where the Japanese have developed significant innovations in the manufacturing processes to offset high wages in advanced countries, particularly in the United States.

The case of the Toyo Bearing Company, which has recently established plants in the United States and West Germany, illustrates the point. The company's move abroad has been partially motivated by the very nature of the product and the industry. Ball bearings have virtually become an international commodity, and the industry is dominated by the two major multinational corporations, S.K.F. and Timken. The Japanese ball-bearing industry has made a substantial inroad into the export market in recent years and is now challenging the preeminence of the two leading world enterprises. The entry of the Toyo Bearing Company into the United States and Europe has been based on the company's ability to design a highly efficient and capital-intensive production unit with automated manufacturing processes. The system developed specifically for advanced countries can be installed as a unit. Each unit is designed to have a maximum of forty employees. To keep management problems to a minimum, the company's policy is to install new units in different parts of the market instead of expanding the existing facilities. While production in the United States has become feasible only through the ability to design a production process appropriate for the environment, local production offers a number of advantages, including the avoidance of various types of import restrictions and proximity to end users. Entry is clearly based on process rather than on product innovations.

Another condition under which Japanese investment in the manufacturing sector has occurred and is likely to grow is when a manufacturer has successfully captured a significant share of the market based on a strong brand position and quality image. When such a company is confronted with a decision to build another plant, it may well consider the possibility of locating it outside of Japan where a large export market is found. The recent decision by Sony to build a plant in Southern California is a good example. Local production will provide a certain insurance against the possibility of further deterioration of the U.S. climate for Japanese imports. Moreover, while the labor cost in the United States is considerably higher than in Japan, at least at present, wages are rapidly increasing in Japan and another round of revaluation is almost certain. Given its outstanding brand position and strong appeal to the quality market, the company has some flexibility in its pricing structure to absorb higher production cost.

Still a third case is an attempt by the American and European subsidiaries of major Japanese trading companies to seek out growth opportunities on their own outside of the traditional fields and somewhat independent of their Japanese parent companies. The sales of a number of these subsidiaries exceed $1 billion, and the subsidiaries are quite capable of diversifying into promising areas, including manufacturing activities.

Having operated in the United States for some time, they have become familiar with American concepts and techniques of diversification and are anxious to apply them to their own benefits. This is a clear case of a large growth-oriented subsidiary in a major market developing independent strategies in response to a unique set of stimuli in that market.[2]

The conditions cited above, however, are rather special cases, and massive investments by large-scale Japanese manufacturing firms in the United States and Europe are not likely to occur in the near future.

Notes

1/ Keiichi Yokobori, "Chushō Kigyo no Kaigaitoshi" [Foreign investment by small-medium size firms], *Chushō Kigyo to Kumiai* (December 1971), pp. 2–7.

2/ Raymond Vernon, "The Location of Economic Activity" (unpublished paper), pp. 8–9.

10.

JAPAN AS HOST TO
THE INTERNATIONAL CORPORATION

M. Y. Yoshino

FOREIGN INVESTMENT IN JAPAN, particularly direct investment, has been comparatively small even in recent decades despite the attractive features that the country offers to potential investors. Japan is now a major industrial nation with a large internal market. There is a well-educated and trained labor force. Moreover, there is a high degree of political stability unknown in the rest of Asia. Thus, in many respects Japan is a very desirable country for international investment. Why, then, has investment by foreigners been so small?

The cumulative book value of all types of foreign investment made in Japan since World War II stood at $23.8 billion at the end of 1972. The details are even more revealing. The combined total of portfolio and direct investment accounts for roughly 52 percent of the total foreign capital inflow during the postwar years; the rest is in some form of loan. But direct investment is only slightly more than $1 billion or about 4.2 percent of the total investment.[1]

The small amount and proportion of foreign direct investment is, of course, due largely to the restrictive policy which had been adopted by the Japanese government until quite recently. While limiting foreign direct investment, Japan has aggressively sought advanced foreign technology. Between 1950 and 1972, Japanese firms signed over 17,600 licensing contracts with foreign firms, for which they paid a staggering sum of $3.3 billion. Indeed, foreign technology has played an important role in Japan's great postwar economic growth.

Historical Sketch

Historically, Japan has not been a very hospitable host to companies based in other countries. This policy, which is now being changed, evolved for very understandable reasons. During the early Meiji era (1868–1912), the development of an industrial society was not an end in itself, but a means of maintaining national independence in the face of serious foreign threats. The strategy that Japan pursued in achieving rapid industrialization was particularly noteworthy for its intense determination to maintain economic as well as political independence.

The Meiji leaders deliberately restricted the entry of foreign capital. With singleness of purpose, they avoided foreign direct investment in Japan. This policy was in part motivated by their desire to protect struggling Japanese industries against foreign competition. What they feared most, however, was foreign ownership and management of Japan's industries through direct investment. Whenever foreign capital was absolutely necessary, they strongly preferred to borrow it.

The Japanese spirit and foreign technology. This cautious attitude with which the Meiji leadership treated foreign direct investment was in striking contrast to the aggressiveness with which the nation sought advanced foreign technology. The Meiji leaders realized in the very early phase of industrialization that advanced technology could be imported without foreign ownership or control. In this they saw the possibility of achieving rapid progress without compromising their overriding goal. A popular slogan of the early Meiji era, *Wakon Yosai* [the Japanese spirit and foreign technology], aptly describes the Japanese attitude toward foreign direct investment throughout the prewar decades.[2]

The tight restrictions against foreign investment were slightly relaxed beginning around the turn of the century. As the nation achieved rapid industrialization, foreign competition became less threatening. Direct foreign investment remained rather small in absolute sum, and much of it took the form of joint ventures. The Zaibatsu-dominated business community shared the view of the political elite and zealously guarded its independence. Even during this period, the most important reason for Japanese firms to seek foreign joint ventures was to obtain advanced foreign technology, which they then adapted to their particular requirements.

The foregoing brief review of the historical attitude toward foreign investment prior to World War II is intended to give the reader a perspective for examining subsequent developments in Japanese policy toward foreign direct investment. Times and policies are different, but there are some significant parallels between the pre- and postwar years.

Postwar Changes in Policy

In 1949, Japan enacted the Foreign Exchange Control Law and in 1950 the Foreign Investment Law. These laws have served as the chief instruments for controlling foreign direct investment. The basic policy that was to prevail for some time was clearly articulated in Article 1 of the Foreign Investment Law. It stated that direct foreign investment was permitted in Japan only when it contributed to (1) the attainment of self-sufficiency and the sound development of the Japanese economy and (2) the improvement of Japan's balance of payments. As long as foreign investment met these requirements, the law unconditionally guaranteed the remittance of principal and profits overseas regardless of Japan's foreign-exchange position. Significantly, the law explicitly recognized the eventual desirability of free entry of foreign capital and pledged that restrictions would be removed as circumstances permitted. The 1950 law also established the Foreign Investment Council (FIC) under the jurisdiction of the minister of finance as the chief advisory body on matters relating to direct foreign investment.

During the first several years after enactment of the law, the Japanese government vigorously adhered to the two requirements indicated above. As Japan achieved economic recovery and began her drive for rapid growth in the latter half of the 1950s, the government began slowly to relax the very strict provisions against foreign investment. The criteria for screening underwent a significant change from admitting only investments making positive contributions to prohibiting those deemed harmful or less desirable. By the early 1960s, foreign investment in Japan was permitted as long as it did not (1) unduly oppress small-size enterprises, (2) seriously disturb industrial order, or (3) seriously impede the domestic development of industrial techniques.

In 1956, the government made an important exception to the screening requirement: As long as foreign firms were willing to forgo the explicit guarantee of repatriation of principal and profit, they could invest in Japan without specific government approval. The subsidiaries established under this provision came to be known as "yen companies." Notwithstanding the obvious disadvantages, there were some advantages to this provision. International companies in consumer-related industries which had experienced difficulty in obtaining government approval were now able to enter the rapidly growing Japanese market and establish wholly owned subsidiaries in Japan. During the six-year period 1956–1963, 316 yen companies were established. The provision was abolished in 1963 in anticipation of Japan's acceptance of Article 8 of the International Monetary Fund (IMF), which required all subscribing nations to guarantee repatriation of principal and earnings of international corporations.

During the earlier years, the maximum foreign ownership allowed was 49 percent, but by 1963 joint ventures on a 50-50 basis became commonplace. Firms in consumer-related industries were now permitted entry under the Foreign Investment Law. Moreover, the government began to allow joint ventures in vital industries in which only licensing had previously been possible. Still, each investment application had to go through individual screening and was rigorously examined by FIC.

Evaluation of policy to the mid-sixties. Thus, Japanese policy toward direct foreign investment before the mid-1960s had several noteworthy features. First, it was highly restrictive, both as to types of industries and extent of foreign ownership. The maximum foreign ownership allowed was 50 percent, reflecting a strong and long-held Japanese aversion to foreign control of its industries. Second, the criteria for screening foreign investment were stated with characteristic vagueness, giving the government officials and FIC considerable latitude. Along with complex bureaucratic machinery and administrative procedures, this presented a formidable obstacle and served as an informal, but nevertheless real, deterrent to international firms contemplating entry into Japan.

At the same time, the administrative latitude given to the bureaucracy in the selection of foreign investment gave it considerable power (albeit informal) vis-à-vis the Japanese business community. Finally, the Japanese government consistently and persistently encouraged, through formal and informal means, technical licensing rather than direct investment.

Japanese strategy toward foreign investment through the mid-1960s was sound in that it gave sufficient protection to domestic industries to enable them to achieve initial recovery and rapid subsequent growth. It also provided necessary protection and encouragement for newly emerging technically oriented industries to let them get well established. By the mid-1960s, however, changing domestic and international situations began to build up pressure for further relaxation of foreign-investment regulations.

Forces leading to change of historical policy. The primary reason for a changed policy lay, of course, in Japan's phenomenal success in achieving rapid economic growth in the postwar years. Within a decade and a half after her defeat in 1945, Japan emerged as a leading industrial nation of the world. In 1964, Japan accepted Article 8 of the IMF regulations and also joined the Organization for Economic Cooperation and Development (OECD). Japan had indeed become one of the world's advanced nations, and with this came a set of obligations. Not the least important of these was to liberalize restrictions against direct foreign investment.

Since Japan had the most restrictive policy toward foreign investment among its member nations, OECD, at the insistence of the United States, began to prod Japan about this. The United States, having an important stake in Japan, also intensified its pressure on Japan independently through formal as well as informal channels. As important as these external thrusts were, there were equally intense, though less obvious, internal pressures for capital policy liberalization. By the mid-1960s, the Japanese themselves began to recognize that some liberalization would be in their own national interest.

In early 1967, FIC was reorganized and turned into a blue-ribbon committee consisting exclusively of distinguished persons from the private sector. Also, a special advisory committee was organized to assist the council. The reorganized FIC was instructed by the finance minister to recommend a policy of capital liberalization. Each relevant ministry was charged with the responsibility of designating those industries in which a less restrictive policy might be feasible. The ministries, particularly the Ministry of International Trade and Industry (MITI), were far from enthusiastic about liberalization, but after intense consultation and negotiation with various industry groups, each submitted a list to FIC. The council held a number of public hearings, consulted with various interest groups, and in the best Japanese tradition sought as broad a consensus as possible.

The council made its recommendations to the finance minister on June 2, 1967, in two parts. In the first part, the council articulated the basic policy that Japan should follow foreign-investment liberalization. In the second part, the council made specific recommendations regarding the first phase of liberalization for immediate implementation.

General Policy Recommendations

First, let us examine the salient features of the general policy recommended. The council stated in no uncertain terms that Japan was determined to carry out the policy of capital liberalization at its own initiative, because it was deemed to be consistent with long-run national interest. The report clearly stated that liberalization did not mean totally unrestricted access to the Japanese market by multinational corporations. While 100 percent foreign ownership would be allowed in some industries, liberalization would proceed primarily on the basis of joint ventures. It was to be carried out in a series of steps to be consummated by the end of fiscal year 1971.

The council's report also suggested what steps the government and Japanese firms had to take in the face of a more liberal policy toward foreign investment. The report urged the government to take the following steps: (1) to prevent economic and social disorder or imbalances that might result from large-scale entry of foreign capital into Japan; (2) to create and sustain an economic environment in which Japanese enterprises could compete with large multinational firms on equal terms; (3) to strengthen the competitive capacity of individual Japanese enterprises and reorganize the structure of Japan's key industries so as to withstand competition from large-scale international corporations.

The council cautioned Japanese firms against their past tendency complacently to seek government protection and emphasized the importance of careful investigation and planning in entering into any collaborative arrangements with multinational firms. The report also exhorted Japanese firms to approach foreign ventures with confidence based on equal partnership.

Also included in this report were guidelines to be followed by international corporations operating in Japan. This was the first time that guidelines applying to all foreign firms had been formally stated. While suggestions for the Japanese government and enterprises were indicated with characteristic vagueness, the guidelines for foreign firms were expressed with unusual specificity. They consisted of the following ten points:

1. Seek coexistence and prosperity with Japanese enterprises through joint ventures on an equal partnership basis.
2. Avoid concentration of investment in specific industries.
3. Avoid suppressing small enterprises when entering into industries characterized by small firms.
4. Cooperate voluntarily with the Japanese effort to maintain proper industrial order.
5. Avoid entering into unduly restrictive arrangements with parent companies abroad, and do not resort to unreasonable restrictions concerning transactions or to unfair competition.
6. Take positive steps toward developing Japanese technology, and do not hamper the efforts of Japanese industries to develop their own technology.
7. Contribute to the improvement of the nation's balance of payments through exports and other means.
8. Appoint Japanese to the board of directors and top management positions and make shares of company stock available to the public.
9. Avoid closures of plants, or mass dismissal, and unnecessary confusion in employment and wage practices by paying due regard to the prevailing Japanese practices.
10. Conform to the government economic policy.

Indeed, these guidelines are extensive, touching on almost every aspect of the conduct of multinational corporations in Japan.

Recommendations for first stage of liberalization. The council in its report made three important policy decisions, setting the tone for subsequent stages. These decisions were: (1) Liberalization will proceed on an industry basis; (2) distinction will be made according to the degree of foreign ownership; and (3) distinction will also be made between establishment of new enterprises and acquisition of existing Japanese firms.

For the first stage, the council designated fifty industries in which at least some measure of liberalization would be carried out. These industries were further grouped into two categories. In the first category were industries in which a maximum of 50 percent foreign ownership would be allowed without individual screening, provided that the venture satisfied certain basic conditions. Thirty-three of the fifty industries were placed into this category, including household appliances, sheet glass, phonograph records, cameras, acetate, pharmaceuticals, and restaurants.

The council imposed three specific conditions that had to be met by the first category of industries to qualify for automatic permission. These stipulations were to provide additional safeguards to ensure equality in joint ventures. They were:

1. The Japanese partner (or partners) that owns at least 50 percent of the shares in the joint ventures must be engaged in the same line of business as the contemplated joint venture. Moreover, one Japanese partner must own at least a third of the total shares of the joint venture.
2. The Japanese representation on the board of directors in the contemplated joint venture must be greater than the proportion of Japanese ownership in the venture.
3. The joint venture must operate under Japanese commercial law, and there should be no provision that the consent of a particular officer or a stockholder be required to execute corporate affairs.

Joint ventures even in first-category industries had to go through individual screening if they did not meet the foregoing three conditions. As noted earlier, the council made a clear-cut distinction between newly established operations and acquisitions of going indigenous concerns. The foregoing first-stage recommendations applied only to newly established operations. Reflecting the extreme sensitivity of the Japanese toward takeover of existing firms by foreign interests, the council recommended only a very limited liberalization for them. Specifically, automatic permission was granted if the total foreign ownership of a company was not more than 20 percent and any single foreign stockholder's share did not exceed 7 percent.

The council recommended that in the second category, consisting of seventeen industries, 100 percent foreign ownership be allowed. Major industries included in this category were ordinary steel, motorcycles, beer, cement, pianos, cotton and rayon spinning, hotels, and shipbuilding of limited size.

The council recommended that application procedures be streamlined for the liberalized industries. Similarly, the council urged the simplification of both application and screening procedures for nonliberalized industries and recommended that the time required for individual screening be shortened.

The first year's results. The council's report was approved in its entirety by the cabinet on June 6, 1967, and the first stage of capital liberalization went into effect on July 1, 1967. The first stage produced few results. The great majority of first-category firms did not hold much appeal for foreign firms. More than a year went by before the first joint venture was established under the liberalized program. Moreover, it was unlikely to think that foreign steel firms or manufacturers of motorcycles would have rushed to Japan, even if highly prized 100 percent ownership were permitted. FIC deliberately had taken a very cautious first step. The government ministries, as well as industrial groups that might be adversely affected by more extensive liberalization, had shown strong resistance. The council, anxious to achieve a broad consensus, had settled for a token liberalization.

The first round, though of limited effect, was significant in that it was a clear expression of Japan's intention to allow more foreign capital and it made clear the basic approach and timetable. It also served notice to nonliberalized industries that a change was indeed imminent and that they should make serious efforts to prepare themselves for this eventuality. In response, a number of significant mergers and joint actions among various firms in several key industries have taken place since 1967, most of which were designed to strengthen the companies' competitive capacity. By June 1968, Japan had effected liberalization by technical licensing in all but a few key product categories such as atomic energy, defense, computers, and petrochemicals.

Planning the second stage. Beginning around mid-1968, the second round of capital liberalization came under serious consideration.

All concerned fully expected that the second round would produce considerably more results than the first. New pressures in this direction began to mount. Particularly noteworthy was the pressure brought by the American automotive industry to break down ironclad restrictions, both in regard to imports and to direct investment. A series of intense negotiations between the two nations resulted in Japan's agreeing, among other things, to remove import restrictions on engines and parts by 1972 and to give consideration to foreign automobile firms for manufacture of parts in Japan.

Equally significant was the leadership of the Japanese business community in becoming more favorably inclined to capital liberalization. A growing positive sentiment toward admitting foreign capital was particularly noticeable among the leadership of the powerful Federation of Economic Organizations (FEO). Several reasons can be cited for this new attitude. First, forward-looking Japanese business leaders became increasingly concerned over the negative attitude of the government as well as of some industry groups toward capital liberalization. This, they felt, had given an impression to the rest of the world that Japan was reneging on its international obligations. Progressive business leaders realized the importance of exerting their leadership in planning for the second stage of liberalization, to prevent the future course from being determined predominantly by the bureaucrats.

Second, they sensed the inevitability of capital liberalization. With their characteristic pragmatism, they concluded that it would be more advantageous for Japan's long-run national interest to seize the initiative rather than to react reluctantly to exogenous pressures. Third, the federation leaders also expressed their serious concern over what they considered excessive government protection of certain industries. They became increasingly convinced that well-planned and well-managed capital liberalization would stimulate industrial reorganization and increase productive efficiency. Perhaps their most fundamental reason was their growing confidence in the dynamism of Japanese industries and their ability to withstand foreign competition.

Amid these pressures and counterpressures, formal deliberations began in the fall of 1968 on the second phase of capital liberalization. Again, FIC, whose membership was now increased to fifteen, was instructed by the finance minister to present specific recommendations. As previously, the various ministries engaged in extensive consultations and discussions with various industry groups under their respective jurisdictions to designate specific industries that could be liberalized.

Increasingly favorable attitude toward capital liberalization. FIC, now consisting almost exclusively of prominent business leaders, and reflecting the attitude of the mainstream of business leadership, took a considerably more positive attitude toward capital liberalization than previously. It prodded the ministries, particularly MITI, to do likewise. As before, the various business and industry associations had also undertaken intensive studies of their own and made their views public. On February 5, 1969, the council made the final recommendations to the finance minister. In doing so, the council basically followed the same approach as it had in the first round. The council designated an additional 135 industries or product groups as Category I, and 20 as Category II. The second phase went into effect on March 1, 1969.

Additional industries now designated as Category I, where up to 50 percent foreign ownership is allowed, included meat processing, instant coffee, farm machinery and implements, precision measuring instruments, toys, wigs, and automobile tires. Also newly added to this category were a number of service industries such as insurance, parking lots, amusement parks, and single-unit specialty retail establishments.

Those designated as Category II (in which foreign ownership may be 100 percent) included sausage made from fish, animal fats, tinplate, *sake* brewing, steel sheets and pipes, fluorescent lamps, and a number of service industries such as barbershops and beauty parlors. Also, nine industries previously designated as Category I were shifted to Category II. Included in this group were restaurants, electrical machinery and equipment, tape recorders, and large-scale shipbuilding.

The second round of capital liberalization was somewhat less extensive than anticipated, particularly in view of the changing sentiment among the leadership of the Japanese business community. FIC deliberately included a few reasonably attractive industries in the second phase of liberalization (the Japanese aptly describe these as "loss leader" industries), but the great majority of those included on the list held little appeal to foreign firms. In the face of vigorous opposition from the ministries and specific industry groups, FIC decided to settle for a less ambitious program. A number of strategic industries came under deliberation, including detergents, cosmetics, aluminum refining, and the three most critical industries: distribution, petrochemicals, and automobiles. The final list, however, included none of these.

The most controversial issue in the second-stage deliberations was the status of the automobile industry. This pitted FIC and FEO against Japan's rapidly growing automobile industry, which was vigorously supported by MITI. The federation leaders became seriously concerned over the highly protective environment in which Japan's automotive industry was operating and the industry's persistent resistance to capital liberalization. They were concerned over the strained relations, even bordering on hostility, that had characterized the United States–Japan automobile negotiations mentioned earlier.

The federation leadership felt that Japan's automobile industry had developed to the point where it could withstand foreign competition and urged the industry to take positive steps toward liberalization. The federation leaders and FIC were fully aware that immediate acquiescence would be out of the question, but they urged the industry to make a definite commitment as to when it would agree to accept foreign capital. The industry group argued that, although Japan's automobile industry is the second largest in the world, its total output was less than half that of General Motors, whose annual sales were larger than Japan's national budget. It also pointed out that total outstanding shares of Toyota Motors at current market value were only about one-fifth of the annual profit of General Motors. Based on these arguments and others, the automobile industry, though not always able to present a unified front, steadfastly resisted the mounting pressure. While neither the federation nor the council was able to extract a definite commitment from the industry, the latter informally agreed to some measure of liberalization prior to 1972.

FIC initially planned to include in its report to the finance minister definite plans and timetables for the subsequent stages; but in the face of strong opposition from MITI, and because of certain technicalities, it did not make this part of the formal report. Instead, FIC made its views known in the form of an opinion attached to the main report. In this opinion, the council urged some measures of liberalization in two of the critical industries—automobiles and distribution—as early as feasible.

Further responses to intensifying pressures. The Japanese government and the business community began to prepare for a third round as they became increasingly sensitive to the mounting criticism that the previous two stages had been only tokens. Such criticism was justified, judging from the fact that between June 1967 and August 1970 the number of investments made in the liberalized industries was no more than nine. Only three of these investments were capitalized at more than ¥100 million.

The third stage reflected sensitivity to this criticism. In terms of the number of product categories included, the results were significant. FIC designated 315 products, nearly twice the combined number of the first and second rounds, for inclusion. In addition, the council moved 17 products that were previously classified Category I into Category II (100 percent foreign ownership). Some key products included in the third round were synthetic rubber, cosmetics, soap, detergents, and electric desk calculators. To the disappointment of foreign interests, the two of the critical industries—automobiles and distribution—as early as on the list.

Liberalization of automobile industry. The third stage of capital liberalization went into effect in August 1970. After the third stage was announced, pressure on the automobile industry for liberalization intensified. Several weeks later, a cabinet meeting approved the action to be effective April 1971, thus moving up the original schedule by six months.

Changing conditions. As FIC began to prepare for the fourth —and what was at that time presumed to be the last—round, Japan faced a new situation. Rapid, sustained growth over the preceding decade and a half had propelled the country into a very strong international competitive position, and some of the earlier constraints, notably Japan's heretofore precarious foreign-exchange position, had been removed.

A more competitive and assertive Japan in the world economy began to present increasingly difficult problems for the rest of the world, particularly for the United States. Notably, trade imbalance between Japan and the United States became quite serious. To correct this situation, the United States pressured Japan into entering into bilateral negotiations to curb Japanese exports to the United States in several key industries. The celebrated textile negotiations provide an excellent case in point. Pressures exerted by the United States on Japan, on one hand, and Japan's persistent resistance to the liberalization, on the other, resulted in further deterioration in the relationship between the United States and Japan. There had never been a time, at least in the postwar period, when the relationship between the two nations had become so strained as in the period between 1970 and 1971. In addition, there were two other critical considerations: (1) The yen had come under serious pressure for revaluation and (2) Okinawa had reverted to Japan.

The convergence of all these circumstances led to a redefinition of the Japanese national interest. No longer was the sole consideration the protection of domestic industries against foreign competition. Much broader goals began to dominate the thinking of the Japanese leadership: namely, to prevent international ostracism, to minimize tensions, and, if possible, to improve Japan's international image. Thus, political rather than economic considerations became overriding. The Japanese leadership had become aware of the nation's new role as a major power in the world economy. The mainstream of business leadership began to espouse a much more positive and liberal view in the matter of capital entry. The political leadership became more concerned about the liberalization program. At the same time, the cries of particular industry groups which were under consideration for liberalizing began to lose their earlier volume and effectiveness. These industry groups were urged by their colleagues in the business community and their political allies to cooperate in the name of the broader national interest.

Adoption of negative-list approach. Reflecting the foregoing record, the fourth round of capital liberalization was the boldest and most sweeping. It departed from the past in that, for the first time, Japan adopted a negative-list approach. In other words, FIC identified those industries that required individual screening and approval instead of singling out product categories to be liberalized. The significance of this change lies in the fact that among the OECD countries, Japan had been the only positive-list country up through July 1971. By becoming a negative-list country in the fourth round, Japan joined the ranks of Spain and Portugal.

FIC identified seven product categories requiring special approval. These included agricultural and fishery products; oil refining and distribution; manufacturing of leather products; manufacturing, selling, or leasing of computers; the information-processing industry (including computer software); retail chain operations; and real estate.

In addition, FIC shifted 151 product classes from Category I to Category II. The third provision called for increasing the ceiling of the percentage of ownership by a single foreign investor in an existing industry from 7 percent to 10 percent. However, the ceiling of the total shares that could be acquired in an existing enterprise by foreign interests remained unchanged.

Pressure for liberalization of computer industry. In the fourth round, the major attention was focused on the status of the computer industry. The computer was among the few industries in which import restrictions, as well as capital investment, had not been liberalized. Given the attractiveness of the computer market in Japan throughout the period immediately preceding the fourth round, considerable pressure was exerted by foreign, particularly American, interests to liberalize the computer industry.

Despite the intense pressure, the industry was confident of MITI's ability to protect it. The situation changed suddenly, however, just a few weeks before the fourth round was to be announced, when Prime Minister Eisaku Sato, realizing the seriousness of the matter, directed Kakuei Tanaka, then the MITI minister, to liberalize the computer industry at the earliest feasible date. In this directive, Sato urged MITI to give serious consideration to including the computer industry in the fourth round. The directive was issued in early July, roughly three weeks prior to the scheduled date of announcement of the fourth round. The industry was caught by surprise, and MITI was placed in the uncomfortable position of persuading the reluctant industry to soften its uncompromising position.

Prime Minister Sato's decision to issue such a directive was extraordinary, and it was based solely on broad political concerns. As noted earlier, the American and Japanese relationship was at perhaps its lowest ebb. The government was confronted with a difficult trade-off on one hand. The Okinawan issue was under active consideration, and the pressure on the yen for revaluation was mounting. The computer industry was a key growth industry for Japan and represented exactly the kind of industry in which Japan wanted to excel in the world. But, in the end, political considerations prevailed over the interests of a particular industry.

The industry leaders, trade associations, industrial companies, and of course MITI began frenetic and intense negotiations. The process was a familiar one, that of a concentrated search for consensus and compromise. MITI skillfully maneuvered for an acceptable compromise that partially satisfied both the industry's need and the government's political imperatives. As a result, partial liberalization of the integrated-circuits industry was included in the fourth round. But the industry succeeded in preventing the immediate liberalization of the manufacturing and distribution of computers and of the data-processing industry, although it had to agree tentatively that these industries would be liberalized as of July 1, 1974. In return, the industry extracted a commitment from the government that it would receive ¥51 billion annually for the coming three-year period to strengthen it in preparation for eventual liberalization.

Departure from past attitudes. Only weeks after the fourth round was announced, the so-called Nixon shock hit Japan—his new economic doctrine and his plan to visit China. In the ensuing several months, the relationship between the United States and Japan deteriorated further, and the pressures for more liberalization intensified. The United States and other OECD member countries objected that Japan's liberalization was yet far from complete on two counts. One was the rather stringent restrictions on the acquisition of shares in the existing enterprises, and the other was the continued adherence to the 50 percent ceiling placed on investment in the attractive industries. In the fall of 1971, the Japanese government made it known that it would undertake another round of liberalization. Almost a year later, FIC began formal deliberation on the next round.

Preparation for the last round of capital liberalization proceeded in an atmosphere radically different from that of the earlier rounds. By early 1973, there was almost total consensus within the leadership as to the inevitability of sweeping liberalization measures. In the face of growing resentment against Japan's still restrictive attitude toward foreign investment, political and business leaders as well as senior bureaucrats began to discuss the need for drastic liberalization for the sake of the national interest—with the same urgency that had characterized their earlier commitment to the need for protection.

Sweeping changes in fifth round of liberalization. Prime Minister Tanaka openly urged FIC to take bold steps. The leadership of the *Keidanren* [Japan federation of economic organizations] made a similar plea. The editorials of leading newspapers likewise strongly favored extensive liberalization. Behind this newly discovered enthusiasm for admission of foreign capital was the recognition that most Japanese industries had, in fact, become competitive and needed no further protection. Moreover, it was increasingly apparent that the cost of maintaining the restrictive posture was becoming prohibitively high for Japan. Final recommendations were made on April 1, 1973. They were subsequently approved by the cabinet and went into effect on May 1.

As noted in the statement made by the chairman of FIC in announcing its recommendations, the fifth round was epochmaking. Indeed, this round marks a basic departure from the past. First, except for a small number of specifically designated product categories, 100 percent ownership is to be automatically allowed. The general principle of allowing 100 percent foreign ownership is thus established.

The five nonliberalized product categories which will continue to require individual screening are the agriculture, forestry and fishery industry; petroleum refining and sale of leather; retail chains; and mining.

Seventeen industries have been designated for inclusion at predetermined schedules within three years. They are integrated circuits; meat products; processed food; manufacturing of precooked food for restaurants and other institutional users; apparel manufacturing and wholesaling; ferroalloys; hydraulic equipment; packaging and wrapping machines; electronic precision instruments; phonograph records; manufacturing, marketing, and leasing of computers; computer software; fruit juice; photographic film; pharmaceuticals; agricultural chemicals; and real estate. Some of these products are already partially liberalized.

Among the seventeen product categories, the most critical, of course, are the computer and computer-related industries. They will be handled in two stages. The first stage (up to 50 percent foreign ownership) went into effect on August 4, 1974; as of December 1, 1975, they will be totally liberalized to all 100 percent foreign ownership.

Another sweeping change in this round is the removal of the rather stringent restrictions on acquisition of existing enterprises. Foreign interests are now allowed to acquire the stock of existing Japanese enterprises up to 100 percent. The only stipulation is that acquisition must be made with the consent of the Japanese interests being acquired. Fearful of negative repercussions and dislocations that takeover bids could cause, the Japanese government, particularly MITI, insisted on this condition.

The fifth round is not likely to be the last. In fact, FIC's report to the foreign minister includes the need for continuing exploration of removing the remaining restrictions. Indeed, considering the highly restrictive policy it had maintained for the preceding two decades, Japan has come a long way during the past several years, particularly during the past year or two. Of course, during this period, Japan's position in the world economy has undergone a dramatic change.

There is no doubt that Japan's liberalization programs have been strongly influenced by external forces, particularly by the persistent and ever-increasing pressure from the United States. However, it is important to recognize that the ultimate decisions were made by Japanese leaders as they reexamined their own national interests.

Notes

1/ *Economic Statistics Annual, 1973* (Tokyo: The Bank of Japan, 1974) p. 208.

2/ For details of the magnitude and role of foreign direct investment in prewar Japan, see S. Okita and T. Miki, "Treatment of Foreign Capital—A Case Study for Japan," in J. Adler and P. W. Kuznets, eds., *Capital Movements and Economic Development* (New York: St. Martin's Press, 1967), pp. 139–156; and W. W. Lockwood, *The Economic Development of Japan: Growth and Structural Change, 1868–1938* (Princeton: Princeton University Press, 1954), pp. 321–323.

CONTRIBUTORS

Isaiah Frank, William L. Clayton Professor of International Economics at Johns Hopkins University School of Advanced International Studies, is the director of international economic studies for the Committee for Economic Development. He was deputy assistant secretary of state for economic affairs and has been a consultant to the World Bank, the United Nations, the Institute for Latin American Integration, the Department of the Treasury, the Department of State, and the Agency for International Development. His writings include *The European Common Market: An Analysis of Commercial Policy.*

Haruhiro Fukui is associate professor of political science at the University of California at Santa Barbara. He has been a research associate at the Brookings Institution, a visiting lecturer at the University of Adelaide, and a research assistant at the Center for Japanese Studies at the University of Michigan. He studied at the University of Michigan and received his Ph.D. from the Australian National University in 1968. He is the author of *Party in Power: The Japanese Liberal-Democrats and Policy Making* (1970).

Donald C. Hellmann is associate director for Japan and Korea at the University of Washington's Institute for Comparative and Foreign Area Studies. He is a consultant to the National Security Council, the Arms Control and Disarmament Agency, the Department of State, the Commission on Critical Choices for Americans, and other organizations. His most recent publication is *Japan and East Asia: The New International Order* (1972).

Leon Hollerman served as an economist with the Supreme Command for the Allied Powers in Tokyo after World War II and began his teaching career at the University of California in 1952. He is now professor of economics at Claremont Men's College and Claremont Graduate School. His numerous publications on Japan include *Japan's Dependence on the World Economy* (1967).

J. J. Kaplan, now a consultant in international finance and economics, was director of the international organizations staff of the Agency for International Development from 1961 to 1964. He also served in the Department of State as an assistant coordinator for foreign assistance programs and as a member of the U.S. delegations to the annual ministerial meetings of the North Atlantic Treaty Organization, the Organization for European Economic Cooperation, the World Bank, and the International Monetary Fund. He has taught at Iowa State College, Yale University, George Washington University, and the University of Pittsburgh and is author of *The Challenge of Foreign Aid* (1967).

Yoichi Okita has worked in both the planning and the econometric sections of the Economic Planning Agency of the Japanese government. He attended Tokyo University and received his Ph.D. in economics from Harvard University in 1974. He is currently with the overseas research section of the Economic Planning Agency.

William V. Rapp is a financial services representative for the Morgan Guaranty Trust Company in Japan and the Far East. He was a consultant for the Boston Consulting Group in Boston and Tokyo and an economist for the Agency for International Development in Korea and Vietnam. He received his Ph.D. in economics from Yale University as a National Science Foundation fellow and undertook Far Eastern studies at Stanford University. Among his published works are *A Theory of Changing Trade Patterns under Economic Growth: Tested for Japan* and *Effective Protective Rates for Korean Industries.*

C. Tait Ratcliffe received his A.B. from Harvard and his Ph.D. in economics from the University of California at Berkeley. He later pursued Japanese-language studies at Keio University, Tokyo, and served as a visiting research associate at the Keio Institute for Management and Labor Studies. He has also been a member of the economics faculty of Stanford University and a consultant with the Boston Consulting Group in Tokyo. He is now vice-president of International Business Information, Tokyo.

Kozo Yamamura is a member of the Institute for Comparative and Foreign Area Studies and the Department of Economics at the University of Washington. He has taught at the Harvard Graduate School of Business Administration and the University of Hawaii and has received awards and fellowships from the Brookings Institution, the National Science Foundation, the National Institutes of Health, and other organizations. His writings on Japan include *Postwar Economic Policy of Japan: Growth vs. Economic Democracy* (1967).

M. Y. Yoshino is professor of business administration at Harvard University. He is consultant to the Ford Foundation and a number of U.S., European, and Japanese business enterprises. He is the author of *Japan's Managerial System: Tradition and Innovation* (1968) and *The Japanese Marketing System: Innovation and Adaptation* (1971).

INDEX